Praise for

THE END OF REALITY

"Smart and essential. *The End of Reality* shows how four Silicon Valley evil geniuses, freed of democratic oversight, have accumulated vast fortunes and power by becoming the oligarchs of the new industrial complex behind America's transformation into fantasyland."

—Kurt Anderson, author of *Evil Geniuses*

"Reading Taplin's invigorating *The End of Reality* is akin to attending a huge outdoor feast. There is so much nourishment in his book, so much provocative thinking, so much vivid writing, so much thought that went into the book's vast menu, that by the final page the reader is left in awe. Taplin is a delightful iconoclast and a daring thinker."

—Ken Auletta, author of *Hollywood Ending*

"*The End of Reality* is incredibly timely and powerful. The technologists pushing us into a world dominated by AI need to abandon their Ayn Rand mindset of 'who's going to stop me' and consider the power of the new, regenerative economics tool set Taplin proposes."

—John Seely Brown, former director, Xerox PARC

"I've followed technology, and politics, for decades. But I found a tremendous amount of new information and insight in *The End of Reality*. Anyone interested in where culture is headed, and how democracy can survive, will want to read this book."

—James Fallows, national correspondent, *The Atlantic*

"A wake-up call as to what happens when a society elevates people who don't have the public's best interests in mind. Jonathan Taplin has a gift for storytelling that turns the bitter pill (reality check) into a fascinating read."

—Scott Galloway, NYU Stern professor of marketing
and bestselling author of *Adrift*

"Taplin takes us to the inner sanctum of the plutocratic insurgency: where libertarian billionaires, resentful that they are not universally acclaimed as heroes, are spinning a 'populist' technophantasmagoria designed first and foremost to distract the rest of us from the vast anti-democratic power and privilege they have amassed for themselves."

—Nils Gilman, senior vice president,
the Bergggruen Institute

"Tech culture has to improve for the sake of humanity, and that's not going to happen without critiques like *The End of Reality*. Please take the time to read this carefully, especially if you are sure it must be wrong."

—Jaron Lanier, author of *Who Owns the Future?*

"Taplin understands true creativity comes from real people, not the lazy musings of the super-rich or the idea factories of the giant corporation. That's why he's fought so hard for so long to protect every human who dreams of making a better world—or just singing a more beautiful song—from the dystopian projects of America's new autocrats. Want a future that works for you and your family? Here's your guide."

—Barry Lynn, director of the Open Markets Institute
and author of *Liberty from All Masters*

"For those who profit from our polarization, isolation, and extremism, a failed democracy is not a bug but a feature. *The End of Reality* is an urgent warning about the concentration of power and privilege in America, an alarm that seeks to break through the captivating distractions of our age."

—Beto O'Rourke

"Once again, Taplin has cut to the core of a heartless techno-oligarchy. If names like Musk, Thiel, and Zuckerberg only cause you distress, Taplin's careful exposé will move you to outrage, though with hope the hyper-barons can be curbed."

—Sean Wilentz, George Henry Davis 1886
Professor of American History, Princeton University

"Persuasive and insightful. This cutting portrait of America's slide toward oligarchy hits home." —Publishers Weekly (starred review)

THE END
OF REALITY

THE END OF REALITY

HOW FOUR BILLIONAIRES
ARE SELLING OUT OUR FUTURE

JONATHAN TAPLIN

torva

TRANSWORLD PUBLISHERS
Penguin Random House, One Embassy Gardens,
8 Viaduct Gardens, London SW11 7BW
www.penguin.co.uk

Transworld is part of the Penguin Random House group of companies
whose addresses can be found at global.penguinrandomhouse.com

Penguin
Random House
UK

First published in Great Britain in 2023 by Torva
an imprint of Transworld Publishers

A CIP catalogue record for this book
is available from the British Library.

ISBNs
9781911709497 hb
9781911709503 tpb

Printed and bound in Great Britain by Clays Ltd, Elcograf S.p.A.

The authorized representative in the EEA is Penguin Random House Ireland,
Morrison Chambers, 32 Nassau Street, Dublin D02 YH68.

Penguin Random House is committed to a sustainable future
for our business, our readers and our planet. This book is made
from Forest Stewardship Council® certified paper.

MIX
Paper | Supporting
responsible forestry
FSC
www.fsc.org   FSC® C018179

For Manuel Castells & John Seely Brown
For their wisdom and guidance

CONTENTS

Reality has had 5,000 years to get good, and is clearly still woefully lacking for most people. We should build—and we are building—online worlds that make life and work and love wonderful for everyone, no matter what level of reality deprivation they find themselves in.

—MARC ANDREESSEN

To abandon facts is to abandon freedom. If nothing is true, then all is spectacle. The biggest wallet pays for the most blinding lights.

—TIMOTHY SNYDER, *ON TYRANNY*

INTRODUCTION

This book seeks to understand the role of four very powerful billionaires—Elon Musk, Peter Thiel, Mark Zuckerberg, and Marc Andreessen—in creating a world where "nothing is true and all is spectacle." If we are to inquire how we got to a place of radical income inequality and the looming potential for a second American Civil War, we need look no further than these four—"the biggest wallets paying for the most blinding lights." Herein, I'll call them the Technocrats, in recognition of the influence of the technocracy movement, founded in the 1930s by Elon Musk's grandfather, Joshua Haldeman. The Technocrats make up a kind of interlocking directorate of Silicon Valley, each investing in or sitting on the boards of the others' companies. And the Eurasia Group, the highly respected consulting firm headed by Ian Bremmer (author of *Us vs. Them: The Failure of Globalism*), aptly describes the world the Technocrats have created as one in which

your personal information will be hacked. Algorithms fed with biased data will make destructive decisions that affect how billions of people live, work, and love. Online mobs will create chaos, inciting violence and sparking runs on stocks. Tens of millions of people

1

will be dragged down the rabbit holes of conspiracy theories. The
one thing that all of these realities have in common is that they ema-
nate from digital space, where a handful of big tech companies, not
governments, are the main actors and enforcers.[1]

A poll conducted by the Benenson Strategy Group in late October
2022 shows the results of this digital anarchy.[2] The share of registered voters who believe "the federal government is controlled by a secret cabal"
was 44 percent; 63 percent of Republicans believed this central tenet of
the QAnon philosophy, as did, more surprisingly, 41 percent of Indepen-
dents and 37 percent of Democrats. The rise of fantastical thinking tracks
the rise of social networks.

I use the term *techno-determinism* to describe the path the Technocrats have dictated for our country because they have sold, and we have
bought into, the idea that they are going to deliver us a bright future,
and we tend to ignore any facts that seem to contradict this story. The
future they are now selling us—crypto fortunes, living to two hundred,
spending our lives in the Metaverse or on Mars—is a lie, just as historian
Timothy Snyder has shown that Donald Trump "was lying not so much
to deny the truth as to invite people into an alternative reality." But when
we surrender to the lies of a Trump or a Musk, we yield power to those
with the fortunes and magnetism to create spectacle in the place of truth.

Much of the spectacle takes place on the social networks that all four
Technocrats have been involved with either as executives or investors.
In May 2009, when Facebook crossed the 250-million-user mark, the
Gallup survey of the dissatisfaction of Americans with their country's
direction stood at 62 percent. Today it is 87 percent. The rise of social networks correlates with the metastasis of social distrust, and as you will see,
political polarization could get worse in the new world the Technocrats
are planning for us.

For years there has been a myth that the Big Tech leaders are progressive heroes, but I will show that the Technocrats are actually part

of a broader antidemocratic, authoritarian turn within Big Tech, deeply invested in preserving the status quo and in keeping their monopolies unchallenged and their multibillion-dollar fortunes secure from higher taxes. But their digital oligopolies are now morphing into political oligarchies. The Technocrats *are* the American oligarchs, controlling online access for billions of users on Facebook, Twitter, Instagram, and WhatsApp. Progressive pundits often blame people like Tucker Carlson for the disinformation that has flooded our society. But in reality Carlson is lucky if he reaches 1 percent of the American public on any given evening (his show reaches 3.3 million people on a good night). By contrast "the number of social media users in the USA at the start of 2022 was equivalent to 80.9 percent of the total population."[3] Elon Musk has 112 million followers who read his tweets. Conservative commentator and *New York Times* columnist Ross Douthat argues that Musk is "arguably the most important right-leaning figure in American life."

The political partisan divide and gridlock that frustrate so many Americans is a feature for the Technocrats, not a bug. Twitter's new owner, Elon Musk, has already allowed Donald Trump and other right-wing propagandists like Marjorie Taylor Greene back on his platform, so the partisan divide will only increase. And, as the election of 2022 showed, their monetary support of an authoritarian Republican Party endangers our democracy but fattens their wallets, as partisan anger leads to more "engagement" on their social media platforms. After the 2022 midterm setback for the Republicans, Peter Thiel delivered a strong rebuke to the party at the Reagan Library. He called for a Republican Party that could unite "the priest, the general and the millionaire," a phrase that could have come out of the mouth of Vladimir Putin. And the new Republican political establishment (under the sway of the Technocrats) will do their best to comply: to ban abortion (the priest), increase the defense budget (the general), and lower taxes (the millionaire).

As Peter Thiel once admitted, "Competition is for suckers." The Technocrats want nothing more than for the digital world to have complete autonomy. The late activist John Perry Barlow, who founded the Electronic Frontier Foundation and called himself a cyberlibertarian, provided an early statement of what became the technocratic credo of autonomy in his 1996 "Declaration of Independence of Cyberspace": "Governments of the Industrial World, you weary giants of flesh and steel, I come from Cyberspace, the new home of Mind. On behalf of the future, I ask you of the past to leave us alone. You are not welcome among us. You have no sovereignty where we gather."[4] But Barlow, who once wrote songs for the Grateful Dead, possessed a certain hippy naïveté that blinded him to a future in which raw corporate power would be the only force in cyberspace.

The four Technocrats are part of an ideological movement that can only be characterized as anarcho-libertarian and that drives a lot of their plans for our future. They are interested in replacing our current reality—an imperfect economic system—with something far more opaque, concentrated, and unaccountable, which they will control. To make this a reality, they supported, during the election year of 2022, authoritarian Senate candidates like J. D. Vance, Blake Masters, and Eric Schmitt, all of whom hewed closely to Donald Trump's stolen-election narrative. Although Masters lost, ninety Republicans who denied the results of the 2020 election won congressional seats in the 2022 midterms. They will constitute a powerful Make America Great Again (MAGA) caucus within the new Republican House majority. As *Axios* reported, "This hard-right flank could command outsized influence in a narrow GOP majority." The Technocrats' social media platforms are the fuel for the post-truth Republican Party. And, as you will see, the Technocrats plan to feed at the government trough to finance some of their more outrageous schemes. Their plan for your future involves four projects that will need tens of trillions of dollars of (mostly public) investment capital over the next two decades. They are confident we will give them that money.

The first project is Web3, a virtual world (the Metaverse) accessed by a virtual reality (VR) helmet, which will convert the free web into an online theme park in which every door requires a crypto token to open. Mark Zuckerberg's business plan projects that a user will spend seven hours a day in the Metaverse (unable to look away from the billboards), thus radically increasing his ad revenue. Supporters like Zuckerberg, Thiel, and Andreessen claim Web3 will democratize the web, but as you will see from the evidence provided later, this is one of the great con jobs of the twenty-first century. As Twitter's founder, Jack Dorsey, recently tweeted, "You don't own web3. The VC's do. It will never escape their incentives. It's ultimately a centralized entity with a different label." Dorsey sees through the fantasy that a company like Meta, accused by the Federal Trade Commission of monopoly, is now pretending that it's new platform—the Metaverse—will be open and decentralized.[5]

The second project is the support of crypto currency. Crypto is basically a pyramid scheme, with early investors dumping their tokens when the price rises. Professor Scott Galloway of New York University (named one of the Global Leaders of Tomorrow by the World Economic Forum) has shown that the top 2 percent of accounts own 95 percent of the $800 billion supply of Bitcoin. In June 2022, a group of computer scientists and cryptographers wrote a letter to congressional leadership warning of the potential economic disaster crypto currencies may cause: "The catastrophes and externalities related to blockchain technologies and crypto-asset investments are neither isolated nor are they growing pains of a nascent technology. They are the inevitable outcomes of a technology that is not built for purpose and will remain forever unsuitable as a foundation for large-scale economic activity."[6] Adam Fisher, Israel's top-ranked venture capitalist, pointed out, "Crypto is not so much an investment idea that aligns with the libertarian political ideology, as it is a virulent strain of libertarian political ideology leveraging human greed through the blockchain."[7]

(While crypto currency was developed using blockchain technology, I will not be dealing with the legitimate uses of blockchain by companies like IBM to develop more effective supply chains, such as Maersk's TradeLens.)

The third project involves getting the government of the United States to pony up at least $10 trillion to fund Elon Musk's *Star Trek* pipe dream of sending humans to live on Mars.[8] In the face of the existential climate crisis, Musk wants to abandon our planet and start all over in an incredibly hostile environment where humans would live inside an enclosed bubble with oxygen shipped from Earth. To what end, Musk will not explain, other than to say, "We should be a multi-planet species."

The final project, led by Peter Thiel, is called *transhumanism*, which the *Encyclopedia Britannica* defines as "a social and philosophical movement devoted to promoting the research and development of robust human-enhancement technologies."[9] The near-term goal for Thiel is to live to age 160. Thiel has reached out to both the United States and Saudi Arabia for government support. But access to these technologies, which have not yet been invented, will be incredibly expensive, so only the millionaires will survive well into their second century. As one of Marc Andreessen's early partners, Balaji Srinivasan, wrote of the Technocrats' goals, "Immutable money, infinite frontier, eternal life." This combination of untraceable crypto wealth, space colonies on Mars, and the ability to live forever is a perfect summation of the fantasy world the Technocrats think they can manufacture.

~

These four projects—the Metaverse, crypto currency, human travel to and colonization of distant planets, and transhumanism—are an existential risk to the world in moral, political, and economic terms. The moral danger comes from the fact that they are all the first steps toward a realized transhumanism—one that all four men support. The transhumanists believe that technological and biological enhancements will allow humans to live to age two hundred or more, migrate to other planets, and merge our brains with computers so that our individual consciousnesses can live forever. Web3 is the first step to a wearable human technological augmentation. Living on Mars would require a permanent technological augmentation, and transhumanism envisions a point at which human and machine merge into some new species of cyborg. As this book was going to print, the generative AIs like ChatGPT and DALL-E were released to the public. They are part of the transhumanist project, but also equally unconnected to reality. What ChatGPT hasn't learned from ingesting all of the internet, it makes up. AI researchers call this "hallucinations."

Philosopher Francis Fukuyama, most famous for his essay "The End of History," labeled transhumanism "the world's most dangerous idea." Fukuyama argued that the whole classical liberal idea embodied in the Declaration of Independence could be undone. He wrote in *Foreign Policy*, "Underlying this idea of the equality of rights is the belief that we all possess a human essence that dwarfs manifest differences in skin color, beauty, and even intelligence. This essence, and the view that individuals therefore have inherent value, is at the heart of political liberalism. But modifying that essence is the core of the transhumanist project."[10] The question of whether humans can turn themselves into machines, cheat death, and rule over nature will be at the heart of this book. Clearly Thomas Jefferson's ideal that "all men are created equal" would have no meaning in a transhumanist world in which wealth would determine the length of your life or the genetic attributes of your children.

To understand the political and societal danger lurking in the Technocrats' schemes, we should recognize that two views of America's future are on offer. One argues that the collective investment priorities of our society should go toward solving issues like the climate crisis, the mental health emergency, and the lack of affordable housing. But the other view, the one held by the Technocrats, is much darker. In this version of the future, artificial intelligence and robots, ruled by the Technocrats, will do most of the work, and a large portion of the population will sit at home, living a fantasy life in the Metaverse, subsisting on government-paid crypto universal basic income, which would cover your broadband bill and your Metacoin micropayments for all the concerts and clubs you attend virtually. Anyone who thinks this is some kind of dystopian fantasy should visit Amazon's research and development facility to see the future of whole warehouses operated by five humans and five thousand robots.[11] In April 2022, the Association for Advancing Automation reported that US orders for workplace robots had increased 40 percent in the first quarter, compared with the same period in 2021. Amazon's willingness to fire eleven thousand workers right before Christmas 2022 indicates that it believes the robots can pick up the slack.

Science fiction like Aldous Huxley's *Brave New World* has often depicted a future in which humans don't have much to do and end up blissed out on drugs and immersive entertainment. For Huxley's idealized government, controlled by the plutocrats, this is an ideal situation because it prevents what Huxley called "the proles" from invading the mansions of their oligarchs. But we are no longer dealing in fiction. These plans for the Metaverse have already attracted billions of dollars of investment. The central question I want to pose is why we, as a society, would invest $20 trillion in fantasy worlds (Mars, crypto, and the Metaverse) when real-world solutions to the critical problems of our planet are currently available. As climate-crisis chronicler David Wallace-Wells (*The Uninhabitable Earth*) recently wrote, "Thanks to astonishing declines in the price of renewables, a truly global political mobilization, a clearer picture of the energy future and serious policy focus from world leaders, we have cut expected warming almost in half in just five years."[12]

This positive change is happening in part due to a new way of thinking about the economy—*regenerative economics*—radically different from the libertarian Right's fetishization of the individual, which makes a virtue of selfishness. Regenerative economics is based on the idea that businesses that utilize natural resources should restore those precious resources rather than treat them as natural capital to be used up. Central to regenerative economics is the idea that America is best when citizens imagine themselves as part of an intergenerational movement to preserve our planet and our democracy. But the Technocrats have given up on that. As Elon Musk has said, "Either we spread Earth to other planets, or we risk going extinct." For them, the next two decades are about escape. Escaping Earth for Mars or escaping reality for the Metaverse.

One question I try to answer is why this culture of escape from reality is so popular right now. In their book *Pastels and Pedophiles: Inside the Mind of QAnon*, Sophia Moskalenko and Mia Bloom have shown that consumers of conspiracy theories become addicted, and "because, like a drug of addiction, QAnon content doesn't actually take the underlying pain away, bigger 'highs' are needed to distract from the root causes of despair. Consumers of QAnon content thus experience cravings for new and exciting conspiracies."[13] Meta's own employees are deeply skeptical of escaping into the Metaverse. The post most upvoted in an employee forum was "How could we avoid a dystopian reality, where the Metaverse is used as an opium for the masses?"[14] And of course, like the Sackler family pushing OxyContin, a small group of very powerful people—the Technocrats—are benefiting financially and politically from amplification of the conspiracy theory addiction on their social media platforms.

The young skeptics at Meta have it right. To check into the Metaverse is to check out of the real struggle that confronts our country: the fight for a decent health care system, for infrastructure that does not collapse, and for real solutions to the climate crisis. The people who are building the Metaverse or planning to live on Mars have surrendered to the nihilism of dystopia. They have forsaken any responsibility for reality in return for a permanent escape into a world of virtual porn and unlimited lives in a constant first-person shooter game.

From an economic standpoint, the four projects of Metaverse, crypto, space, and transhumanism will require an astonishing amount of capital. Elon Musk estimates it will cost at least $10 trillion to build the first colony on Mars, most of which would come from you, the taxpayer, funneled through NASA to Musk's SpaceX.[15] Of course none of Musk's previous projects have come in on budget, so we must be skeptical of the $10 trillion figure. That's almost two years of the entire federal budget.

Realizing a complete version of the Metaverse will require at least $3 trillion over the next twenty years, though that will flow from private capital. Of course, if Zuckerberg is right, those universal basic income payments will provide much of the revenue to Meta. No one can say how much will be poured into the transhumanism project, but it's in the billions.[16] The Technocrats' hype machine can undoubtedly attract that kind of investment from the government and the private sector, and they could subsequently hire the best scientists in the world to work for them. But putting money into virtual reality or a space race to Mars does not solve any of the problems actually facing America. It's a modern version of the Roman "bread and circuses," used to divert attention from epic inequality.

In the late 1920s (tellingly, just before the Great Depression), Italian philosopher Antonio Gramsci wrote, "The crisis consists precisely in the fact that the old is dying and the new cannot be born; in this interregnum a great variety of morbid symptoms appear."[17] Gramsci was sitting in an Italian prison cell, arrested and convicted by Benito Mussolini for anti-fascist activities. The idea of an interregnum is a good way to understand America's current political and social crisis. It began in early 2007.

The first week of January 2007 was awash in optimism. The S&P 500 stock index was on its way to an all-time record. In California, Elon Musk was planning the third launch of his Falcon rocket (the first two had failed) in hopes of beginning his dream of a mission to Mars, where he planned to construct a greenhouse and grow plants. On the other side of the country, another young man, Barack Obama, had equally audacious dreams. He was writing a speech in which he would announce his candidacy for the presidency of the United States.

But beneath this sea of calm as the new year began, three highly secret projects were being birthed that would dramatically disrupt America's economy, culture, and politics. The success of the projects would make the three men that conceived them into billionaires and change the meaning of "life, liberty, and the pursuit of happiness."

In San Francisco's cavernous Moscone Center, Steve Jobs yelled at a group of engineers trying to prepare his presentation for the unveiling of the first iPhone prototype in three days. "You are fucking my company," he screamed as the demo kept crashing.

In Manhattan, John Paulson was pushing a group of mathematicians and analysts to uncover the riskiest pools of subprime mortgages in the country in order to construct a $10 billion bet that the American housing market would collapse.[18]

In Palo Alto, Mark Zuckerberg led a team of designers to create software that would blend personalization and algorithmic amplification to create "engagement-based ranking" on your Facebook Feed.

All three men believed that they saw things their peers did not understand and that this perception would be the key to their fortunes. Within a year these extraordinary bets paid off as the housing market crashed, Bear Stearns and Lehman Brothers were liquidated, Apple sold almost 12 million iPhones, and Facebook's monthly average users grew from 30 million to 150 million.

The old that was dying in early 2007 included the bedrock institutions that had been a certainty in American life for a century. The first was the American Dream: the belief that home ownership was the secret to financial security. Paulson made $4 billion in a couple of months proving that was an illusion. The second was the notion that the major American media corporations could "manufacture consent" by pushing a narrative of the conventional wisdom—that average citizens would open their newspapers in the morning and watch the network news at night and assume they knew what was going on in the world. Steve Jobs and Mark Zuckerberg destroyed that system by giving citizens a powerful handheld communication device and a way to broadcast their opinions to billions of people. The rise of Barack Obama unmoored many white Americans, undermining their assumptions about their place in a changing multiracial America. And, finally, Elon Musk began to build what would become the world's largest fortune based on a utopian fantasy. But here was the problem that Gramsci understood: the transition from the old (extractive economy, white rule, top-down media) to the new (renewable energy, pluralistic society, bottom-up media) is full of "morbid symptoms," ranging from political violence, to exploitive politicians like Trump, to unexpected economic dislocations as the creative destruction of the disrupters sets in. In the midst of this chaotic interregnum, both businesspeople and politicians have created fantasies to help guide the society toward the ends they seek.

History has proven that fantasy is both a brilliant marketing tool and a powerful political tool. The Technocrats are employing it in both spheres. In the commercial realm Musk floats the notion that we will escape our planet's inevitable extinction by building a new civilization on Mars. Mark Zuckerberg promises you can escape the dreary reality of your life by putting on the Meta Quest 2 VR helmet. Marc Andreessen suggests we can fight wars without human casualties with the autonomous weapons he is developing and you can get rich just by purchasing the Bored Ape nonfungible tokens he is selling. And Thiel markets the greatest fantasy of all: you can live forever.

But it is in politics that Trump has used fantasy ("Obama is not an American"; "I won the 2020 election") to fuel his political rise since 2011. Today the hard-right amplification of the fantasy that a "woke" socialist and communist cabal has taken over the Democratic Party, the news media, education, and even many large American corporations poisons our possibility for political reconciliation. This is straight out of the Nazi Party playbook of the early 1930s that inflated the power of the German socialists. Adolf Hitler blamed the burning of the German parliament, the Reichstag, on the communists and then immediately banned them from political participation. In 1977 German writer Klaus Theweleit, in his book *Male Fantasies*, set out to understand the appeal fascism had for the average German male who joined the Nazi Freikorps (equivalent to our Proud Boys) in the 1930s.[19] *Guardian* writer Laura Smith, reviewing *Male Fantasies*, notes, "To modern readers, the Freikorpsmen's fantasy life will be familiar: a country in decline, a nationalistic call to purge it of disorder, a clear separation between men and women, rich and poor, your kind and the other."[20]

So for the Technocrats, this is not just an economic project. It is a political movement that sees the modern economy as corrupt, harmful, and in need of sweeping transformation. In the spirit of their anarcho-libertarian heroes, like Ayn Rand, the four Technocrats believe that the "administrative state" needs to be killed off. If they achieve their aims, by 2035 they will be living in a semi-stateless economic system where no one even knows how much Bitcoin they own, because it can be legally held under a pseudonym or in a shadow company account. As Peter Thiel has stated, "The ability to move money fluidly and the erosion of the nation-state are closely related."[21]

In this project, Trump and other Republicans are the Technocrat's supplicants. Just as Vladimir Putin has pleased his oligarch allies by using oil export revenues to prop up the ruble and the Russian stock market, instead of providing the tools needed for a credible military, so our own oligarchs will be able to depend on the Republicans to cut their taxes and protect their monopolies. Trump already has associates (some working with Peter Thiel) creating a plan for his second term that would involve firing much of the federal bureaucracy and replacing it with MAGA-compliant functionaries at all of the regulatory agencies.[22] Are the Technocrats divorced from reality, or is this a darker plot that is employing fantasy to enact a right-wing political coup that will kill our majoritarian democracy and lead us into an era of economic unrest and civil war? For the Technocrats, Web3 puts their wealth, data, and resources beyond the reach of the state. It helps them sidestep anti-money-laundering regulations, sanctions, and taxation. And as you will see, Thiel and some of his brethren have had a kind of apocalyptic view of the future for some time. Maybe that's why they all own "bolt-hole" estates in distant lands like New Zealand.

In a long view of history, the United States has of course gone through periods that feel like collective schizophrenic breaks. Episodes ranging from the Salem witch trials to the 1950s obsession with extraterrestrial invasions to the emergence of QAnon display the classic symptoms of loss of contact with reality and delusional thinking. Perhaps we can attribute today's psychological angst to the seeming endlessness of the Covid-19 pandemic. Yet this period of time feels different. In the earlier manias, the symptoms were confined to a small minority of believers, not 60 percent of one of our two major political parties.

We have always had con men like P. T. Barnum, but they never won the presidency or ran the most valuable automobile company in the world. Creating a political economy in which the wealthy minority rules over the middle- and lower-class majority is a hard task. It requires mechanisms for voter suppression and for propaganda that convinces middle-class voters that cultural division is more important than economic equality. MAGA Republicans' convincing the working class to vote for them is really an artful trick, for, as Paul Krugman has shown, "despite its populist rhetoric, the G.O.P. is still very much a party of and for the rich."

In creating the fantasy that the Republicans represent the working class, control of Twitter and Facebook has been key to the Technocrats' success. But these social networks are also the nexus of right-wing anger. And particularly troubling about this period is the rise of political violence. Over the past decade (according to the Anti-Defamation League) political extremists have committed 450 murders in the United States; most of these perpetrators self-identify with a kind of neofascism.[23]

Harvard political scientist Steven Levitsky, coauthor of *How Democracies Die*, has said, "In a stable democracy politicians unambiguously reject violence and unambiguously expel from their ranks antidemocratic forces."[24] But the Trumpist Republican Party refuses to push out its neofascists. And the mainstream media refuses to put that name on the disease. Fascism has relied on propaganda, myth, and a sense of the unreal. Democracy in an age where everyone has a microphone to express his or her outrage becomes a very fragile system. And, as I will show, the libertarian philosophy the Technocrats were raised on has morphed into coercive fascism in the past. As Jason Stanley points out in his book *How Fascism Works*, "Tech giants and media benefit from the dramatic clash of friend and enemy. Fear and anger get people to the polls, but they also keep people online and glued to the media."[25]

It is important to justify my use of the term *fascism*. Geoff Eley, the Karl Pohrt Distinguished University Professor of History at the University of Michigan, has defined fascism well: "As a politics, I have suggested, fascism can be distilled into the following: it wants to silence and even murder its opponents rather than arguing with them; it prefers an authoritarian state over democracy; it pits an aggressively exclusionary idea of the nation against a pluralism that values and prioritizes difference."[26]

Tucker Carlson and the Trumpist Republicans hate the whole idea of pluralism and exalt nationalism and race as a path back to power. The threat of political murder from the Right increases every week. I have no doubt that if Trump returns to the presidency, we will see a forcible suppression of the opposition as we have never experienced in this country. But whether Trump returns to power or not, our country is really two countries as deeply divided as during the period leading up to the Civil War, with a June 2022 poll reporting a majority of Americans agreeing that America would one day "cease to be a democracy."[27] Even President Joe Biden has expressed deep concern, saying, "What we're seeing now is either the beginning or the death knell of an extreme MAGA philosophy. It's not just Trump, it's the entire philosophy that underpins the—I'm going to say something—it's like semi-fascism." While the term *semi-fascism* may seem like an artful dodge, academics have actually used it for years to describe the early years of regimes like that of Spain's Francisco Franco, whose fascism was somewhat constrained within the Catholic and semipluralist structure of the conservative movement. Only after Franco had won the Civil War and consolidated all state power did the regime's true authoritarian fascist character emerge.

So a critical question for me is *why*? Instead of the bounty of tech's promised productivity, why has the internet brought middle-class wage stagnation, the hollowing out of many American towns, a radical increase in income inequality, and unbounded public acrimony? The so-called digital revolution is rooted in a profound paradox. On the one hand, it *is* revolutionary in that it has brought the promise of truly open democratic communication into being. There are no more gatekeepers, and the average (sometimes clueless) citizen has access to the global microphone of Facebook or Twitter.

But the other side of the digital revolution paradox is that it is not really a revolution at all. At least since the dawn of the Industrial Revolution, much of our collective wealth has been derived from an extractive economy that treats all local economies and natural resources as sources of capital to be used up. Such economies are dominated by rent-extraction firms. *Rent* is defined as outsized economic reward sustained through control of assets that cannot be quickly and widely replicated. John D. Rockefeller's extraction of rents through monopolizing oil assets is the classic case studied in business school, but Zuckerberg's rent extraction from controlling the Facebook accounts of three billion people is far more lucrative. Extractive economies tend to produce great concentrations of wealth, and they tend to corrupt the institutions meant to police them.

Somehow the Technocrats got us to believe that the digital economy is different from the extractive one that America was built on. But that is a lie. The idea expressed in the phrase "data is the new oil" is true. In 1998, in the oil extraction business, ExxonMobil was the largest company in America (by market cap). Today the data-extraction businesses Google, Facebook, and Amazon sit atop the S&P 500, accounting for nearly 14 percent of the market value of the entire index. Even crypto is part of the extractive economy. Mining Bitcoin requires as much electricity per year as powering the Netherlands.[28] And as for Elon Musk, who portrayed himself for years as the spiritual leader of an environmental movement, you will see that much of that is hype. He plans to be the extraction king of outer space. When he gets to Mars, he told Mining.com, "mining robots will be a key part of the planned colonization of the red planet."[29] And as for their being factories of innovation, the Big Tech industries haven't actually come up with a new profitable business in years. Google and Meta are milking the ad business they invented years ago. Even Apple hasn't had a new breakthrough product since it introduced the iPhone fifteen years ago.

But the old businesses are so profitable that today Big Tech dominates the economy in a way that Rockefeller could have hardly imagined. Harvard historian Jill Lepore says of Elon Musk, "He sees himself as above the presidency." The Technocrats have left us with a feeling that "there is no alternative" to the future they are offering us. But history is not a linear progression toward a technological utopia. In fact, as historians like Arnold Toynbee and Edward Gibbon have written, history is a cyclical process of genesis, growth, breakdown, and disintegration. American democracy is in danger of breakdown. Peter Thiel has said, "I no longer believe that freedom and democracy are compatible."[30] The libertarian choice of the Technocrats' freedom over our democracy puts not only our country at risk but also our planet.

The process of growth followed by breakdown mimics natural systems. I've come to realize that the really important scientific breakthroughs of our age revolve not around augmenting humans with technology but around taking the rules by which living systems sustain and replenish themselves and applying them to nonliving systems, including economies and polities. This is what is meant by regenerative economics. It involves moving away from extractive economics and toward systems that restore the Earth rather than destroy it. But it will also mean abandoning our seventy-year reign as global policeman in order to provide the funds needed to rebuild America in a sustainable fashion. One would think that the supposedly environmentally conscious Technocrats would understand this. But they don't. So in the final chapters of the book, I'm going to begin developing a thesis about the regenerative economy as an alternative to the destructive transhumanist economy of the Technocrats.

To understand our present dilemma and begin to answer the question of what we do about it, we need to understand that the libertarian ideology that technology, freed from government regulation, can solve all the world's problems has a more than one-hundred-year history.

PART 1
The Past

1

TECHNOCRACY'S LIBERTARIAN ROOTS

We intend to sing the love of danger, the habit of energy and
fearlessness.

—FILIPPO MARINETTI, FOUNDER OF FUTURISM, 1913

Technological revolutions are not always openly embraced by ruling elites. It is in the transition points between eras that things get dicey—Antonio Gramsci's morbid symptoms. The worst of those symptoms to come out of the early-twentieth-century crisis of democracy was fascism. The Italian dictator Benito Mussolini threw Gramsci into prison in 1926 for his vocal opposition to the Fascist Party of Italy. Given that Gramsci first published the idea of the interregnum in his *Prison Notebooks*, it seems clear that Gramsci was thinking about the wrenching upheavals that began in 1900, led to World War I, and presaged the arrival of fascism in Italy and his own imprisonment.[1] When the old was clearly dying but the new could not get control, a society was open to the clarion call of autocrats who promised social order.

The funeral of Queen Victoria in February 1901 can be seen as a clear marker of the old order dying. As the assembled crowned heads of Europe marched in the funeral procession, they marked the end of the Age of Empire, during which European colonial powers ruled over more than half the world's population. The three emperors, two kings, and assorted archdukes and princes were, of course, unaware that their time was up, but as they walked in the cold London morning, the fires of a technological revolution were burning in laboratories from Geneva to London to Menlo Park, New Jersey. Within a decade, radio, cinema, physics, the automobile, the phonograph, and the airplane would remake the world the monarchs had controlled for centuries. These technologies presaged the death of distance. They extended knowledge and democratized culture. They provided mobility for the average citizen. They ushered in an interregnum.

But Gramsci was right when he wrote that "the new cannot be born"—all across Europe, the resistance to modernity was fighting hard. Governments tried to control technologies like the radio (the three first radio networks in Europe—BBC in England, URI in Italy, and Radio France—were all government owned), and the arbiters of high culture looked down on the vulgarity of popular music and cinema. As historian Eric Hobsbawm has written, Europe was facing a crisis of the bourgeoisie:

> For the bourgeoisie had believed not only in individualism, respectability and property, but also in progress, reform and a moderate liberalism. In the eternal battle among the upper strata of nineteenth-century societies, between the "parties of movement" or "progress" and the "parties of order," the middle class had unquestionably stood, in the great majority, for movement, though by no means insensitive to order. Yet progress, reform and liberalism were all in crisis.[2]

In Italy in 1908, this crisis took the form of both the rise of nationalism and the beginnings of an avant-garde cultural revolution that left most middle-class Italians mystified. The nationalism was propelled by Italians who were tired of ceding their northern territories to the Austro-Hungarian Empire. For centuries, Italy had been nothing more than a group of small kingdoms, many controlled by Spain or Austria.

Austrian chancellor Franz Metternich noted that the word *Italy* was nothing more than "a geographic expression." Napoleon Bonaparte briefly united the country, but when he was driven into exile, the Austro-Hungarian rule of northern Italy returned. And for the young Italian avant-gardists, the reign of King Victor Emmanuel (1861–1878) and the style of his era were symbolic of a dead culture, one afraid of the future.

Into this interregnum came a brash young artist and poet named Filippo Marinetti. He created a movement called futurism, declaring, "We want no part of it, the past, we the young and strong *Futurists!*" He started the movement with a manifesto, which bristled with the same kind of arrogance John Perry Barlow would bring to his Declaration of Cyber Independence almost a century later.

> We are on the extreme promontory of the centuries! What is the use of looking behind at the moment when we must open the mysterious shutters of the impossible? Time and Space died yesterday. We are already living in the absolute, since we have already created eternal, omnipresent speed...
>
> We want to demolish museums and libraries, fight morality, feminism and all opportunist and utilitarian cowardice...
>
> It is in Italy that we are issuing this manifesto of ruinous and incendiary violence, by which we today are founding Futurism, because we want to deliver Italy from its gangrene of professors, archaeologists, tourist guides and antiquaries.[3]

Certain words recur in this populist manifesto: *invention, modernity, speed, industry, disruption, brash, energetic, combative.* The marriage of innovation, disruption, and violence in Marinetti's work created a template that is familiar to this day. Compare Marinetti's rage against feminism with Peter Thiel's thoughts on women's suffrage. As Thiel wrote, "Since 1920, the vast increase in welfare beneficiaries and the extension of the franchise to women—two constituencies that are notoriously tough for libertarians—have rendered the notion of 'capitalist democracy' into an oxymoron."[4]

As in the prewar era in Italy, today we also find liberalism in crisis; the path Marinetti took to cultural power is therefore instructive. Just as John Perry Barlow started as a radical (Grateful Dead songwriter) and slowly moved to the right politically, so too Marinetti and the early members of the futurist movement, who were initially more identified with anarchism, would in time move to the right, toward fascism.

This early anarchist futurism was an artistic expression of impotent fury and a desire to upend the status quo, not only in the world of art but in the real world. The manifesto illuminates the ease with which Italian futurism merged with fascism. Like Barlow, Marinetti approached technology as an aid to a new kind of art. Futurism glorified war, power, disorder, and devastation as ways of forcing humankind into newness. The manifesto states, "We will glorify war—the world's only hygiene—militarism, patriotism, the destructive gesture of freedom-bringers, beautiful ideas worth dying for, and scorn for woman." As World War I began, Italy saw an opening, a chance to regain its lost territory; its leaders secretly negotiated the Treaty of London in the spring of 1915, joining Britain and France against her old allies Germany and Austro-Hungary. When the final armistice was signed in 1918, however, the Italians realized that the Allies were not going to keep to the Treaty of London. Though the Italians got back most of the Tyrol in the north, some other concessions were abandoned, much to the resentment of many Italians.

Felipe Fernández-Armesto's *Out of Our Minds: A History of What We Think and How We Think It* beautifully depicts this interregnum moment for Italian culture: "Destruction and despair leave citizens stakeless, with no investment in tranquility and no allegiance amid wreckage; so the terrible expenditure of money and mortality bought not peace but political revolutions."[5]

After the war the futurist movement turned political. A thirty-two-year-old Italian army veteran named Benito Mussolini formed a new political group called Fasci Italiani di Combattimento (Italian Combat Squad), known simply as the Fascisti. Their basic idea was *spazio vitale* (vital space), meaning that Italy should control all of the Italian-speaking territories along the Adriatic that had been part of the Roman Empire. This notion appealed to Marinetti, and he joined the Fascisti. By 1921, Mussolini had been elected to the Chamber of Deputies; in 1922, he staged the famous March on Rome with thirty thousand of his Blackshirts, demanding the resignation of the prime minister and the appointment of a Fascist government. King Victor Emmanuel, fearful of the street battles, gave in and appointed Mussolini prime minister. A lesson perhaps relevant for our current age: if you are going to attempt a coup d'état, you'd better succeed. A year later, Adolf Hitler made a similar move (the Beer Hall Putsch), failed, and was sentenced to five years in prison.

Many historians believe that Mussolini used the futurist manifesto to build the philosophical scaffolding of fascism. Certainly the ideas first expressed in the manifesto of 1909 show up by 1919 in the early Fascist manifestos. These ideas include extreme nationalism, glorification of violence, war and imperialism, fetishization of masculinity, blatant misogyny, opposition to parliamentary democracy and socialism, anti-intellectual rhetoric, and the creation of scapegoats. By the time Mussolini became prime minister, he had garnered the support of both the military and the business elite, who were afraid that the large Socialist Party in Italy might follow the recent example of the Russian socialists: seize power and nationalize their businesses. Mussolini was eager to paint his administration as a technocratic ally of Fiat, Olivetti, and the other Italian business powers. He stated, "Fascism should more appropriately be called Corporatism because it is a merger of state and corporate power." The futurist architects were put to work building their vision of *la città nuova*. The popular appeal of fascism in the 1920s was its claim to technocratic excellence—Mussolini "made the trains run on time."

Marinetti became, in essence, a Fascist courtier and was convinced that Mussolini shared his irreverence for the Renaissance past of Italian culture. More importantly, he recognized that the government could be a key source of patronage, especially for the coterie of architects who had allied themselves with futurism. As Professor Gabriel Rubin of Washington University has argued,

> Reconciling the chauvinistic conservatism of Fascism with the blitz-krieg (Futurist) speed of modern industry poses fewer problems than might be expected. Slavoj Zizek, in his examination of Nazi propaganda, explains that in times of huge disruptions to the social order (from agrarian to urban, religious to secular, manual to mech-anized), the populace is highly susceptible to the appeal of both nostalgia and utopia. At first glance those two concepts seem anti-thetical, but both rely on the myth of the supremacy of the nation.[6]

We should keep in mind that this is still a useful formula. It is exactly what Elon Musk and Jeff Bezos are selling: nostalgia (put Captain Kirk on your rocket) and utopia (colonies on Mars).

But another aspect of Marinetti's persona will seem somewhat famil-iar: he was a wild man, often drunk and out of control. Here is his account of his encounter with two bicyclists while driving his new Fiat at sixty miles per hour after a night of drinking.[7]

> The words were scarcely out of my mouth when I spun my car around with the frenzy of a dog trying to bite its tail, and there, sud-denly, were two cyclists coming toward me, shaking their fists, wob-bling like two equally convincing but nevertheless contradictory arguments. Their stupid dilemma was blocking my way—Damn! Ouch!...I stopped short and to my disgust rolled over into a ditch with my wheels in the air.

Clearly, as Friedrich Nietzsche suggested, revolutions are often spurred on by people with Dionysian personalities. He believed that the emotion, intoxication, disorder, and ecstasy of the Dionysian were necessary to liberate men. Certainly an observer in the early 1920s watching either Hitler's or Mussolini's rallies would have understood that.

Futurism yields two lessons for our present investigation into how technology ultimately allies itself with political power and centralization. Like a young Mark Zuckerberg, Marinetti could have easily chosen "Move Fast and Break Things" as his mantra. But that's simpler to say when you are outside the tent of power. Once the Fascists seized power, Marinetti was much more interested in joining the ruling party (he was elected to the Italian Academy) than in being a disrupter. Once in power the futurists argued that innovation should never be hindered, whether by government, moral objections, or private-sector initiatives. The idea that quickening technological change undermines elites is one of the main lessons to be learned from this history of the early twentieth century. And it clearly applies to our contemporary crisis. When Breitbart News is as accessible as the *New York Times*, the notion of elite opinion makers is relegated to the trash bin of history.

The second lesson is that culture leads politics. The futurists started their movement before World War I, and early statements of futurism were made through painting and music. (Hitler also started out as an artist.) It's easy to express ideas like the glorification of violence in a futurist painting in 1911, when you are a poor and unrecognized artist. Only later do those ideas migrate into the larger culture. As an avant-garde artist, Marinetti could get away with such statements as "Speaking personally, I much prefer the anarchist's bomb to the cringing attitude of the bourgeois." Once he became part of the mainstream Fascist culture, he was much more careful with his rhetoric.

As Nicholas Goodrick-Clarke's *The Occult Roots of Nazism* demonstrates, the intellectual roots of Nazism were not conceived of by Hitler;

rather, they can be traced back to a number of influential occult and millenarian sects that arose in the Habsburg Empire during its waning years.[8] This same obsession with the dark side of the occult lurks in the hearts of Peter Thiel and Elon Musk. Take for example Thiel's commentary on *Lord of the Rings*; he's all in with Sauron, the dark lord of Mordor: "Gandalf's the crazy person who wants to start a war ... Mordor is this technological civilization based on reason and science. Outside of Mordor, it's all sort of mystical and environmental and nothing works."

⤳

Herbert Hoover carried the banner of the Technocrats in America. Having served as secretary of commerce in both the Calvin Coolidge and Warren Harding administrations, Hoover believed that new technologies like commercial airlines and radio networks would totally transform American business and life, and to a certain degree, he was right. Historian Jill Lepore has described Hoover's theory as "technological utopianism." Like many before him, Hoover believed that technology and the associated rise in productivity would create a bounty of societal wealth. In the summer of 1928, as he was campaigning for the presidency, Hoover said, "We in America today are nearer to the final triumph over poverty than ever before in the history of any land." But Hoover's technological utopianism did not prove out, and within eighteen months, millions would be standing in breadlines.

The Technocrats like Hoover didn't really realize that there was a growing reaction to modernity, especially in the South. The vanguard of that reaction was the Ku Klux Klan, which had all the rhetoric of fascism but lacked a charismatic leader like Mussolini or Hitler. Perhaps the white robes and masks were not the ideal garb for a populist leader to emerge. Still, the Klan had a powerful piece of propaganda in the film *Birth of a Nation*, directed by D. W. Griffith and premiered at President Woodrow Wilson's White House in the fall of 1918. Much like today's right-wing propaganda about the Proud Boys, Griffith's film depicts the Klan as a group of freedom fighters freeing the southern white man from the tyranny of Lincoln's Emancipation Proclamation—the very document that had brought many Black lawmakers into local and federal legislatures. Wilson, a dyed-in-the-wool segregationist, praised the film, which is now seen as the first American film epic, albeit one that would embarrass scholars for a century. Of course, like most fascist propaganda, *Birth of a Nation* had no connection to reality. Its version of Reconstruction was a complete illusion. Clearly right-wing partisans have been partial to media that carries comforting fantasies for decades.

Herbert Hoover won the presidency in 1928 as voters (and investors) bought into his boosterism. Many went broke a year later in the greatest stock market crash in history. If we believe, like Mark Twain (supposedly) did, that "history doesn't repeat but it rhymes," then we should spend some time looking at the Wall Street "touts" of 1928 and 1929. Are the cyber currency promoters of today singing from the same score? Certainly the overnight crash of a crypto exchange like FTX has parallels with 1929.

The hot technology stocks of the 1920s were radio companies. That radio would become an advertising medium was not a foregone conclusion at the end of World War I, when the US government turned over control of the Guglielmo Marconi radio patents to General Electric, its radio subsidiary RCA, and Westinghouse Electric. For the contemporary multitasking media consumer, images of whole families gathered around a massive radio box must seem odd indeed. Initially, RCA and Westinghouse believed that the function of a radio network was to provide just enough programming to sell the radio sets they manufactured. Westinghouse owned stations WBZ in Boston and KDKA in Pittsburgh, which became the first station to go on the air in America when it broadcast the results of the 1920 presidential election on the night of November 2. In Great Britain, the government had already decided that an independent government corporation would run the new medium of radio, free of advertisements and financed by a small "license fee" levied on the sale of radio sets.

As early as 1922, Commerce Secretary Hoover said, "It was inconceivable that we should allow so great a possibility for service, for news, for entertainment, for education, and for vital commercial purposes, to be drowned in advertising chatter." Hoover felt from the outset that some sort of federal regulation of the airwaves would be necessary, but the business boosterism of the Harding and Coolidge administrations (he served in both), plus a conservative Supreme Court that regularly struck down commercial regulation, frustrated his attempts. By July 1926, Hoover had abandoned his regulation ideas. As Paul Starr points out in his definitive *The Creation of the Media*, "A free-for-all then broke out as more than 200 new stations appeared, while others jumped to new frequencies, changed their hours, or increased their power."[9] The result was radio anarchy: one station's signal impinged on another's, leaving the customer with static and chaos. Outraged citizens who had spent $200 on a radio set complained to Congress. And in 1927, Congress formed the Federal Radio Commission (FRC), not wanting to give Hoover—who was openly planning to run for president—power over the airwaves. The FRC was thought of as a temporary solution, but its successor, the Federal Communications Commission, still regulates broadcasting eighty years later.

Here again the lessons of the past inform our present. Google's Larry Page swore to his early investors that advertising would ruin Google, but the realities of Wall Street finance forced him to abandon his idealistic stance. In the same way, Hoover's belief that radio could be a public service used to educate our nation died in its infancy because Wall Street wanted RCA (the Google of the 1920s) to sell advertising on its radio networks. But radio advertising remained a fairly small business until the entrance of Edward Bernays. Bernays swore he invented the word *propaganda* while working with Walter Lippmann to build support for

America's entrance into World War I, but it was in applying these propaganda lessons to the selling of products that he made his fortune.

In the early 1920s, George Hill, president of American Tobacco, engaged Bernays in a critical campaign: break the taboo on women smoking in public.[10] Bernays, using his connection to his uncle, Sigmund Freud, urged advertisers to look for the strong "motives, which men and women conceal from themselves." After consulting with A. A. Brill, the leading American Freudian analyst, Bernays told Hill that women saw cigarettes as a "substitute penis" and that smoking in public would give them power in the "war between the sexes." Hill was skeptical but told Bernays that successfully breaking the taboo would "be like opening a new gold mine right in our front yard." Hill paid Bernays to arrange for a group of debutantes, walking in the Easter Parade on Fifth Avenue in 1929, to pull out cigarettes and light up their "torches of freedom" in front of photographers whom Bernays would alert.

The stunt was tremendously successful, appearing on the front page of the *New York Times* the next morning. As Bernays later said, "Age old customs, I learned, could be broken down by a dramatic appeal [and] disseminated by the network of the media." Hill's next move was to appeal to women's desire for the new slim flapper silhouette with the slogan "Reach for a Lucky instead of a sweet." Bernays's Freudian influence could also be seen in ads for Camel cigarettes, which showed a young man lighting a woman's cigarette over the caption "Pleasure Ahead."

The very notion that these women marching in the Easter Parade had to hide their cigarettes under their skirts shows you how far we have traveled. But why the sudden surge of interest in the magic of advertising? The revolution in mass production grew out of the new production line systems introduced by Henry Ford in 1912 and adopted by most major auto and appliance manufacturers. Soon the capacity for productive output was potentially exceeding the population's consumption appetite. As Lehman Brothers partner Paul Mazur would write, "Men's appetite for goods must be quickened and increased if their standard of living is to be improved sufficiently to absorb increasing quantities of goods and thereby maintain private competitive enterprise. The American way of life simply cannot afford a state of stagnation."[11] In 1920, in the aftermath of World War I, there had been a deep recession. Many senior executives could remember the panics of 1897 and 1907 and were anxious to find any way to stimulate customer demand.

This same need underlies the pitches Facebook and Google serve up to corporate executives every day. In trying to convince clients that they should build Metaverse ad capabilities, Accenture chief technology officer Paul Daugherty says, "If companies don't act now, they'll find themselves operating in worlds designed by, and for, someone else."[12] American policymakers have always been afraid of any restrictions on advertising because they believe people's need to consume must be constantly fed. Studebaker's chief designer, Brooks Stevens, said in the early 1920s that it was critical to "instill in the buyer the desire to own something a little newer, a little better, a little sooner than is necessary." Thus began the notion of "planned obsolescence."[13]

So Hoover's efforts to make radio ad-free bumped up against the reality of post–World War I capitalism. It's important to remember about Hoover's embrace of "technological utopianism" that there was never any role for the government in this scheme other than to regulate which station got which frequency to operate on. In a way Hoover came to embrace an early form of libertarianism: the market ruled. This set the United States apart from much of the world in terms of communications regulation policy. And ever since, the libertarian imperative has ruled US communications regulation for a century.

⤳

The American roots of libertarian thought exist in the 1915–1940 work of Albert Nock, whom many credit with coining the term *libertarian* in its contemporary sense. Nock believed that the pursuit of human ends could be divided into two forms: the productive or economic means and the parasitic, political means. Ayn Rand subsequently adopted this in her "Makers and Takers" dialectic, infamously appropriated by Mitt Romney during the 2012 presidential race. Nock is important to this book in that most leading thinkers of modern conservatism consider him the founder of the libertarian movement. William F. Buckley, Ayn Rand, H. L. Mencken, Murray Rothbard, and Leonard Read all cite Nock as a primary influence.

Like many characters in the history of libertarianism, Nock started on the left. He wrote antiwar editorials for *The Nation* in the run-up to America's involvement in World War I; when the war was over, he published a book, *Myth of a Guilty Nation*, that accused men like Walter Lippmann and Edward Bernays of conspiring to create a public media campaign about the "German menace" that the diplomatic cables of their own government completely contradicted.[14] Lippmann and Bernays worked for the Committee on Public Information, our first government-run propaganda office. Lippmann, in his book *Public Opinion*, had used the phrase "manufacturing consent." Both he and Bernays had a dim view of what they called "the democratic doctrine" and believed the masses could only be educated by reducing complex ideas to slogans and clichés.

From 1920 to 1924, Nock edited his own magazine, *The Freeman*, financed by Helen Swift, the heiress to the Swift meatpacking fortune. Swift had married a dashing English actor named Francis Neilson, a devotee of Henry George; George's 1879 *Progress and Poverty* had become one of the best-selling political treatises in American history. The book, which spawned a movement called Georgism, propounded the belief that people should own the value they produce themselves but that the economic value derived from land should belong equally to all members of society. The solution was a single tax on land rents (in the economic sense of unearned excess profit), which would accrue to the whole society and help mitigate the incredible income inequality that marked the end of the nineteenth century.

Nock and Neilson coedited the magazine, but in 1923 Nock began to pull away from what he considered the "collectivist" bent of the Georgist movement. When Nock resigned, *The Freeman* folded. Nock spent the next few years writing a biography of Thomas Jefferson, then watched in dismay as the United States plunged into the Great Depression.

By the time Franklin Roosevelt was elected, Nock had moved as far right as was possible in mid-1930s America. In 1935, he published *Our Enemy, the State*, which he later described as a plea for "philosophical anarchism." He wrote, "The practical reason for freedom is that freedom seems to be the only condition under which any kind of substantial moral fiber can be developed. Everything else has been tried, world without end. Going dead against reason and experience, we have tried law, compulsion and authoritarianism of various kinds, and the result is nothing to be proud of."[15] He denounced the New Deal (which he called a "coup d'état"), noting that FDR "turns every contingency into a resource for accumulating power in itself, always at the expense of social power." Nock believed that Americans were being conditioned to accept their lost freedom and social power as normal. Any student of modern libertarian thought can hear echoes of his thought. This notion that "freedom" is the only value worth defending lives with us still when we are told that mask mandates rob us of our liberty.

But Nock became increasingly alienated. By 1936, he had given up trying to persuade the general public of the correct course and had begun arguing that libertarians should focus on nurturing what he called "the Remnant," a group of true believers who would emerge after liberalism failed. His publication of the essay "The Jewish Problem in America," which argued that as an Oriental people, Jews will forever be strangers "to Occidental Mass-man," marked the end of his career as a social critic. Nock retired to quietly lead the Remnant, leaving his protégé, Ayn Rand, to be the public face of libertarianism.

Nock was not alone in writing about "the Other." By 1939, aviation hero Charles Lindbergh was leading an American fascist group called

America First, which opposed the country's entrance into the war against Nazi Germany. Writing in the *Reader's Digest* (then America's most popular magazine), Lindbergh argued, "It is time to turn from our quarrels and to build our White ramparts again. This alliance with foreign races means nothing but death to us. It is our turn to guard our heritage from Mongol and Persian and Moor, before we become engulfed in a limitless foreign sea."[16] So we have confronted before fascist ideas like the "great replacement" theory—which Tucker Carlson is always referencing—in the writings of those who gave birth to American libertarian thought.

⸙

While Albert Nock was privately sinking into a well of despondency, Elon Musk's grandfather, Joshua Haldeman, was working to create a vibrant anti-Roosevelt movement in America. He called his movement technocracy. Howard Scott, Haldeman's coleader, set out the principles of technocracy in a speech given during the depths of the Great Depression, saying, "Technocracy is the science of social engineering, the scientific operation of the entire social mechanism to produce and distribute goods and services to the entire population of this continent."[17]

Haldeman is a fascinating character, and given that certain traits pass down through the generations, you would have to conclude that young Elon Musk got a lot from his grandfather. To begin with, they bear a striking resemblance. But Haldeman also suffered from the same attention deficit disorder that seems to plague Musk (who has been quite open about some of the symptoms of his Asperger's). Although Haldeman was born in Minnesota, his family moved to Saskatchewan, Canada, in 1906. He seems to have attended six different colleges without ever earning a degree. He eventually trained as a chiropractor at a school in Davenport, Iowa; during the late 1920s, he moved from town to town in Saskatchewan, trying to establish a practice. In early 1929, he moved back to Iowa and bought a farm, but in January 1931 the bank that had loaned him money for his farming equipment foreclosed, and he lost the property. This set him on the political path that was to change his life. Haldeman believed that financial institutions were inherently corrupt and that the state did nothing to protect the citizen. In May 1931 he joined up with Howard Scott to form Technocracy, Inc.

The basic concept of technocracy was that engineers, not elected politicians, should run society. In essence, it was a dictatorship by engineers—the Technate. At the top of the organization chart was a continental director (the chief engineer of the country), who controlled the armed forces, continental research, social relations, and foreign relations. For all of Haldeman's lack of success up to that point, his managing to convince tens of thousands to join the organization was quite remarkable. Amid the depths of the Depression, some people were desperate enough to willingly surrender to this kind of thinking, and Haldeman and Scott began to have rallies all over the country. The events had a fascist tinge, featuring uniformed men and women and lots of salutes.

Haldeman and Scott then started a magazine, which advanced the idea of a universal basic income, and a radio show, which aired in fifteen cities. But the fervor would not last. The *New York Times* wrote about the movement in June 1932, and critics of its antidemocratic stance formed a growing chorus. In an attempt to quiet the doubters, Technocracy, Inc. paid for a nationwide radio address on January 13, 1933. It was a disaster. Scott sounded confused and defensive, and as Howard Segal wrote in *Technological Utopianism in American Culture*, "The technocrats made a believable case for a kind of technological utopia, but their asking price was too high. The idea of political democracy still represented a stronger ideal than technological elitism. In the end, critics believed that the socially desirable goals that technology made possible could be achieved without the sacrifice of existing institutions and values and without incurring the apocalypse that technocracy predicted."[18] The question of whether we must sacrifice the existing institutions of democracy to accommodate the Technocrats' desires lives with us to this day.

The technocracy movement stumbled on for a few more years, but Hitler's invasion of the Soviet Union caused a huge spilt between Haldeman and Scott. In early 1940, the government of Canada declared Technocracy, Inc. an illegal organization, owing to its sympathetic outreach to the Nazis. Scott's US organization immediately pledged to support the Allies. According to Haldeman's obituary from the Canadian Chiropractic Society,

> Haldeman resigned from Technocracy, Inc. sometime in 1941, when its New York–based central office changed its policies from "unequivocally opposed to Communism, Fascism, Nazism and Socialism" to "complete economic and military collaboration with Soviet Russia" following Hitler's invasion of the USSR. Always a man of strong convictions and principles, Joshua Haldeman could find no justification for any alliance with Stalin's godless dictatorship.[19]

Like Nock, Haldeman eventually gave up on changing society. In 1950, he left for the security of apartheid South Africa, saying, "The political system in Canada had deteriorated with a rapid growth in the power of government to control the lives of individuals." He spent much of the rest of his life searching for the Lost City of the Kalahari Desert. Despite five expeditions, he was unsuccessful. Elon Musk, who was born in South Africa, never forgot his grandfather's legacy. In 2019, Musk tweeted, "Accelerating Starship development to build the Martian Technocracy." If Elon made it to Mars, his colony would be ruled by the engineers.

A few Technocracy, Inc. chapters exist and operate to this day. But the lesson learned from Marinetti, Hoover, Nock, and Haldeman was that technological libertarian philosophy did not transition easily into a mass political movement—especially in the United States during the

Great Depression. Given the choice between freedom (as meant by libertarians) and bread, Americans chose bread.

⤶

Ayn Rand never wanted to lead a political movement. But after she had
toiled for years in obscurity, her objectivist philosophy became the guiding light for an American libertarian movement that is with us to this day.
Ayn Rand, the pen name of Alisa Zinovyevna Rosenbaum, was born in
Saint Petersburg, Russia, on February 2, 1905. When she was twelve, Vladimir Lenin and his Bolshevik cadres took control of the city (renamed
Petrograd), thus beginning the Russian Revolution. The Bolsheviks con-
fiscated her father's pharmacy business, and the family fled to the Crimea
region of Ukraine. Her father failed to establish a new life in Crimea, and
in 1921 they returned to their home city. Rand was one of the first group
of women to enroll in Petrograd State University but was purged before
graduating for making anti-Soviet remarks. A visiting group of foreign
scientists protested the purge, and Rand and her classmates were rein-
stated and allowed to graduate in 1924.

Entranced with the movies, Rand enrolled in the State Technicum for
Screen Arts, writing her first long paper on the actress Pola Negri. The
Technicum was the pinnacle of Soviet film culture at a point when the
techniques of Sergei Eisenstein were being hailed around the world. But
curiously, young Miss Rosenbaum was already looking to Hollywood, as
Elizabeth Blake of Saint Louis University writes.

> Strangely absent from her movie diary are these cinematic classics
> whose innovative techniques (most notably montage) and positive
> portrayal of Revolutionary reality define the Golden Age of Soviet
> film (1924–29). Rand's critical de-construction of montage in her
> early autobiographical novel *We the Living*, her early admiration of
> the star system in *Pola Negri* and *Hollywood: American City of Movies*,

and her focus on Western cinema suggest a conscious rejection of the prevailing film theories on revolutionary content and form that informed the budding industry in both Leningrad and Moscow.[20]

Within a year Rand managed to get a visa to visit relatives in Chicago; four months later, in the fall of 1926, she was on a train to Los Angeles, convinced she could be a screenwriter. Within two weeks of her arrival in Hollywood, she somehow convinced Cecil B. DeMille to cast her as an extra in his production of *The King of Kings*. When the movie was over, DeMille allowed Rand to stay on the lot as an "apprentice screenwriter." All through 1927 Rand worked for DeMille, but he never showed any interest in filming her work. At Christmas in 1927, Rand, like much of the country, became fascinated by a horrific tale. A teenager named William Edward Hickman drove to Mount Vernon Junior High School in Los Angeles and, as school was letting out, kidnapped a pretty young girl named Marion Parker. Hickman knew that Parker's father was a prominent banker in Los Angeles. He demanded ransom of $1,500 (a year's working-class salary in the 1920s), signing the ransom note "The Fox." Parker's father quickly agreed to pay the ransom. Rand began to obsessively follow this story. Much of the appalling narrative was only revealed by a *Pittsburgh Press* reporter who managed to get to Hickman after he was arrested.[21] The day before the exchange, Hickman strangled Parker to death. He told the reporter, "It was while I was fixing the blindfold that the urge to murder came upon me. I just couldn't help myself. I got a towel and stepped up behind Parker. Then, before she could move, I put it around her neck and twisted it tightly. After she was dead I carried her body into the bathroom and undressed her, all but the underwear, and cut a hole in her throat with a pocket knife to let the blood out."

He then arranged her dead body in his car, sewed her eyes open to appear like she was alive, and went to collect the ransom. Keeping the father some distance from the car with a shotgun, he took the $1,500, got back in the car, and kicked Parker's lifeless corpse to the curb. He was caught in Oregon three days later and eventually sentenced to be "hanged until dead." Most people, like the *Los Angeles Times*, thought this was "the murder of the decade."

But not Ayn Rand. When he was caught, an unrepentant Hickman said, "I am like the state: what is good for me is right." Rand wrote in her diary that these words were "the best and strongest expression of a real man's psychology I ever heard."[22] During the trial she wrote, "It is not the crime alone that has raised the fury of public hatred. It is the case of a daring challenge to society…It is the amazing picture of a man with no regard whatever for all that society holds sacred, with a consciousness all his own."

For Rand, the lonely iconoclast who defies the mob is the hero. She would eventually create a fictional version of Hickman in her first popular novel (*The Fountainhead*), but that would take fifteen years to accomplish. In early 1928 Rand began seeing an actor who had also appeared in *The King of Kings*, Frank O'Connor. DeMille immediately dismissed her (was it jealousy?). Determined to stay in the movie business, she went to work in the wardrobe department at RKO. Writing at night, she turned out a screenplay for a spy thriller titled *Red Pawn*, set in the Soviet Union at a gulag for political prisoners on an island in Siberia. In 1929, Rand and O'Connor married.

Like many Rand plots to follow (including her real life), *Red Pawn* involves a love triangle. An American woman, whose husband has been imprisoned by Joseph Stalin, enters the Soviet prison under the pretext that she has been sent by Stalin to be the new wife of the prison warden. She seduces the warden while she works to free her husband, all the while fooling the prison staff. In classic melodramatic style, the woman eventually convinces the warden to escape with her and her husband from the island and Soviet tyranny. Rand sold the script to Universal for $1,500, but the movie was never made; Rand blamed the "Fellow Traveling Reds" in Hollywood for blocking its production.

Rand described herself as a romantic realist, defining the genre as a "category of art based on the recognition of the principle that man possesses the faculty of volition…The method of romantic realism is to make life more beautiful and interesting than it actually is, yet give it all the reality, and even a more convincing reality than that of our everyday existence." But her pursuit of romantic realism did not pay off for many years. The longer she remained in America, the more right-wing her views became. For instance, she thought the genocidal conquest of the Native American tribes by the Europeans was totally justified, as the Native Americans did not conceptualize a private right of land ownership. She justified most American and European imperialism under this same cultural imperative theory.

Her first novel, *We the Living*, another anti-Soviet tract, failed to sell well, and the publisher let it go out of print. Undaunted, Rand tried to mount a New York stage production of the work, but it closed after one week. In 1943, she finally found success with the publication of *The Fountainhead*.

The Fountainhead is the tale of an individualistic architect, Howard Roark. Rand depicts Roark as a superior man, struggling against the suffocating mob. Begun in 1935, at a point when Rand was identifying herself with a small band of anti-Roosevelt partisans like H. L. Mencken and Nock, *The Fountainhead*, along with Rand's later novel, *Atlas Shrugged*, became the key texts of the libertarian movement. The early libertarians formed the core of an intellectual opposition to Roosevelt's New Deal. As Mencken wrote, "I believe that all government is evil, in that all government must necessarily make war upon liberty, and that the democratic form is as bad as any of the other forms."[23] During World War I, Mencken had so admired the German kaiser's authoritarian regime that he submitted an essay to the *Atlantic* titled "After Germany's Conquest of the United States." The *Atlantic* editor returned the essay, saying he was not interested in being tried for treason. In the mid-1920s Mencken and

Nock also endorsed the Liberty League, which was originally an anti-Prohibition movement. But after Roosevelt pushed through the constitutional repeal of Prohibition in 1933, the Liberty League evolved into a right-wing, big-business-funded, anti-Roosevelt group that called FDR's proposed Social Security "the end of democracy." Rand's biographer, Jennifer Burns, while noting that Rand was only peripherally involved, described the Liberty League as "a secretive cabal of wealthy businessmen hoping to wrest control of the government from the masses."[24]

I will not dwell on Rand's literary efforts. Most serious critics dismissed her work, and Rand harbored resentments against the literary establishment her whole life. Typical of the reviews was that of the *New York Times'* Orville Prescott, who called *The Fountainhead* "disastrous," with a plot containing "coils and convolutions" and a "crude cast of characters." But we should not locate Rand's philosophy in her novel. Her ethos truly lies in the numerous aphorisms that populate her political nonfiction. Here are three examples:

> *If any civilization is to survive, it is the morality of altruism that men have to reject.*

> *Achievement of your happiness is the only moral purpose of your life, and that happiness, not pain or mindless self-indulgence, is the proof of your moral integrity, since it is the proof and the result of your loyalty to the achievement of your values.*

> *We are fast approaching the stage of the ultimate inversion: the stage where the government is free to do anything it pleases, while the citizens may act only by permission; which is the stage of the darkest periods of human history, the stage of rule by brute force.*

Over the years, the ideas of Ayn Rand have continued to gain followers in Republican circles. Paul Ryan, during his tenure as Speaker of the House, urged every member of his caucus to read Rand. And in 2017 President Donald Trump called *The Fountainhead* his favorite book, saying, "It relates to business, beauty, life and inner emotions. That book relates to…everything."[25] Many senior Republicans followed Trump in believing Rand to be the major intellectual influence on their politics. As Paul Krugman has written, the Republican elite is "too committed to an Ayn Rand storyline about heroic job creators versus moochers to admit either that trickle-down economics can fail to deliver good jobs, or that sometimes government aid is a crucial lifeline."[26]

But for the hard-core libertarians, it wasn't enough to rail against the moochers. Murray Rothbard, who declared himself an "anarcho-capitalist" in 1950, contended that all services provided by the "monopoly system of the corporate state" could be delivered more economically by the private sector; the state, he wrote, is "the organization of robbery systematized and writ large." Rothbard fought a long battle against the civil rights movement, writing that opposition to Martin Luther King Jr., whom he demeaned as a "coercive integrationist," should be a litmus test for all libertarians.

September 4, 1974, when Alan Greenspan introduced his good friend Ayn Rand to President Gerald Ford, was a sea change moment in the intersection of libertarian politics with the Republican Party elite. As in our current moment, the arrival of inflation had undercut the liberal economic orthodoxy that had ruled America since the Great Depression. Greenspan, who had been part of Rand's inner circle since the early 1950s, saw an opening for her laissez-faire economics to break the hold of Keynesianism. As chairman of Ford's Council of Economic Advisors, Greenspan held great influence with the president. According to the *New York Times* reporting at the time, Greenspan was more loyal to Randian philosophy than to the Republican party line: "In articles for Miss Rand's Objectivist Newsletter, he [Greenspan] had opposed the anti-trust law ('Inhibits businessmen from undertaking what would otherwise be sound productive ventures'); deficit spending ('a scheme for the "hidden"

confiscation of wealth'); consumer protection laws ('It is precisely the
"greed" of the businessman or, more appropriately, his profit-seeking
which is the unexcelled protector of the consumer')."[27]

Ford's meeting with Rand signaled to one and all that the libertarian moment had arrived. Rand's view of taxes as "confiscation" would
become Republican orthodoxy, and an era of deregulation that has now
lasted almost fifty years was initiated. This in turn led to startling gains
in wealth for the top 1 percent. After the crash of 1929, the share of US
wealth held by that echelon had fallen from 46 to 20 percent. With the
beginning of libertarian deregulation, followed by Ronald Reagan's tax
cuts in 1981, the wealth share of the top 1 percent began to climb. Today it
sits at over 40 percent. In October 2008 Alan Greenspan testified to the
House that his libertarian views had been misguided. "Those of us who
have looked to the self-interest of lending institutions to protect shareholders' equity, myself included, are in a state of shocked disbelief," he
told the House Committee on Oversight and Government Reform.

Clearly Greenspan based his free market orthodoxy of neoliberalism on a theory of economic upward mobility and meritocracy. But in a
winner-takes-all society, where the top 1 percent own more wealth than
the bottom 90 percent, these nostrums of the free market are nonsense. As
economists Elena Mitrea, Monika Mühlböck, and Julia Warmuth write,
"The experience of upward mobility has become less common, while the
fear of downward mobility is no longer confined to the lower bound of
the social strata, but pervades the whole society."[28] As we will explore
later, this fear of downward mobility fuels conspiracies like the "great
replacement" or QAnon, which are the precursors of a new fascism. The
downwardly mobile working class has often looked for a scapegoat. In
Germany in 1933 it was the Jews. In America today it is immigrants and
people of color.

For years I have heard a paraphrase of lines from Rand's *The Fountainhead* repeated endlessly at Silicon Valley gatherings: "The question
isn't who is going to let me; it's who is going to stop me." I used to treat it

as a kind of crank obsession, rich men imagining themselves as Howard Roark. After all, when David Koch (another Howard Roark fanboy) ran for vice president on the Libertarian Party ticket in 1980, he received only 1.06 percent of the vote. So I dismissed the political power of the libertarian ideology.

I did not realize that in a period of less than four years, a few true believers in Rand's system (Peter Thiel, Jared Kushner, and President Trump) could take libertarianism from a fringe belief to the core philosophy of the Republican Party. And they did it with the help of the Technocrats. As Marc Andreessen's partner, Ben Horowitz, said, "Libertarianism has got a lot of the false positives that Communism had, in that it's a very simple solution that solves everything." And like communism, the theory doesn't work very well in practice.

When the pandemic hit, I realized that the Republican Party had adopted Rand's philosophy, full stop. In her 1961 book *For the New Intellectual*, Rand wrote, "The man who speaks to you of sacrifice is speaking of slaves and masters. And intends to be the master."[29] A straight line can be drawn from this statement to the mask and vaccine refusal of 2020.

And behind all of this resistance is Facebook. Ethan Zuckerman, director of the Initiative for Digital Infrastructure at the University of Massachusetts, Amherst, recently wrote about this problem in a way that mirrors my thinking:

> Facebook can claim originality in at least one thing. Its combination of scale and irresponsibility has unleashed a set of diverse and fascinating sociopolitical challenges that it will take lawmakers, scholars, and activists at least a generation to fix. If Facebook has learned anything from 17 years of avoiding mediating those conflicts, it's not apparent from the vision for the Metaverse, where the power of human connection is celebrated as uncritically as it was before Macedonian fake-news brokers worked to sway the 2016 election.[30]

What is the legacy of this one hundred years of libertarian thought, which has twisted the very notion of the human condition? T. M. Scanlon, one of the world's preeminent moral philosophers, the Alford Professor of Natural Religion, Moral Philosophy, and Civil Polity at Harvard University until his retirement, wrote a book titled *What We Owe to Each Other*.[31] Scanlon believes that morality comprises being able to justify your conduct to others. Doing right by other people means treating them in ways they cannot "reasonably reject." To the followers of Ayn Rand, this is nonsense. The great irony is that more and more decisions on the internet are being made by algorithms. Clearly moral philosophy is not a subject that artificial intelligence has been able to parse. Algorithms are completely indifferent to the kinds of values that Scanlon discusses. As we move deeper into a world run by machines, we will move further from the values that brought us to this point in human history. We will also move closer to the world the techno-libertarians have envisioned for a century.

2

THE RISE OF THE TECHNOCRATS

Musk thinks Peter is a sociopath, and Peter thinks Musk is a fraud and a braggart.
—An acquaintance of Peter Thiel and Elon Musk[1]

The early pioneers of what we now call Silicon Valley were very different from our Technocrats. Men like Douglas Englebart and Stewart Brand combined a love of computers and a delight in the Acid Tests staged by Ken Kesey with ample supplies of LSD and music from the Grateful Dead. The early personal computer era was an offshoot of the counterculture—as much a break from the IBM suit-and-tie era as Jimi Hendrix was from Elvis Presley. All of this came together in the person of Steve Jobs, who told the *New York Times'* John Markoff that "he still believed that taking LSD was one of the two or three most important things he had done in his life, and he said that because people he knew well had not tried psychedelics, there were things about him they couldn't understand."[2] Steve Jobs became an icon because he truly believed he was inventing tools that would transform people's lives—and maybe even the world. That kind of idealism is far removed from the spirit that animates the four men I'm calling the Technocrats: Peter Thiel, Elon Musk, Marc Andreessen, and Mark Zuckerberg.

Max Chafkin, Peter Thiel's biographer, describes the zeitgeist that now animates Silicon Valley: "To start a company was no longer to help people reach their true potential; it was to flaunt norms, then change them, and, in changing them, set yourself up to get rich off the new order. Facebook would develop a monopoly on social media and use that monopoly to crush competitors, charging progressively higher fees to advertisers—while telling the world that this predatory behavior was a social good."[3]

Today's Technocrats also remind me of the take-no-prisoners corporate raiders I encountered in the mid-1980s as a vice president at Merrill Lynch Investment Banking Media Mergers and Acquisitions Group. I had spent my twenties and thirties producing music with Bob Dylan, The Band, and George Harrison and movies with Martin Scorsese. An act of fate led me to help the Bass Brothers save Walt Disney from a corporate raid, and at their suggestion I went to work at Merrill Lynch in the media merger business. While there for four years, I came across a lot of hard characters, like Ivan Boesky, Mike Milken, and Ron Perlman. Known as "corporate raiders," they were real buccaneers and took no prisoners. I see the same character traits in the Technocrats. Zuckerberg's willingness to crush (or buy out) rival social networks, Musk's flaunting of Securities and Exchange Commission (SEC) rules, Thiel's secret financing of a suit to bankrupt Gawker, and Andreessen's backing of the nonfungible token (NFT) marketplace OpenSea (where over 80 percent of the content is pirated) are just a few examples of the similarities between these two groups. All four of them seem to take the attitude that the ordinary rules of civility, law, and business conduct don't apply to them. Peter Thiel, Elon Musk, Marc Andreessen, and Mark Zuckerberg are obviously men of extraordinary talent and ambition, but like the corporate raiders who ruled the business landscape in the mid-1980s, they operate with no sense of obligation to the collective good. They are the Michael Douglas character in Oliver Stone's *Wall Street*—"greed is good."

The one thing the Technocrats understand that idealists like Jobs failed to grasp was that a global network like the internet is not the democratizing, decentralizing force men like Stewart Brand described. Brand was a true iconoclast. He made the *Whole Earth Catalog*, which was kind of like Google on paper in the late 1960s, with the slogan "access to tools." The catalog was incredibly wide-ranging and allowed the new "homesteaders" of the 1960s to find all the devices that might make life off the grid enjoyable and rewarding. It was all dedicated to the collective good.

In early 2003, as a professor of digital communications at the University of Southern California's Annenberg School, I was invited to attend a scenario-planning workshop hosted by the Global Business Network, a think tank in San Francisco. Stewart Brand and Peter Schwartz, men who literally wrote the book on scenarios, led the workshop. The attendees were a mix of academics, corporate futurists, and "government officials" who would only give you their first name. We were still in the shadow of 9/11, and the scenario task was to look out ten years and see where the United States might fit in this rapidly changing world. This was the scenario matrix presented.

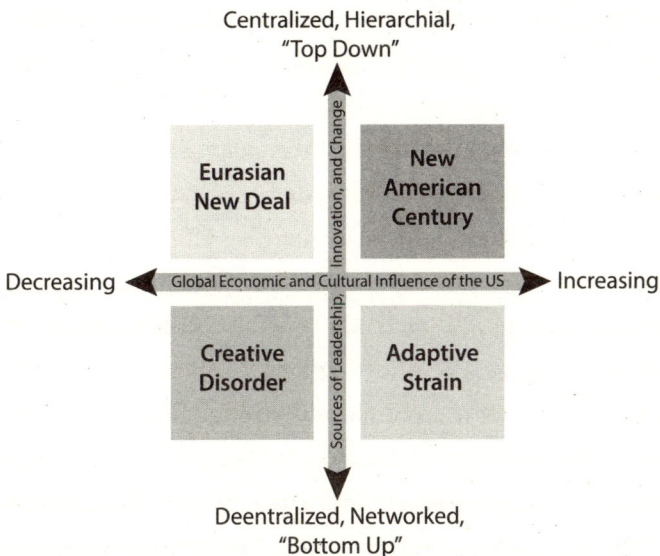

Centralized, Hierarchial,
"Top Down"

Eurasian New Deal	New American Century

Innovation, and Change

Decreasing ← Global Economic and Cultural Influence of the US → Increasing

Sources of Leadership,

Creative Disorder	Adaptive Strain

Deentralized, Networked,
"Bottom Up"

Copyright 2023 Deloitte Development, LLC

Critical for this discussion in *The End of Reality* is our assumption that the opposing forces in "Sources of Leadership, Innovation and Change" (vertical axis) would be "Centralized, Hierarchical, Top-Down" or "Decentralized, Networked, Bottom-Up." Twenty years later, we can see how wrong we were. Our networked world has led to *more* centralization. Seeing Google as a tool to decentralize knowledge, we didn't realize that it would become a monopoly with a 90 percent share of the search business. But the Technocrats understood this long before anyone else. As the brilliant technology analyst Ben Thompson (who writes the *Stratechery* subscription newsletter, read by most tech leaders) has pointed out with his "aggregation theory," "When services compete without the constraints of geography or marginal costs, dominance is achieved by controlling demand, not supply, and winners take most."[4] Facebook, Pay-Pal, and Amazon all benefited greatly from this dynamic because they all share the three qualities Thompson assigns to the aggregator: (1) a direct relationship with users; (2) zero marginal costs for serving users, and (3) demand-driven multisided networks with decreasing acquisition costs.

My whole life in the media rested on the idea that content was king. If you wanted to build a successful media company, you would spend a lot of money making good records or movies, which you would then sell to distributors (record stores or movie theaters), and hopefully the audience would find your content and buy it. Facebook turned the whole idea on its head. It made no content (relying on users to post their cat pictures and favorite news articles), instead spending all its energy and money signing up subscribers. Once it had a billion users, it controlled demand, and a content provider like the *Cleveland Plain Dealer* was helpless. It had to let its content be available to Facebook's billions of subscribers. The winner, Facebook, took most of the advertising revenue.

To understand this shift—and how the Technocrats grasped it before anyone else—it is important to understand the education and early career of each man. The following brief character sketches will help frame and contextualize discussion of the Technocrats' moves in the rest of the book.

I want to start with Peter Thiel, because even though he is not the rich-est of our four Technocrats (with a net worth, according to *Bloomberg*, of "only" $7.2 billion), he is certainly the most influential. While Musk, Andreessen, and Zuckerberg would have called themselves progressives during the Barack Obama campaign of 2008, Thiel has been a hard-core right-wing fighter since the age of sixteen. And today Musk, Andreessen, and (to some extent) Zuckerberg are aligned with Thiel's radical right libertarian philosophy.

More than Zuckerberg, Thiel represents the "move fast and break things" mentality, the idea that nothing should stand in the way of tech-nological progress. And because he currently has such outsized political influence in the Republican Party, he can influence legislation and pol-icy. In 2015 Thiel said, "One of the things I like about technology is that when technology's un-regulated you can change the world without get-ting approval from other people. At its best, it's not subject to democratic control, and not subject to the majority, which I think is often hostile to change."[5] In essence, Peter Thiel does not believe in democracy. He also doesn't like competition. "It's for suckers," he told the *Wall Street Journal*. "If you want to create and capture lasting value, look to build a monopo-ly."[6] Even in the face of the "techlash," the Technocrats have been able to fight off regulation. Senator Amy Klobuchar's American Innovation and Choice Online Act passed through the Judiciary Committee with bipar-tisan support. The bill would prevent the monopoly social networks and commerce sites from favoring their own content over that of third-party providers. And then, as the *New York Times* reported, Big Tech "poured tens of millions of dollars into lobbying against the bill. Groups funded by the companies put ads on the air in swing states, saying the legislation was ill-advised at a time of rampant inflation."[7] The bill has yet to come to the Senate floor, as Majority Leader Charles Schumer (whose children work for Big Tech) doubts it can overcome a filibuster. I don't want to impugn Schumer's motive here, but we need to note that Big Tech's sway with politicians of both parties has increased as these companies have come to dominate the S&P 500 stock market index.

A brief biography of Thiel's rise to power is in order. He was born in Germany in 1967; when he was a year old, his father, Klaus, a chemical engineer, moved the family to Cleveland, Ohio. Before Peter's ninth birthday, the family moved to the town of Swakopmund in Southwest Africa (now Namibia), where Klaus was employed by the most important new uranium-mining operation in a generation. At the time, Southwest Africa was part of the greater South Africa, which was under an apartheid regime. A report from the Namibia Support Committee later described workers "dying like flies" in 1976, while the mine was under construction, due to radiation poisoning.

For most of its history, German immigrants had occupied Swakopmund. Peter was sent to a very strict German school, which required uniforms and doled out a good deal of corporal punishment. He would later tell friends that it was the beginning of his quest for a libertarian philosophy of life. Despite his school experience, he loved South Africa. Even in college he went out of his way to defend apartheid. As his biographer Max Chafkin puts it, "An African-American student, Julie Lythcott-Haims, confronted Thiel about his pro-apartheid stance... Thiel looked at her blankly and, according to Lythcott-Haims's account, told her that South Africa's systematic denial of civil rights to Black people was economically sound. Any moral issues were irrelevant."[8]

Upon returning to the United States in 1977, the family wound up in Foster City, California, a lower-middle-class suburb of San Francisco. These years were a source of pain for the young Peter. He did not play sports and was a constant target of bullies, who teased him for his slightly effeminate manner. In chess, he found a pursuit that he could dominate and spent hours honing his game. He eventually started a school chess club and found a few friends. He graduated high school with honors in math, aced his SATs, and was class valedictorian. He arrived at Stanford

University at the height of the Ronald Reagan era, having read everything Ayn Rand had ever written.

Stanford, of course, was an oasis of conservative thought, with the Hoover Institution dominating the local academic discourse. The book that has subsequently shaped Thiel's political thinking, *The Sovereign Individual* by James Dale Davidson and William Rees-Mogg, depicts the collapse of the nation-state as an exciting possibility for elites, who, freed of regulation, would interact "on terms that echo the relation among the gods in Greek myth."[9] Private militias would protect the oligarchs, as the rest of humanity descended into destitution and random violence.

But Thiel was not content to move into the conservative academic establishment. More a bomb thrower than a consensus builder, he started the *Stanford Review*, modeled after the *Dartmouth Review*, edited by another right-wing agitator, Dinesh D'Souza. From the outset, Thiel's publication set out to destroy Stanford's efforts to introduce diversity and multiculturalism into the curriculum.

Like the other three men in this story, Thiel is a mass of contradictions, among the strangest being the *Stanford Review*'s outrageous homophobia. One of Thiel's editors went so far as to suggest that the *Review* relabel its antigay bias as "miso-sodomy—to focus on deviant sexual practices." Although Thiel did not admit his homosexuality until 2007, it does seem strange that he and many of his friends on the *Review* staff were both closeted and militantly homophobic. It went so far that Thiel's best friend, Keith Rabois, was taken into custody by campus police for standing outside the dorm residence of one of his instructors and shouting over and over, "Faggot! Faggot! Hope you die of AIDS."[10] Rabois, like Thiel, was a closeted homosexual and didn't publicly come out until 2018, when he married Jacob Helberg.

Was this homophobia a kind of self-hatred, the behavior of young men afraid to reveal their orientation? Or was it a way to get noticed in the far-right circles that Thiel and Rabois longed to join? Years later, after Gawker Media outed him in 2005, Thiel was unrelenting in his quest for revenge, secretly financing a scheme to bankrupt the online media company. In May 2016, he admitted to the *New York Times* that he had financed Hulk Hogan's invasion-of-privacy suit against Gawker, which resulted in its demise.[11] The backstory was this: in the wake of the 2008 Great Recession, Thiel's hedge fund Clarium Capital suffered significant losses, and many key investors pulled out, reducing the value of Clarium's assets from $7.3 billion to $350 million (two-thirds of which was Thiel's money). Thiel believed that the pulling of so much Arab money from his fund could be traced to the Gawker revelations about his sexuality. His anger and loss of confidence were all tied up in his quest for revenge. One of his traders at Clarium noted, "The way I think about it is he had a terrible crackup. He got wrong-footed, and it was hard to get right." Clearly the combination of making wrong financial bets in the crash of 2008 and the loss of all his Saudi backers broke Thiel's storied self-confidence.[12]

Thiel's desire to win at all costs could also be glimpsed in his first major business triumph, PayPal, the company he founded with Elon Musk. Musk and Thiel started out as rivals for the same online-payments space. Musk's X.com had the backing of Sequoia Capital, one of the premier venture capital firms in Silicon Valley. Thiel's startup, PayPal, had a narrow focus on sending money electronically between users of the PalmPilot, the early handheld computer. Working literally across the hall from each other in Palo Alto, Musk and Thiel realized that a merger was the only rational path to profitability. The dot-com crash of the early 2000s increased the necessity of merging. But Musk had the upper hand: Thiel's company was almost out of money; X.com had lots of cash and the backing of Sequoia. In the merger, Musk ended up with the controlling stake and the CEO job.

But Musk was a somewhat reckless manager. The company, now called X PayPal, was growing fast, partially because of incentives to join but also because anyone could get an account. At a standard bank, I can't open an account in the name of Tom Brady without some proof that I'm

Tom Brady. On X PayPal, that was not an obstacle. Within months the fraud numbers were off the charts. Peter Thiel's original libertarian ideal for PayPal was that it could provide Swiss-like anonymous bank accounts for anyone, all out of sight of Big Government. But the reality was that tax cheats, money launderers, weapons dealers, and international criminals were the ones needing anonymity. Low-level con artists were also big early adopters, especially after eBay became a huge market for PayPal. Users would buy something on auction and send the money via PayPal; then the goods would never show up.

Worse still, the basic idea that Thiel had sold to investors—that people would leave their money in PayPal, which could then earn interest on the float—never materialized. At one point, when they were on the verge of bankruptcy, Musk drove Thiel to a meeting at Sequoia Capital in his brand-new $150,000 McLaren sports car. Showing off the awesome acceleration, Musk crashed into an embankment a half mile from Sequoia. As they pulled themselves out of the totaled car, Musk turned to Thiel and said, "You know, I had read all these stories about people who made money and bought sports cars and crashed them. But I knew it would never happen to me, so I didn't get any insurance."[13] Thiel began to feel that Musk was out of control.

For his part, Musk began to assert his power and suggested they drop the PayPal name in favor of X.com. Many of the staff suggested that this sounded like a porn site; besides, eBay users, now a huge part of the user base, loved the PayPal name. Musk, not sensing a growing rebellion, decided to embark on a honeymoon to Australia with his new wife. Within hours of his departure, most of the staff delivered to the board and to Thiel a letter saying that if Thiel did not replace Musk as CEO, they would walk. Thiel met with Sequoia and agreed to step into the job. Musk loyalists contacted him in Sydney, and he immediately flew back to San Francisco, saying, "This activity is heinous." But it was too late. The board sided with Thiel, and Musk was shown the door.

Thiel immediately set out to rewrite the story of PayPal's founding, basing it on his own libertarian philosophy. He gave a speech in 1999, saying, "PayPal will give citizens worldwide more direct control over their currencies than they ever had before. It will be nearly impossible for corrupt governments to steal wealth from their people through their old means because if they try the people will switch to dollars or Pounds or Yen, in effect dumping the worthless local currency for something more secure." He gives the same speech today to support Bitcoin. He told a crypto conference in November 2021 that Bitcoin's $60,000 price was proof that the "Federal Reserve was in crisis."[14]

Even worse, as far as Musk was concerned, Thiel got Eric Jackson, one of his employees, to write a book titled *The PayPal Wars*. Jackson's book set Thiel's version of the story in stone, portraying Musk as an egomaniacal CEO bent on destroying the company. In response, Musk wrote a two-thousand-word blog post on Gawker's *Valley-wag*. He called Jackson "a sycophantic jackass, one notch above an intern," then added, "Since Eric worships Peter, the outcome was obvious—Peter sounds like Mel Gibson in *Braveheart* and my role is somewhere between negligible and a bad seed."[15]

But even if Thiel won the PR wars, one action he took ultimately made Musk much richer than him. Thiel introduced the concept of "blitzscaling," which essentially meant that PayPal would spend all its available cash to take over the online-payments market and crush its competitors. Once PayPal achieved dominance, the company could raise prices, which is exactly what it did to eBay sellers after PayPal put eBay's own payment processor, Billpoint, out of business. Once eBay realized how much of each transaction PayPal was taking, eBay basically had no choice but to buy PayPal.

The transaction for $1.5 billion in eBay stock closed in October 2002. Musk received $175 million for his controlling stake in PayPal and moved immediately to Los Angeles to start a rocket company. Thiel divided his

$55 million between his hedge fund (Clarium) and a new venture fund called Founders Fund. In a move that tax accountants marvel at to this day, Thiel had put founders shares of PayPal (valued at pennies per share) into a Roth IRA. When the company was sold to eBay those shares were worth millions. As ProPublica reported, "Using stock deals unavailable to most people, Thiel has taken a retirement account worth less than $2,000 in 1999 and spun it into a $5 billion windfall." Subsequently, he made many of his investments (including in Facebook) from that tax-free vehicle. All of this, of course, was legal but hardly the intent of a law that was meant for middle-class wealth preservation.[16]

In the midst of the post-9/11 fear of terror attacks, Thiel saw a market opportunity to build a company that used advanced data analytics to find terrorists. It would require access to phone, internet, and social media data on all Americans. Thiel figured the CIA's venture capital fund, In-Q-Tel, would be an ideal investor and assumed it could get him access to CIA data. Even though all the other Silicon Valley venture firms refused, In-Q-Tel invested $2 million. Thiel named the company Palantir after the "seeing stones" in *Lord of the Rings,* which could tell the future. The company flourished during the George W. Bush administration, but under Obama, due to a certain skepticism about the cost-benefit of Palantir's technology, some projects were cancelled. Thiel turned on Obama and began his foray as a major funder of Republican candidates. At one point, convinced that the Obama administration was going to look closely at his use of the Roth IRA to shield his capital gains, he contemplated leaving the country. He convinced the government of New Zealand to give him a passport. Although he bought a home in New Zealand and made one investment there, he has not been seen in the country for ten years. Of course, the Obama administration never followed through with the investigation of the misuse of Roth IRAs, so Thiel never had to flee America. Thiel has also recently applied for a Maltese passport.[17]

⌣

Elon Musk is the most complex of our Technocrats. His opening monologue when he hosted *Saturday Night Live* explains some of these
complications:

> I'm actually making history tonight as the first person with Asperg-
> er's to host *SNL*... So, I won't make a lot of eye contact with the cast
> tonight. But don't worry, I'm pretty good at running "human" in
> emulation mode... Look, I know I sometimes say or post strange
> things, but that's just how my brain works. To anyone who's been
> offended, I just want to say, I reinvented electric cars, and I'm send-
> ing people to Mars in a rocket ship. Did you think I was also going
> to be a chill, normal dude?[18]

The definitive *Harvard Health Letter* defines some aspects of Asperger's:

> Despite normal and sometimes superior intelligence, people with
> Asperger's have difficulty understanding social conventions and
> reading social cues. As a result, they often seem tactless or rude, and
> making friends can be hard for them... They may be unable to take
> hints, keep secrets, or understand metaphor, irony, and humor...
> They stand too close, talk too loudly, and don't make eye contact.
> They have one-track minds that focus narrowly but intensely, some-
> times producing long-winded lecturing on subjects of interest only
> to themselves.[19]

Anyone who has studied Musk sees most of these traits, though it
must be said he is more transparent than his fellow Technocrats. It could
be that being the richest man in the world has freed Elon Musk to talk
about the autistic spectrum in a way that none of his compatriots feel free
to do. And ironically, Peter Thiel saw Musk's Asperger's as an advantage,

saying, "Many of the more successful entrepreneurs seem to be suffering from a mild form of Asperger's where it's like you're missing the imitation, socialization gene."[20] Thiel sees Asperger's as a secret power: "We need to ask what is it about our society where those of us who do not suffer from Asperger's are at some massive disadvantage because we will be talked out of our interesting, original, creative ideas before they're even fully formed."

Of the Technocrats, Musk is the only one who could be considered an inventor at the level of Thomas Edison or Alexander Graham Bell. But Edison and Bell were inventing to make the lives of the general public better; that has not been Musk's ambition. The electric light or the telephone was a mass-market invention, priced to be available to one and all. By contrast, the Tesla Roadster, priced at $109,000, was specifically aimed at rich liberals interested in virtue-signaling their environmental concerns. Musk understood that market because he lived and worked in Silicon Valley, an area filled with that specific demographic. As for sending people to Mars in a rocket ship, this too is only for the very rich or (more importantly) for the very deep pockets of NASA and the Department of Defense.

That said, Musk is clearly a seminal figure of our age. As you will see, he has taken extraordinary risks, and with his own funds as opposed to OPM (other people's money), a philosophy that his three fellow Technocrats operate by. He did invest early in Tesla and helped reinvent the electric car and make it cool, in the same way that Steve Jobs reinvented the phone. And in space he broke the monopoly of Lockheed-Martin on rocket production, and for that alone he deserves credit.

However, it has become clear to me in researching this book that colonizing Mars is the sort of classic unreachable goal Musk uses to motivate his workforce. The original SpaceX presentation said that the company would first launch the Falcon 1 rocket in November 2003. In March 2006 its first attempt blew up twenty-five seconds after liftoff. The first successful launch didn't come until December 2010. As *New York Times* columnist Farhad Manjoo notes, "Sometimes [Musk's] big talk pans out, but it rarely seems to matter if the promises never come true. After all, not delivering only ramps up the drama, and with Elon Musk, the drama is the point."[21]

There may come a day when Musk designs a "people's electric car," but he seems to be in no rush. Tesla's cheapest Model 3 now sells for $46,990; with needed added features, it's about $55,000. Musk's biographer, Ashlee Vance, notes that for much of Silicon Valley, Musk is a polarizing figure. For the nonbelievers, "Musk is a sci-fi version of P. T. Barnum who has gotten extraordinarily rich by preying on people's fear and self-hatred. Buy a Tesla. Forget about the mess you've made of the planet for a while." Musk's desire to paint himself as the prototype of the progressive CEO took a hit in May 2022, when the S&P took Tesla off its ESG Index (of companies that are socially responsible with respect to environmental, social, and governance issues). The S&P mentioned racial discrimination and poor working conditions at Tesla's factory in Fremont, California, as well as Tesla's treatment of an investigation by the National Highway Traffic Safety Administration after multiple deaths and injuries were linked to the Full Self-Driving System. The highway safety regulator said that of the four hundred crashes attributed to the use of advanced driver assistance, two-thirds happened in a Tesla. In response, Musk, who had been touting Tesla's ESG rating, tweeted, "I am increasingly convinced that corporate ESG is the Devil Incarnate."[22]

Elon Musk grew up in South Africa, and, like Peter Thiel, he was an awkward, introverted kid who was often bullied. He once had to go to the hospital after being thrown down a flight of stairs by a group of classmates. His mother said, "I do think Elon was always a little different, but in a nerdy way. It didn't endear him to his peers." He took refuge in books. And unlike Thiel, he never tried to defend apartheid. In fact, he escaped South Africa at the age of seventeen in 1988, at the height of the apartheid struggle, to avoid conscription into the security forces, which were violently putting down Black efforts for freedom. He arrived in Toronto (his

mother was a Canadian citizen) hoping to live with a relative, but the relative had moved to Minnesota. Musk bummed around Canada, doing odd
jobs, and eventually got accepted at Queens University in Ontario. Two
years later, he transferred to the University of Pennsylvania and graduated in 1995 with a BA in physics and a BS in economics. He was accepted
to the PhD program at Stanford in materials sciences but dropped out
in the first week to start an internet company with his brother. Elon said
that when he and his brother couldn't agree on a business decision, they
would stage a wrestling match in the middle of the office to decide.

The company, Zip2, was an internet city guide for the newspaper
publishing industry, with maps, directions, and yellow pages. Within a
year, Zip2 had deals with both the *New York Times* and the *Chicago Tri-
bune*. One of the newspaper executives Musk negotiated with recalled,
"He slept under his desk and he didn't smell very good. He didn't have
any inherent interest in newspapers. He told me he wanted to do this so
he could make money and then do what he really wanted to do, which
was design spaceships."[23] In a move that would presage his later career
choices, Musk persuaded his board to reject an offer from City Search,
then the dominant site in the category Zip2 was looking to disrupt.

Three years later—and just ten months before the 2000s dot-com
crash—Musk and his brother sold Zip2 to Compaq for $307 million
in cash. Elon walked away with $22 million. With the money from the
sale, Elon plunged into the world of online banking, forming X.com, the
business that became X PayPal. The PayPal experience is instructive for
what Musk learned from it: he was fired from his own company, only to
emerge a few years later with $175 million. The lesson seemed to be that
no matter how badly he behaved, he was a graced individual who would
end up making money regardless. It gave him a license to be careless that
he embraces to this day.

After the sale of PayPal to eBay, *Fortune* wanted to do a story titled
"The PayPal Mafia"—the idea being that the all-male coterie of nerds
surrounding Thiel were now starting all sorts of companies in Silicon

Valley (Yelp and YouTube being the most prominent). Thiel organized a photo shoot in a dark bar, with him playing the Don Corleone role. Musk refused to participate, saying, "Peter's philosophy is pretty odd. It's not normal. He's a contrarian from an investing standpoint and thinks a lot about the singularity."[24] Elon would no longer be part of a team. He was the Lone Ranger of tech.

The Singularity is an important concept in the story of the Technocrats, so I want to pause for a definition of it by British mathematician Irving John Good, one of its inventors. Good surmised that sometime in the mid-twenty-first century, humans would build an "ultraintelligent computer... [T]he first ultraintelligent machine is the last invention that man need ever make, provided that the machine is docile enough to tell us how to keep it under control." We will probe the implications for humanity if the machines are not "docile" later; suffice it to say that if we are slowly turning our decision-making process over to algorithms and machines, we are engaged in the ultimate escape.

But crucially, Musk's exit from PayPal set him on a very different trajectory from that of Thiel, Andreessen, or Zuckerberg, all of whom were firm believers in OPM—other people's money. In 2002, Musk embarked on two of the riskiest ventures in history: the reinvention of the electric car and the complete reimagining of rocket design and manufacture. And he did it with his own money. He had no partners who could throw him out, and he made every major business decision himself. In a best-selling management book, *Built to Last: Successful Habits of Visionary Companies*, Jim Collins and Jerry Porras cite the tactic of setting a "big hairy audacious goal," or BHAG, as a way to drive performance in an organization.[25] Just like Musk used men on Mars as a BHAG for SpaceX, the Tesla goal was fully automated self-driving. In 2016, Musk announced that new Tesla owners would be able to download the self-driving software within six months if they paid extra at the time of purchase. This came as a huge shock to his engineering staff, who knew that the self-driving software was nowhere close to ready for release.

Of course, the software download never arrived, but every year, like clockwork, Musk would announce that self-driving was about to happen. It is still not here. Musk then announced that he was going to build a fully automated Tesla factory that would require no human workers. Musk turned the failure of this ridiculous venture into a semi-heroic story, tweeting that he had slept on the factory floor for six months to drive his team. But as Edward Niedermeyer, author of *Ludicrous: The Unvarnished Story of Tesla Motors*, wrote, "What he left out of his self-aggrandizing was the reality for his employees. His presence brought no real manufacturing expertise to bear, just the overbearing pressure of a boss whose public shaming was punctuated by declarations like 'I can be on my own private island with naked supermodels, drinking mai tais—but I'm not.' "[26]

Setting outrageous goals that will never be met may be a management tactic, but actually listening to employees is not something Musk excels at. Black workers nicknamed Tesla's Fremont factory "The Plantation" due to continued harassment, the menial tasks they were assigned, and racist graffiti on the walls. Female workers who sued over a pervasive culture of groping and sexual harassment received an email from Musk telling them, "It is important to be thick-skinned."

At a certain point, when both Tesla and SpaceX had endured multiple production line failures and Musk was running out of money, he contemplated which company he should save. "I could either pick SpaceX or Tesla or split the money I had left between them," Musk recalled. "That was a tough decision. If I split the money, maybe both of them would die. If I gave the money to just one company, the probability of it surviving was greater, but then it would mean certain death for the other company. I debated that over and over."[27]

In the end, the US government saved Elon Musk, though you wouldn't know it from the libertarian rhetoric he espouses today. In June 2009, the Obama administration announced a $465 million loan to Tesla. This of course was part of the Obama effort to save the American automobile industry, and it pales in comparison to the $10 billion loaned to GM. A year later, NASA and the US Air Force decided to cut their dependence on Russian rockets to lift satellites into orbit, turning instead to SpaceX, and so Musk was able to save both companies.

Through it all, he endured multiple personal setbacks and tragedies. He had married his first wife, Justine Wilson, in 2000 (announcing to her during the traditional first dance at the wedding, "I am the alpha in this relationship"). In the first year of their marriage, while they were on vacation in South Africa, he caught a particularly virulent strain of malaria. When he returned home, Justine convinced him to go to the local hospital. The doctors there misdiagnosed the illness, but fortunately a visiting doctor happened to see Musk's blood work in the lab and sounded the alarm. Heavy-duty antibiotics eventually worked, but by that time Musk had lost forty-five pounds. He took almost six months to recover. His only remark later was "That's my lesson for taking a vacation: vacations will kill you." The visiting doctor told Elon that if he had seen the labs a day later, Musk would have been dead.

Two years later, Elon and Justine's first child, Nevada, suffered sudden infant death syndrome. The child spent three days on life support at Children's Hospital before his parents made the decision to take him off it. A few months later, Justine wrote, "Elon made it clear that he did not want to talk about Nevada's death. I didn't understand this, just as he didn't understand why I grieved openly, which he regarded as 'emotionally manipulative.' "[28]

Musk's ability to endure tragedy and even betrayal by friends like Thiel has turned out to be one of his superpowers. But the ability to maintain a marriage has not. Despite the births of five more kids (twins and triplets, thanks to IVF), the marriage did not survive. Justine, a published novelist, wrote for *Marie Claire* about their split: "He was constantly remarking on the ways he found me lacking. 'I am your wife,' I told him repeatedly, 'not your employee.' 'If you were my employee,' he said just as often, 'I would fire you.' "[29]

Musk's short attention span was reflected in his subsequent romantic relationships. He dated and wed English actress Talulah Riley, but the marriage lasted less than two years. He divorced her in 2012, remarried her in 2013, and divorced her again in 2014. In 2018, he started dating the singer Grimes. They had two children together. The first boy was named "X Æ A-12." The state of California refused to issue a birth certificate, as the name included characters that are not in the English alphabet. Elon finally settled on X as his son's first name. A daughter, born a year later, was named Y. Musk and Grimes split up in late 2021. At one point between girlfriends, Musk told a reporter his life was "10 percent playboy, 90 percent engineer." But not even Musk's friends were protected from Elon's priapic playboy persona. The *Wall Street Journal* reported in July 2022 that Musk "engaged in a brief affair last fall with the wife of Sergey Brin, prompting the Google co-founder to file for divorce earlier this year and ending the tech billionaires' long friendship, according to people familiar with the matter."[30]

On Twitter, Musk often acted like a hormonal teenager. Asked by Twitter founder Jack Dorsey which of his seventeen thousand tweets ranked as essential Musk, he chose one from 2020: "I put the art in fart." After moving to Texas to avoid California taxes, he said he was going to start the Texas Institute for Technology and Science (TITS). "It will have epic merch," he tweeted.

The problem with this formulation is that the teenager/playboy side often messed things up for the engineer. In the summer of 2022, two allegations appeared in *Business Insider*. The first was that "Musk allegedly exposed himself to a flight attendant, sexually propositioned her, offered to buy her a horse, and later settled her claim against him for a quarter million dollars."[31] The second was that he fathered twins with an executive at his artificial intelligence (AI) start-up, Neuralink. Musk and executive Shivon Zilis filed a court petition in Texas to change the names of the children to include both their surnames. In a classic Musk move, after the news broke online that he had fathered nine children, he tweeted, "Doing my best to help the underpopulation crisis. A collapsing birth rate is the biggest danger civilization faces by far."

But the legal ramifications of Musk's playboy tweets could be serious. Case in point: the infamous Tesla tweet that brought the SEC down on his head. On August 7, 2018, at the opening of the stock market, Musk tweeted, "Am considering taking Tesla private at $420. Funding secured." Tesla stock surged 10 percent in two hours. Most people under fifty understood that "420" was a reference to smoking pot, but from the SEC's point of view, the phrase "funding secured" was highly problematic. A month later, the SEC sued Musk for fraud "by making false public statements with the potential to hurt investors." The complaint continued, "In truth and in fact, Musk had not even discussed, much less confirmed, key deal terms, including price, with any potential funding source." It sought to bar him for life from serving as an executive or director of any public company. Faced with this possibility, Musk quickly settled. Both he and Tesla paid $20 million in fines.[32]

Of course, because he is the world's richest man, the story didn't end there. The female rapper Azealia Banks had been brought to Los Angeles by Musk and put up at his house, ostensibly to make beats for Grimes's new record. This happened on the day of the tweet. Never one to shy away from free publicity, Banks started posting a running commentary on Instagram, including this text from Grimes: "He just got into weed cuz of me and he's super entertained by 420 so when he decided to take the stock private he calculated it was worth 419$ so he rounded up to 420 for a laugh and now the sec is investigating him for fraud."

Musk at first denied ever meeting Banks but eventually admitted to the *New York Times* that she had been staying in his house. Banks later said that Musk took her phone and gave it to his lawyer to "eliminate the evidence." She tweeted, "Staying in Elon musks house has been like a real [life] episode of *Get Out*."

But that was not the end of the matter as private investors mounted a class action suit against Musk, alleging that his "funding secured" Tweet had cost them millions. But on the witness stand at the trial, Musk was defiant. "Just because I tweet something does not mean people believe it or will act accordingly," he declared.

Of course this was only the beginning of Elon Musk's transgressions against Wall Street and the SEC. We will look at the saga of his pursuit of Twitter later. The takeaway here is that the lessons learned early have only amplified Musk's need to risk everything on every deal.

⌐

Marc Andreessen does not like to be touched. As a profile by Tad Friend in the *New Yorker* noted, "He hates being complimented, looked at, or embraced, and has toyed with the idea of wearing a T-shirt that says 'No hugging, no touching.' He doesn't grasp the protocols of social chitchat, and prefers getting a memo to which he can e-mail a response, typing at a hundred and forty words a minute."[33] What should we think about the fact that, like his peers, Andreessen is inventing the social networks of tomorrow without any real social skills? Is that why he is so attracted to the Metaverse? In the Metaverse you never have to worry about some rando coming up and hugging you. You literally can deploy a shield around your avatar to keep strangers ten (virtual) feet away.

Perhaps Andreessen's loveless childhood explains some of this hardness as well. Of his Scandinavian-descended parents, he has said, "They didn't like me, and I didn't like them all that much, either," according to Tad Friend, who writes that Andreessen told him, "'The natural state of human beings is to be subsistence farmers, and that was my expectation,'...adding that his world was 'Scandinavian, hard-core, very self-denying people who go through life never expecting to be happy.'"[34] Now, of course, Andreessen owns the most expensive estate in Malibu, California, and lives a life as far from his hardscrabble upbringing as could be imagined.

Andreessen is famous for having created the first web browser, Mosaic, while working at the National Center for Supercomputing Applications (NCSA) and attending the University of Illinois Urbana-Champaign. But this widespread history is not entirely accurate. By

1991, Tim Berners-Lee's invention of the World Wide Web had spread among the scientific community as a way to share information. Tony Johnson, a physicist at Stanford University, created a web browser called Midas, which he used to display scientific formulas and other graphics. Andreessen downloaded the browser and enthusiastically wrote Johnson, "Superb! Fantastic! Stunning! Impressive as hell!"[35] Andreessen then sent a long list of bugs he had uncovered and suggested that he and Johnson collaborate on an improved version. Johnson wrote back that Midas worked for his needs and that he wanted to get back to physics.

Undeterred, Andreessen forged ahead on his own, finding a partner at NCSA in Eric Bina. Bina, known as the most experienced coder at the center, took up the challenge and created a quick demo in a week. He and Andreessen showed it to their superior at NCSA, Joseph Hardin, who gave them permission to drop their other work and create a working browser. Bina concentrated on the visual display while Andreessen used Berners-Lee's library of programs (he had publicly released them) to give the browser the ability to retrieve documents from any kind of server around the world. By January 1993, the two men had a working prototype of Mosaic; on January 30, they released it to the public.

They were not ready for the response. As Andreessen told the story, "It just spread virally from there, to a thousand, to ten thousand, two hundred thousand, to a million...It was just something else. Like you would open the door and here was the universe."

Andreessen knew he had caught lightning in a bottle. He also knew he could never make any money off it inside a university. So, like the other Technocrats, he moved to Silicon Valley. There he met Jim Clark, who had founded Silicon Graphics, the high-end workstation used to create the special effects in Hollywood films such as *Jurassic Park*. Clark agreed to fund a commercial version of the Mosaic browser but made the mistake of naming his company Mosaic Communications Corporation. Even though Clark and Andreessen were careful not to use Mosaic code, the NCSA immediately sued them; they changed the company's name to Netscape and in

October 1994 released the Netscape browser to the public. For the next two years, it was the default browser for the web, enabling Netscape to go public at a $2.9 billion valuation. Andreessen was now worth $58 million.

But Netscape's days were numbered. Microsoft had released the first version of Internet Explorer within a month of the Netscape IPO. Because Microsoft bundled the browser with Windows and gave it away for free, Netscape didn't have a chance. The antitrust suits were decided in Netscape's favor, but by then it was too late. Clark had sold the remnants of the business to AOL, and although Andreessen briefly served as AOL's chief technology officer, he was already on to his next life as a venture capitalist.

He modeled his firm, Andreessen Horowitz, after Mike Ovitz's Creative Artists Agency, with individual partners having specific sector knowledge and acting as a guide for the companies in which they invested. In a few short years Andreessen Horowitz became the most powerful venture capital firm in Silicon Valley. Its portfolio companies included Airbnb, Facebook, Groupon, Lyft, Pinterest, Robinhood, and Slack, among many others. In the last three years it has been the major investor (outside Meta) in the Web3 ecosystem, including crypto exchanges, NFT platforms, and other Metaverse applications. Its NFT platform, OpenSea, is the dominant platform in that space.

Unlike many venture capitalists, Andreessen believed in the value of publicity. From the start, he made a huge effort to be a kind of public intellectual for Silicon Valley. His first major foray was an essay, published in the *Wall Street Journal*, titled "Why Software Is Eating the World":

> My own theory is that we are in the middle of a dramatic and broad technological and economic shift in which software companies are poised to take over large swathes of the economy...In some industries, particularly those with a heavy real-world component such as oil and gas, the software revolution is primarily an opportunity for incumbents. But in many industries, new software ideas will result

in the rise of new Silicon Valley–style start-ups that invade existing industries with impunity.[36]

Andreessen's public intellectual stance has recently manifested in his posting "required readings" on his Twitter feed. His latest obsession is with the work of 1940s Trotskyite turned anticommunist James Burnham. Burnham's most important book was *The Managerial Revolution*, published in 1941. George Orwell was so surprised by Burnham's intellectual evolution that he wrote a long essay on the book. This passage from Orwell's essay hints at what intrigues Andreessen about Burnham's work.

> Capitalism is disappearing, but Socialism is not replacing it. What is now arising is a new kind of planned, centralized society which will be neither capitalist nor, in any accepted sense of the word, democratic. The rulers of this new society will be the people who effectively control the means of production: that is, business executives, technicians, bureaucrats and soldiers, lumped together by Burnham under the name of "managers." These people will eliminate the old capitalist class, crush the working class, and so organize society that all power and economic privilege remain in their own hands.[37]

The four men I am writing about want this outcome—where "all power and economic privilege remain in their own hands." And as Orwell presciently noted, this society would not be democratic "in any accepted sense of the word." Andreessen, Musk, Thiel, and Zuckerberg's disruptions of our notions of both capitalism and democracy are only going to increase in the coming years.

The core notion that disruption is always good remains at the heart of Andreessen's philosophy. And Twitter has been a big part of his disruption strategy. For a while, he was tweeting about one hundred times a day—an output level akin to that of Musk and Donald Trump. As he said of Twitter, "Reporters are obsessed with it. It's like a tube and I have loudspeakers installed in every reporting cubicle around the world."

Andreessen's Twitter output often took the form of tweet storms, like this one, sent when India blocked Facebook's efforts to give a "walled garden" (Facebook companies only) version of the internet called Free Basics:

> *Denying world's poorest free partial Internet connectivity when today they have none, for ideological reasons, strikes me as morally wrong.*

> *Another in a long line of economically suicidal decisions made by the Indian government against its own citizens.*

> *Anti-colonialism has been economically catastrophic for the Indian people for decades. Why stop now?*

Zuckerberg, very irritated with his board member's tweets, asked Andreessen to apologize. Andreessen signed off on the matter on Twitter, saying, "I now withdraw from all future discussions of Indian economics and politics, and leave them to people with more knowledge and experience!"

Although Andreessen supported Obama in 2008, he began to listen to Thiel's complaints about government regulation during the long hours they spent together in Facebook board meetings. By 2012, Andreessen publicly backed Mitt Romney against Obama. During the Trump administration, Andreessen took to liking the tweets of some of the most hard-core white nationalists, figures such as Milo Yiannopoulos, Tucker Carlson, and Mike Cernovich.[38]

Andreessen also watched his friends Musk and Thiel profiting from government defense contracts, and so in 2017 he began investing in what might be called the digital defense complex. He wrote in 2018,

> I believe we are now seeing the creation of a new generation of Silicon Valley–style defense vendors that can move faster and smarter,

and specialize in applying the leading edge of modern technology in original ways. We at Andreessen Horowitz have already been proudly funding companies in this space, such as Shield AI, an AI company co-founded by a former Navy SEAL, which today makes artificially intelligent, autonomous drones that see, reason about, search, and clear spaces to protect military service members in the field.[39]

Shield AI's pilotless drones, which "clear the battlefield" by swarming the enemy, are perhaps the exact example of the superintelligent machine that may be neither docile nor totally controllable. But the company hypes its expertise with the old scary-enemy pitch that has worked for the legacy military-industrial firms for seventy years: "China's military is Netflix; the U.S. military is Blockbuster. China is Amazon; the U.S. is Barnes & Noble. China is Tesla; the U.S. is General Motors."

Andreessen learned something else from Musk, aside from the fact that the Defense Department will keep investing in boom-or-bust cycles. Musk understood that technology investors needed to be promoters as well. No one today has ever heard of Arthur Rock, the first venture capitalist investor in Apple. But Andreessen knew that being the quiet investor in the background was not going to work in an age of social media and online promotion. As Nicole Perlroth wrote in *Wired*, "The biggest catalyst for the attention-seeking atmosphere, venture capitalists say, has been the rise of Andreessen Horowitz." So if Andreessen is not exactly the leader of the Technocrats, he is a fast follower. He has recently embraced Zuckerberg's ideas about the Metaverse, believing that his investments in crypto and NFTs can best be used in a fantasy virtual universe.

⤛

Mark Zuckerberg is clearly the junior partner of the Technocrats. Kara Swisher, the brilliant internet analyst who now writes for *Vox*, watched the evolution of Zuckerberg over the years: "My impression of Zuckerberg was that he was an intellectual lightweight, and he was very easily swayed by Andreessen or Peter Thiel; he wanted to be seen as smart by them so he adopted the changes they suggested and the libertarian mindset they projected."

Zuckerberg's Machiavellian ability to adapt to the prevailing mores would be the key to his success. He grew up the son of a well-off dentist father and a mother with a good psychiatry practice. They lived in a beautiful house in the New York suburb of Dobbs Ferry, and the family belonged to a Reform Jewish temple. He attended the best private schools, but he was a loner nerd and was given a private computer science tutor at an early age. When just twelve he built a messaging program for his family called Zucknet, and he created an early iteration of a music streaming program while at boarding school. He aspired to an upper-class lifestyle, spending hours in the sport of fencing and eventually rising to the captain of the Exeter fencing team. From the age of twelve on, he was an aggressive striver. But he was also a pragmatist. He did not take sides in political arguments and gravitated always toward proximity to power.

Mark Zuckerberg didn't invent Facebook. He iterated on two previous versions of a Facebook that he had encountered at boarding school and at college. At Exeter, Zuckerberg's classmate Kristopher Tillery built an online student directory with students' names, headshots, phone numbers, and interests. It was called the "Photo Address Book," but students quickly dubbed it "the Facebook." Zuckerberg, jealous of Tillery, used his hacking skills to "break things" for his rival. Whenever students clicked on Zuckerberg's picture, their computers would crash. Tillery realized that Zuckerberg had inserted a line of code into his own profile to cause the bug. He later said of Zuckerberg, "He was very competitive, and very, very, very smart. He wanted to see if he could push what I was doing a little further. I saw it as a test and just him flagging for people that his skills were, well, better than mine."[40]

At Harvard, the same combination of skill and arrogance led to Zuckerberg's second encounter with an existing Facebook. Harvard had always given every freshman a small book known as "the Facebook";

it had pictures and addresses for every student in every dormitory. Three upperclassmen, Cameron and Tyler Winklevoss and Divya Narendra, hired Zuckerberg to create an online version of the Facebook, to be called the Harvard Connection. Within weeks, he was ducking meetings with them while working to create his own version.

Zuckerberg had already enraged much of the Harvard community by creating a website called Face Mash, which matched two pictures of different female students and asked users to vote on who was hotter. The site was so popular, it crashed a Harvard network switch, and the university forced him to shut it down. Two student groups at Harvard, Fuerza Latina, a pan-Latino cultural group, and the Association of Black Harvard Women, led the campaign against Zuckerberg. He quickly wrote them an apology, which went public: "I understood that some parts were still a little sketchy and I wanted some more time to think about whether or not this was really appropriate to release to the Harvard community. This is not how I meant for things to go, and I apologize for any harm done as a result of my neglect to consider how quickly the site would spread and its consequences thereafter." This was a model for many of the nonapology apologies Zuckerberg would issue in the years to come.

When the Winklevoss twins sued Zuckerberg for stealing their Facebook idea, certain of Zuckerberg's text messages came out in discovery. Two offer unique insight into the young man's character:

Zuck: *i have over 4000 emails, pictures, addresses, sns*

Friend: *what!? how'd you manage that one?*

Zuck: *people just submitted it*

Zuck: *i don't know why*

Zuck: *they "trust me"*

Zuck: *dumb fucks*

He was asked how long he could continue to stall the Winklevoss twins:

Friend: *so have you decided what you are going to do about the websites?*

Zuck: *yea i'm going to fuck them*

Zuck: *probably in the year*

Zuck: **ear*[41]

All of this would come out in David Fincher's searing film portrait of the young Zuckerberg, *The Social Network*. Screenwriter Aaron Sorkin said of the film, "It's a group of, in one way or another, socially dysfunctional people who created the world's great social-networking site." When asked by a *New Yorker* writer if the film was an accurate portrait, Zuckerberg said, "I think a lot people will look at that stuff, you know, when I was nineteen, and say, 'Oh, well, he was like that…He must still be like that, right?'"[42]

Right. Zuckerberg was able to leverage one brilliant idea (partially created by others) when he was nineteen, and it was all he needed to build the world's most profitable business. Facebook's gross profit margin is 80 percent. By comparison, Google's is 53 percent, Amazon's is 41 percent, Apple's is 38 percent, and Walmart's is 24 percent. Zuckerberg's secret was in getting his users to produce Facebook's content for free. The internet then distributed the content for free. And the more time users spent on the site, the more they inadvertently revealed about their desires, their politics, and their hatreds. All this became a gold mine for advertisers.

From the beginning, Zuckerberg was astonished by how easy it was to get all this data. His only job was to convert that data to other uses. As he wrote early on, "In a site where people give personal information for one thing, it then takes a lot of work and precaution to use that information for something else." Needless to say, precaution was not something he paid much attention to.

Zuckerberg quit Harvard after his sophomore year and moved to Palo Alto to grow Facebook in the summer of 2004. Within a year, he had fallen under the spell of Peter Thiel and Marc Andreessen. Thiel provided the first significant capital infusion to Facebook; Andreessen also invested, and both he and Thiel joined Facebook's board of directors. Although conservative commentators have painted Zuckerberg as a staunch progressive, the reality is quite different. Although he supports gay marriage and liberal immigration policy, both help his business recruit the best talent. Like Thiel, Musk, and Andreessen, he has adopted a libertarian stance on content moderation, business regulation, and tax cuts.

Thiel and Andreessen would ensure that the libertarian point of view was sacrosanct when Facebook faced one of its biggest political challenges in December 2015. A Facebook content moderator flagged a video that Republican presidential candidate Donald Trump had posted to the site. It was a speech Trump had just given in South Carolina, during which he excoriated President Obama for treating "illegal immigrants better than wounded warriors." Trump went on to say, "Donald J. Trump is calling for a total and complete shutdown of Muslims entering the United States until our country's representatives can figure out what the hell is going on." The content moderator asked his boss whether this violated Facebook's hate speech rules. By the time the question got to Facebook chief operating officer Sheryl Sandberg's desk, the post had generated one hundred thousand likes and been shared fourteen thousand times. Sandberg convened a video call with her team, including Joel Kaplan, a Republican operative whom she had hired as a Washington lobbyist conservatives would trust. Kaplan was conferenced in from India, where he was working to save Zuckerberg's Free Basics scheme. Sandberg indicated that several senior executives were worried about Trump's speech, but Kaplan was adamant that conservatives would see removal of Trump's speech as censorship. "Don't poke the bear," he advised. When Zuckerberg talked to Thiel, Thiel reinforced Kaplan's point of view.

The security team pointed out that Trump had been flagged on numerous occasions by users for violating the hate speech rules, and multiple strikes were grounds for removing the account completely. But Kaplan, a Harvard Law School grad who had clerked for Supreme Court justice Antonin Scalia, came up with a rationalization for how Facebook could let Trump live by different rules than the average user. He argued that Trump could be protected under a "newsworthiness standard"—in other words, that Trump deserved extra protection because the public could make up their own minds based on the unedited posts.

Kaplan and Zuckerberg did not poke the Trump bear, but it was left to the young CEO of Facebook to defend the policy decision in front of an angry group of employees at one of Facebook's regular town hall meetings. When a young Muslim employee asked why Trump's speech targeting Muslims was not hate speech, Zuckerberg fell back on the talking point Peter Thiel had given him. The issue was hard, he said, but he believed in the First Amendment; free expression was at the core of Facebook's mission.[43]

Over the course of Trump's presidency, Kaplan's role as head of global policy at Facebook became even more critical. And he and Peter Thiel suggested that the newsworthiness standard should not be applied just to presidents. In November 2020, Zuckerberg told an all-staff meeting that Steve Bannon had not violated enough policies to be suspended from Facebook—this after the ex-Trump adviser suggested in a video that FBI director Christopher Wray and Dr. Anthony Fauci be beheaded.

In 2012, when Facebook was about to go public, Zuckerberg had written a letter to prospective shareholders.

Facebook was not originally created to be a company. It was built to accomplish a social mission—to make the world more open and connected...People sharing more—even if just with their close friends or families—creates a more open culture and leads to a better understanding of the lives and perspectives of others. We believe that this creates a greater number of stronger relationships between people, and that it helps people get exposed to a greater number of diverse perspectives. By helping people form these connections, we hope to rewire the way people spread and consume information.[44]

It's hard to know, ten years later, if Zuckerberg was naive or cynical (the "dumb fucks"). Certainly Facebook accomplished none of the things this letter suggested it would. In fact, as I will show, the site did more to destabilize the world than any other factor in the last ten years. As Shoshana Zuboff puts it, "Zuckerberg sits at his celestial keyboard, and he can decide day by day, hour by hour, whether people are going to be more angry or less angry, whether publications are going to live or die."

Beyond the critique of Facebook undermining democracy, Facebook really did "rewire the way people spread and consume information"—just not in the way Zuckerberg implied. From the beginning, privacy was an issue for many people in the company, but not for Zuckerberg, who stated in 2010 that privacy "was no longer a social norm." Such attitudes would be tested in 2013 when former National Security Agency (NSA) consultant Edward Snowden revealed that Facebook had given the spy agency a back door into its servers to check on individual users. Snowden told Kara Swisher, "Facebook's internal purpose, whether they state it publicly or not, is to compile perfect records of private lives to the maximum extent of their capability, and then exploit that for their own corporate enrichment." When the information came out, Facebook declared that the government "did not have direct access to its servers." This turned out to be a classic nondenial denial. As Yahoo News reported,

So the government doesn't have "direct access" to Facebook and Google servers, but there is a process in place so the NSA can request the information, and there's a special, secure place for them to retrieve that information. The NSA wants information on person X so they send a request to Google or Facebook. The tech company gathers all the information it has on person X and deposits that information onto the secure server set up for the NSA. Once the information is in place, the NSA accesses the secure server and retrieves the requested information.[45]

As Zuckerberg's collaboration with the national security apparatus indicates, despite their talk of liberty, every one of the Technocrats is clearly anxious to stay in the good graces of whatever administration holds power in the United States. Thiel, Andreessen, and Musk all own businesses that rely on Pentagon, CIA, and NASA funding. And Zuckerberg is equally comfortable dining with either Trump or Obama.[46]

This leaves us with the question of whether Facebook is a net benefit or deficit to society. Ironically, Peter Thiel himself once saw the problem. As he told a class at Yale, "We wanted flying cars, instead we got 140 characters." He was suggesting that the hype of the tech revolution has dissolved into the proliferation of time-wasting apps like Twitter and Facebook. Certainly, looking at a chart of labor productivity forces one to wonder why the supposed post-1990 computer-fueled productivity boom collapsed in 2007—the moment, of course, when Facebook arrived. If productivity was growing at 2.6 percent between 2000 and 2007, why did it fall to 1.3 percent between 2007 and 2015? Could it be that workers are spending more time checking their Facebook Feed than doing their work? Perhaps. A study by Boston IT advisory firm Nucleus Research found that companies that allow users to access Facebook in the workplace lose an average 1.5 percent in total worker productivity. Every manager knows that Facebook and TikTok are huge time sucks, but they are too afraid of their Gen Z workforce to ban them in the office.

If a worship of freedom and disruption is the marker of our four Technocrats, then we need to ask what differentiates these plutocrats from the
robber barons of the 1890s Gilded Age or the corporate raiders of the 1980s.

To begin with, these tech businesses are profitable on a level the
world has never before experienced. Facebook's gross profit margin is
a staggering 80 percent. When I wrote a December 2016 op-ed for the
New York Times suggesting that Facebook and Google were monopolies
(then a controversial statement), readers were shocked to learn that both
were among the top-five largest companies in the world (by market capi-
talization).[47] Out of these extraordinary market caps came extraordinary
personal fortunes. But what Elon Musk and Mark Zuckerberg have that
John D. Rockefeller and J. P. Morgan lacked is a narrative of openness,
disruption, and enchantment. Musk justifies his $250 billion fortune by
tweeting that he is "accumulating resources to help make life multiplan-
etary & extend the light of consciousness to the stars." But as Evgeny
Morozov wrote, all the Technocrats' talk about being open and disruptive
is a smokescreen: "The open agenda is, in many ways, the opposite of
equality and justice. They think anything that helps you to bypass institutions is, by default, empowering or liberating. You might not be able
to pay for health care or your insurance, but if you have an app on your
phone that alerts you to the fact that you need to exercise more, or you
aren't eating healthily enough, they think they are solving the problem."[48]

My research has led me to believe that all four Technocrats have constructed their companies in a way that stymies the ordinary feedback
loops that help leaders course correct. Michael Maccoby, writing in the
Harvard Business Review, notes, "Narcissistic leaders often say that they
want teamwork. What that means in practice is that they want a group
of yes-men."[49] Maccoby cites Zuckerberg and Musk as prime examples
of narcissistic leaders, characterized by grandiosity, a lack of empathy,
poisonous envy, a sense of entitlement, and a tendency to manipulate and
exploit other people. Think of Peter Thiel spending millions to put Gawker
out of business for writing something that was common knowledge in

Silicon Valley (that he was gay). Or consider Andreessen. The *New Yorker's* Tad Friend, in his reporting about Andreessen, heard such observations as "When he feels disrespected, Marc can cut you out of his life like a cancer." The *New York Times* wrote of Elon Musk's leadership, "To a degree unseen in any other mogul, the entrepreneur acts on whim, fancy and the certainty that he is 100 percent right...To operate this way, Mr. Musk has constructed an insular world of about 10 confidants who mostly agree with him and carry out his bidding."[50] In June 2022, SpaceX fired five employees who had written an open letter criticizing Musk's behavior on Twitter as "a frequent source of distraction and embarrassment." In a recent deposition, Musk acknowledged his narcissism when a lawyer asked him, "Do you have some kind of unique ability to identify narcissistic sociopaths?" and he replied, "You mean by looking in the mirror?"[51]

Indeed, Musk has to be the poster boy for social-media-fueled narcissism. On anointing him its 2021 "Person of the Year," *Time* magazine noted that he seemed to be at the center of all that was hot—solar power, electric vehicles, crypto, and AI. But I think he provides another model for his millions of fans and other young business leaders, a model fallen business heroes like Elizabeth Holmes or Adam Neumann have tried, unsuccessfully, to emulate. Musk understands that success in today's fantasy world is a confidence game—"fake it till you make it," essentially. Take his Hyperloop, meant to carry passengers at three hundred miles per hour in pods between major cities. As the *Daily Beast* reported, when Musk unveiled the project, "Instead of a pod rocketing passengers at high speeds, reporters climbed into electric cars made by Musk's Tesla and were treated to a 40 mph ride along a bumpy path."[52] Musk has subsequently dropped all mention of the Hyperloop from his website. As Edward Niedermeyer, author of the definitive book on Tesla, wrote, "His ability to repeatedly sell such science fiction fantasies to a credulous public is the foundation for a vast empire and fortune."

Musk, like the other famous con man of our time, Donald Trump, is an impulsive creature. On December 14, 2021, he tweeted that Tesla would accept a joke crypto currency called Dogecoin as payment. In two hours, the value of Dogecoin rose 40 percent. Musk did not disclose how much Dogecoin he personally owned before or after tweeting, but he has since been sued for $258 billion for engaging "in a crypto pyramid scheme by way of Dogecoin cryptocurrency."[53] Mark Zuckerberg has recently taken up Musk's "fake it till you make it" formula, with Metaverse ads touting heart surgeons' ability to use the Metaverse to train medical students how to operate on the heart. Of course Meta has built none of this technology.

Nassim Nicholas Taleb, author of *The Black Swan*, recently tweeted, "Elon Musk illustrates my #FooledbyRandomness point: solid financial success is largely the result of skills, hard work, and wisdom. But wild success (in the far tail) is more likely to be the result of reckless betting, extreme luck, & the opposite of wisdom: folly."

Such narcissism isn't just confined to the Technocrats. *New York Times* columnist David Brooks, commenting on a *Washington Post* headline, "America Is a Nation of Narcissists, According to Two New Studies," writes, "But there must also be some spiritual or moral problem at the core of this. Over the past several years, and over a wide range of different behaviors, Americans have been acting in fewer pro-social and relational ways and in more antisocial and self-destructive ways. But why?"[54]

I would answer Brooks's question by saying that social media breeds narcissism and antisocial behavior, and the Technocrats have very little interest in democracy. The four projects (Metaverse, Mars, crypto, and transhumanism) that I discuss next are born—ironically—out of a deep cynicism about the future, which all the Technocrats carry with them. Musk (like Amazon's billionaire head, Jeff Bezos) believes humankind will have to abandon Earth in order to preserve it as a kind of Disneyland, a place humans can visit to remember what life was like in an earlier, less polluted time. Thiel promotes transhumanism because he is deeply afraid of death. Zuckerberg needs the shiny new object that is the Metaverse to lure back Gen Z, because he is afraid the *New York Times* is right in noting that Facebook is turning into "a Boomer-dominated sludge pit filled with cute animal videos and hyperpartisan garbage."[55] As for Andrees-sen, his aggressive behavior can be traced back to childhood trauma. His business partner, Ben Horowitz, told the *New Yorker*, "He reminds me of Kanye, that level of emotional intensity—his childhood was so intensely bad, he just won't go there."

An aspect of the struggle for Americans in the twenty-first century is to make the unreflective parts of our minds reflective. To be conscious of our "unconscious bias" has been an important area of growth for many of us. The goal of the Metaverse is to reverse that process of enlightenment—to make the few parts of our known, conscious identity unconscious. Dean Kissick, in the *New York Times Magazine*, described Facebook's new ad for the Metaverse, which shows children at a museum falling into the Henri Rousseau painting *Fight Between a Tiger and a Buffalo*: "It's a scene that suggests Facebook may be returning to Silicon Valley's coun-tercultural origins: a psychedelic dream of a global community sharing in collective hallucinations."[56] After all, if you can design your own rep-resentation (your avatar) and live in a fantasy world playing poker with robots, what is the meaning of identity? The Metaverse, if achieved, will be the ultimate playground for narcissists.

PART II
The Present

3

TECHNOLOGY AND INEQUALITY

The belief that technological progress will lead to the triumph of human capital over financial capital, capable managers over fat cat stockholders, and skill over nepotism is largely illusory.

—THOMAS PIKETTY

How did we get to a point at which billionaire CEOs spend their money on magical thinking while more and more Americans are being pushed by these same men into the Precariat—a world of temporary gig labor with no social safety net?

To answer this question, we must begin with the obvious. As Thomas Piketty, the celebrated historian of inequality, states, "The distribution of wealth is first and foremost about the distribution of power."[1] Another factor is that the very nature of the software business (the core of tech fortunes) is far more profitable than any business that preceded it. Each Ford car costs about the same to manufacture as the one ahead of it on the assembly line. Sure, there are some benefits to scale, but they are minimal when compared to the scale possible with a product like Windows.

When founded in 1975, Microsoft realized that all of the expense stemmed from writing the original code. Once that was finished, the cost of each additional copy of Windows was negligible. In a world of online distribution, it almost disappeared. When Microsoft went public in 1986, Bill Gates became the youngest billionaire in the history of the United States. As the chart shows, the share of US wealth held by the top 1 percent begins to really rise in the 1980s, and despite a small dip in the great recession of 2008, that growth continues to this day. Most of the richest men in this country are in one way or another involved in software, and so the rise of tech has meant the rise of income inequality.

But beyond financial power, the libertarian worldview held by our four billionaires has changed the role of the capitalist in our society. Each of our Technocrats learned from Ayn Rand that "if any civilization is to survive, it is the morality of altruism that men have to reject." And though conservatives often cite Adam Smith as one of the founders of their philosophy, Rand's elevation of selfish desires lies at a great distance from

Share of US Household Wealth

— Bottom 90%   — Top 1%

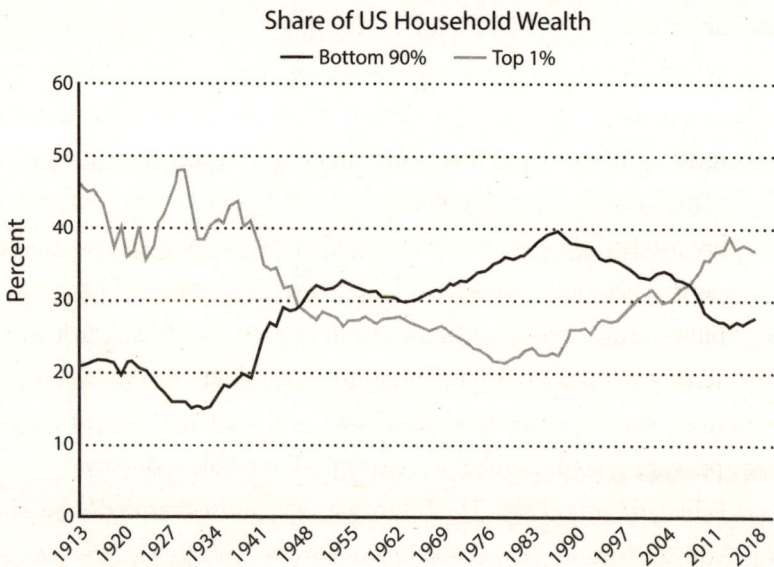

Smith's *The Theory of Moral Sentiments*: "How selfish soever man may be supposed, there are evidently some principles in his nature, which interest him in the fortune of others, and render their happiness necessary to him, though he derives nothing from it except the pleasure of seeing it."

In the golden age of American capitalism (1948–1970), people of vast wealth were taxed at marginal rates as high as 90 percent on income above a certain very high threshold. Even in the earlier age of the robber barons, the wealthiest used philanthropy to try to deal with their society's most pressing problems. To this day, foundations created out of the great fortunes of Henry Ford, John D. Rockefeller, and Andrew Carnegie are working to assuage poverty and health concerns.

But our libertarian plutocrats reject all of that. Someone once said libertarians are like house cats: they believe they are fiercely independent but are completely oblivious of the fact that their entire existence is dependent on a support system they do not perceive or understand. Elon Musk views the whole notion of altruism as a joke, replying to a tweet by Senator Bernie Sanders demanding that "the extremely wealthy pay their share" with "I keep forgetting that you're still alive." When Senator Elizabeth Warren raised the same concerns, featuring Peter Thiel and Musk in a political ad about greedy billionaires, Musk tweeted, "You remind me of when I was a kid and my friend's angry Mom would just randomly yell at everyone for no reason. Please don't call the manager on me, Senator Karen." Thiel simply said that Warren's whole premise was wrong. His taxes were too high.

But as the *New York Times* reported, "When Tesla awarded Elon Musk a multibillion-dollar pay package in 2018, the landmark deal helped to vastly increase the potential compensation of the chief executives at many of America's biggest public companies."[2] Not only is Elon Musk greedy, but his pay package is setting a bad precedent for the whole economy.

In February 2015, Peter Thiel told the *Economist* that the Food and Drug Administration was basically a worthless agency. "You would not be able to invent the polio vaccine today," Thiel said.[3] He has never retracted this opinion, not even after the Covid-19 vaccine was developed in record time. The Technocrats believe that science can solve society's problems if only government will get out of the way. Of the Covid pandemic, Marc Andreessen recently wrote, "Technology helped save the world." He went on to tell economist Noah Smith, "The private sector can and does deliver even under considerable duress, and even when much of our political system is devoted to stifling it with regulatory handcuffs and damaging it with misguided policies." These libertarian views grew out of the theories of Milton Friedman and others and have become known as neoliberalism—which advocates for the privatization of the public sector, the deregulation of the corporate sector, and the lowering of income and corporate taxes. Policies put into place in the 1980s by Ronald Reagan and Margaret Thatcher exemplifying this neoliberal orthodoxy benefited the Big Tech industries more than anyone.

Today every action the Technocrats take is in furtherance of preserving the status quo. That our country seems chaotic and our political class paralyzed is fine with the Technocrats. For them, the pandemic was all upside. In 1996, ten years after Microsoft went public, the top spot on the Forbes 400 list of the richest Americans was held by Bill Gates, with a fortune of $18.5 billion. Today, Elon Musk sits atop the billionaire list with a fortune of $292 billion. As the *Washington Post* reported, the global pandemic has added about $1 trillion to the net worth of America's tech elite, and "one fifth of that haul flowed into the pockets of two men: Jeff Bezos and Elon Musk."

To understand how we arrived in this precarious position, it is necessary to go back to the early 1970s, when Friedman's libertarian economic theories first began to penetrate the Washington policy consensus. The Arab oil embargo of 1973, an act of retaliation against the US decision to resupply the Israeli military, ignited a surge of inflation far worse than that seen in 2022. Friedman had for years been railing against the Keynesian economics embraced by US policymakers of both parties since the Great Depression. Friedman believed that the government had only one role—to control the supply of money—and the free market, unshackled from government regulation, could take care of the rest.

The Democratic administration of Jimmy Carter bought into Friedman's notions of monetarism, appointing Paul Volcker to run the Federal Reserve. Volcker radically cut the money supply, sending interest rates to record highs. Volcker may not have been a Friedman acolyte, but he used Friedman's policy prescriptions. Carter also took the first steps to deregulate the economy by freeing the airline industry from many regulations and encouraging consolidation. The act that deregulated the airlines stated as one of its purposes "the avoidance of unreasonable concentration which would tend to allow one or more air carriers to unreasonably increase prices, reduce services or exclude competition." When the act was passed in 1978, there were forty-three airline companies. Now there are four major carriers. Deregulation did lead to falling prices from 1980 to 2004, but with increased consolidation, fares are beginning to climb again. In September 2022 the US Labor Department reported that according to the Consumer Price Index, airfare was up 43 percent from a year earlier.

Volcker induced a painful recession by raising interest rates to 12 percent but succeeded in stopping the inflationary spiral. By the time Ronald Reagan was elected in 1980, Milton Friedman's philosophy of neoliberalism had been fully embraced both in the United States and in Margaret Thatcher's United Kingdom. Thatcher famously used the acronym TINA (there is no alternative) to advocate for Friedman's philosophy.

At the same time, the growth of global transportation and communication networks made the concept of "offshoring" incredibly popular in the boardrooms of America's largest multinational firms. General Electric's Jack Welch, the alpha CEO of the 1980s, preached that firms should seek to lower costs and increase profits by relocating operations to whichever locale was cheapest. "Ideally," Welch said, "you'd have every plant you own on a barge to move with currencies and changes in the economy." Welch also urged his suppliers to follow the factories abroad, threatening, "Migrate or be out of business."

The effect of these moves on the American working class was cata-strophic. Between 1974 and 1981, average hourly earnings of production personnel fell from $25 to $21. In the same period the share of wealth in the United States owned by the top 0.01 percent rose from 2 to 12 per-cent. In response, French economist Thomas Piketty wrote *Capital in the Twenty-First Century*, a scathing takedown of the whole neoliberal enter-prise.[4] Piketty argued that the central result of neoliberalism was reflected in the simple statement $r > g$, where r is the average return on capital, and g is the economic growth rate. When the return on capital exceeds the growth rate, the money that rich people make from their stock holdings grows rapidly, while wages rise more slowly—if at all. Piketty points out that this is not the story that economists have told since the 1930s. For example, Simon Kuznets, who won the Nobel Prize in Economics in 1971, had written in the 1950s that inequality moderates as countries become more technologically developed and more people are able to take advan-tage of the resulting prospects.

Kuznets's ideas, which represented the consensus of economists at the time, did not hold up in the face of US history. While the rise of offshoring hollowed out the middle class in America, income inequality didn't become too obvious to ignore until the beginning of the Silicon Valley tech boom in the late 1990s. Notably, the growth in the top 1 per-cent of wealth in America differs after 1980 from that of western Europe. While in the United States the share of national income held by the top 1 percent rose from 11 percent (1980) to 32 percent (2021), in Europe the growth over that same period was from 10 to 17 percent.

Why is that? Venture capitalist Steve Jurvetson, who sits on the SpaceX board, thinks he knows: "It just seems so obvious to me [that] technology is accelerating the rich-poor gap. It's the elephant in the room, stomping around, banging off the walls." Stanford University economist Erik Bryn-jolfsson argues that the leaders of the Big Tech firms are benefiting from the sort of winner-take-all effect Sherwin Rosen described in a 1981 paper titled "The Economics of Superstars." Rosen (who was chairman of the

University of Chicago's famed economics department) argued that, just like LeBron James, a business superstar such as Elon Musk can demand a level of compensation that was unheard of even ten years ago. And this stock-option-driven wealth is being accelerated by the kind of hype cycle the young Technocrats know how to stoke.

For the first eight years of Tesla's life as a public company, the stock price hardly grew at all, never rising above $70. Then, in 2018, Elon Musk took to Twitter up to twenty times a day and accumulated eighty million followers, many of whom bought the stock. By November 2021, the stock was at $1,144. He was aided in his efforts by an army of Tesla bot accounts on Twitter, as David Kirsch, a business professor at the University of Maryland, showed: "Over the 10-year study period, of about 1.4 million tweets from the top 400 accounts posting to the 'cashtag' $TSLA, 10% were produced by bots. Of 157,000 tweets posted to the hashtag #TSLA, 23% were from bots."[5]

The irony of Musk promising to get rid of all the bots on Twitter after taking ownership is not lost on the researchers. Promising Twitter users that he would rid the service of the bots he had used for years to pump up Tesla stock was a unique form of hypocrisy. Of course, this is nothing new from Musk, who constantly criticizes the government for how much money it spends and all the regulations it puts on his companies. He never mentions that in recent years Tesla has sold more than $6 billion in government-mandated electric vehicle (EV) credits—funds that represent the difference between a profitable Tesla and a money-losing venture. He sells these credits to other auto companies that need to lower their average fleet gas consumption numbers for regulators. Now, of course, as California has mandated that all autos sold after 2035 be electric, Musk is going to have a lot more competition in the EV field.

↬

In the midst of the Great Depression, British economist John Maynard Keynes advocated for "the euthanasia of the rentier." By *rentier* (or rent taker), he meant the kind of monopoly business that can extract "rent" from consumers and other companies for a commodity it has cornered. In the case of Facebook, this commodity is the supply of social media advertising spots on its various platforms. For Amazon, its monopsonistic position as the monopoly supplier of online book sales allows it to extract rents from publishers for various add-ons like promotion, search listings, and recommendations. As a result its power with the multiple sellers (the publishing companies) has grown over time. The effect of the Covid-19 pandemic was to only increase the power of the online rentiers.

The pandemic also vastly increased the size of the gig economy that Big Tech both invented and powers. As artificial intelligence (AI) algorithms push deeper into every enterprise, a new class of employees is created: the Precariat. Members of the Precariat are freelancers and gig workers with no unions, health insurance, or 401(k)s. The pandemic has pushed more people into the gig economy such that today one in three US workers does gig work.[6] The lucky ones (relatively), working above the application program interface (API), tell computers what to do. They are the web designers and coders.

But a much larger group lives below the API: computers tell them what to do. They are the Amazon warehouse workers and the Uber drivers. In years to come, the AI and the robots it controls will replace the "below the API" workers. Professor Daron Acemoglu of the Massachusetts Institute of Technology (MIT) has suggested that much of the rush to replace workers with robots is an outgrowth of our tax policy. As the *New York Times* noted, "The tax rate on labor, including payroll and federal income tax, is 25 percent. After a series of tax breaks, the current rate on the costs of equipment and software is near zero."[7] And Silicon Valley has constantly pushed for lowering the tax treatment of computers and software. This has also led to a focus on AI and robotics that can replace humans rather than on how these tools can aid humans. I will never forget my friend John Seely Brown (former director of the famed Xerox PARC lab) telling me, after IBM's Deep Blue computer had bested chess master

Gary Kasparov in 1997, that a human with the aid of a computer would always be able to beat a computer in chess. But the idea of computers as our assistants never caught on other than at Apple when it introduced Siri. Google and Amazon soon followed suit, but at the corporate level, the idea is to have the robot or the AI lower employment costs.

But neither libertarians nor liberals want to talk about the new class that automation is creating. This is the deep irony. Liberals, so married to narratives of identity, have given up on notions of class, even as the greatest creation of the app economy is a new underclass: the Precariat. Thiel and Andreessen (the principal funders of Uber, Lyft, Airbnb, and many other gig companies) designed the gig economy to reset the balance of power between capital and labor. Thiel believes that the protections afforded to workers by the New Deal and subsequent Democratic legislation were "among the worst developments in American history."[8] As his biographer Max Chafkin writes, "Airbnb, Lyft, and the rest of Thiel's portfolio provided an ideology to back up the shift. Stripping workers of their rights wasn't about corporate greed; it was the future."

Andreessen argues that "Luddites" have always said technology would put people out of work, and it has never happened. But others argue that the digital revolution is distinctly different from the nineteenth-century Industrial Revolution. While the Industrial Revolution created many jobs for citizens with little or no education, the revolution in automation is having a contrary effect—crushing the unskilled and quickly working its way up into white-collar jobs. Lawyers have case research software that can accomplish in twenty minutes the same amount as four new hires working in a law library for two weeks. By the end of the decade, the job of a radiologist will be to bring the results from the AI scan reader to the patient—hardly a job that will pay $170,000 a year. Reporting on the research of MIT's Acemoglu, the *New York Times* wrote, "Half or more of the increasing gap in wages among American workers over the last 40 years is attributable to the automation of tasks formerly done by human workers, especially men without college degrees."[9]

The four projects I explore in this book are based on the Technocrats'
assumption that many of us will soon have a lot of time on our hands
and can live in a Metaverse fantasy. Or, if we have a lot of money, we
might dream of space tourism or living to age 160. In support of this idea,
Andreessen argues that the reality of everyday life sucks for many Americans, who are stuck in what the anthropologist David Graeber called
"bullshit jobs." Graeber wrote, "Huge swathes of people, in Europe and
North America in particular, spend their entire working lives performing
tasks they secretly believe do not really need to be performed."[10] Graeber
was clearly onto something. Recently Millennials and Gen Z workers have
been discussing "quiet quitting," where you don't actually quit your job;
you just do the minimum to keep from getting fired.

Graeber didn't really have any solutions to the bullshit jobs problem, but he strongly opposed the idea that we can just automate those
jobs without consequences. Some on the left, like British socialist Paul
Mason in *PostCapitalism: A Guide to Our Future*, have envisioned a world
where AI does all the hard work and most of us are free (on universal
basic income) to write poetry or play video games.[11] Ironically, this is also
the Technocrats' dream. But given the history of capitalism in the age
of information, count me as skeptical of this future. Has thirty years of
computer assistance really cut the number of hours the average person
puts in per day? I would even argue that on average white-collar workers
are putting in longer hours (for the same pay) because they are always
reachable on their mobile devices.

Yet, for the Technocrats, if a job can be automated, it should be. This
leads to what Acemoglu calls "so-so technologies": self-checkout kiosks
in grocery stores or automated customer service over the phone. Such
technologies put a lot of people out of work, but they don't really improve
productivity. By contrast, truly meaningful technologies create new jobs
elsewhere, stimulating employment and wages. The Technocrats are able
to embrace these "so-so technologies" because politicians and commentators alike are afraid to challenge their judgment. In the twenty-five

years since Google and Amazon became an important part of our lives, the Big Tech companies have held unchallenged sovereignty over the digital world.

Case in point is Elon Musk's hostile takeover of Twitter. As the *Wall Street Journal* reported, "Before and during Mr. Musk's breakneck takeover of Twitter, a close-knit group of libertarian-leaning activists and businessmen have been encouraging him to get involved."[12] Leading that group was Peter Thiel, who was anxious for Donald Trump to return to Twitter. The takeover was more of a political act than a wise investment move, as Musk's subsequent attempts to back away demonstrated. It's clear in hindsight that Musk massively overpaid when he bid $44 billion for a company whose current market capitalization is $30.9 billion. The idea that he would overpay just for the privilege of letting Donald Trump back on Twitter seems like another late-night pot-fueled idea, the dark reality of which was clear to both Musk and his advisers within days, when tech stocks fell dramatically. Musk then spent months trying to get out of the deal, only to ultimately fail when a Delaware chancery court found that his excuses lacked merit. One banker commented, "This is like watching a train wreck in slow motion." The fact that Musk had to borrow against most of his valuable Tesla stock to buy a social media company that has hardly ever earned a profit tells you a lot about the performative nature of the Technocrats. As Musk vaporized more than $400 billion from the market capitalization of Tesla in his pursuit of Twitter, Dan Ives, analyst at Wedbush Securities, wrote, "There is just a feeling that the pilot on the plane is watching some Netflix show while you're going through a massive thunderstorm."

Musk believed his Twitter acquisition was a blow for freedom, but if he believes that he can run Twitter without any responsibility to the general public, then all the rules of communication regulation will have to be revisited. Having stated that he was a "free speech absolutist," he then had to backpedal in the face of a mass advertiser exodus. Four days before he took over, he wrote that Twitter could not "become a free-for-all hellscape, where anything can be said with no consequences!" The Far Right began testing Musk's free speech absolutism within hours of his takeover of Twitter. The Network Contagion Research Institute reported that the use of the N-word on Twitter increased 500 percent in the twelve hours after Musk's purchase was finalized. A video montage celebrating Adolf Hitler was liked four thousand times, with the poster commenting, "I hear that there have been some changes around here."[13] Soon after, the Anti-Defamation League reported a coordinated campaign of twelve hundred anti-Semitic tweets.[14] And Musk himself contributed to the right-wing trolling, tweeting about the attack on Nancy Pelosi's husband, "There is a tiny possibility there might be more to this story than meets the eye," and linking to a totally discredited right-wing conspiracy site.[15] He later deleted the tweet.

Of course, in the following week, Musk announced that anyone could buy a verified blue check mark for $8 a month. Having been a great Twitter troll himself, he should have known the outcome. On November 10 a tweet appeared on a verified Eli Lilly account: "We are excited to announce insulin is free now." Within minutes, Lilly stock began to fall as traders assumed this benevolent gesture would cost shareholders a great deal. Lilly's communications team desperately tried to get Twitter to take down the Tweet, but Musk had fired most of the content moderation team earlier in the week, so hours went by before any action was taken. Six hours later, after the stock market had closed with Lilly having fallen 4 percent, Twitter finally took down the tweet, but by that time pranksters had created multiple verified Lilly accounts, along with ones for Lockheed Martin, Chiquita, Tesla, and SpaceX.

The mass trolling continued for days. Lockheed announced it was pausing weapons sales to Israel, Saudi Arabia, and the United States for a human rights investigation. Chiquita announced it had overthrown the government of Brazil. One of the thousands of Twitter trolls who were enjoying their new freedom to punk every corporation in America wrote, "There's a nerd who bought this website cuz he was so desperate to be funny and we have a chance to ruin his fucking life. We have a chance to cost him billions but most importantly we have a chance to really hurt his feelings." As with the kids who tried to ruin the short sellers of GameStop, there was the feeling that if you were not one of life's winners, like Musk, you could at least spoil the game for him. What astonished me was that Musk rolled out a verification system that literally only verified whether your credit card was good for the $8 a month.

The net result was that Twitter did turn into a "free-for-all hellscape" of hate and parody. Advertisers did flee, and Musk's financial problems escalated. He borrowed more than $12.7 billion to acquire Twitter, so his additional yearly debt service is more than $1 billion. The banks that loaned Musk that money have conceded they can't sell that debt and "will probably end up incurring huge losses on the financing package."[16] In 2020 Twitter lost $1 billion, so if the advertiser pullback continues, Musk will have to sell more Tesla stock, just to keep his social media toy afloat, because there is little chance that people like Larry Ellison or Marc Andreessen, having already put in $1 billion and $400 million, respectively, will be interested in throwing more money on this dumpster fire. And if Musk doesn't pay the interest on his debt, then the banks will have to file involuntary bankruptcy and take the company away from him. They might get their $13 billion back, but all of Musk and his partners' $32 billion in equity would be wiped out.

Having said in May 2022 that he wasn't buying Twitter to make money, the possibility of losing his fortune has suddenly focused Musk on finding ways to make money on Twitter. Aside from the proposal to charge for the verified check mark, his two most aggressive moves to get money out of Twitter users seem questionable at best. One would be to copy the OnlyFans model by putting up a paywall whereby content creators could charge users to watch videos, with Twitter taking a cut. OnlyFans has shown that the only significant market for this service is porn, so it will be interesting if the owner of X.com (Musk's holding company) becomes the king of online porn. The second scheme involves charging

Twitter users to be able to send direct messages (DMs) to their favorite celebrities on Twitter. I doubt that LeBron James or Kim Kardashian is going to spend hours a day responding to DMs from rando fans.

By the end of his first week of owning Twitter, Musk appeared to be in a panic. After firing half of his employees, he admitted that Twitter was experiencing a "massive drop in [ad] revenue," which he attributed to woke activists pressuring major advertisers. He called the ad pullback an assault on freedom of speech and said he would punish the advertisers. "A thermonuclear name & shame is exactly what will happen if this continues," he tweeted. Musk failed to understand that advertising spending is a zero-sum game. The amount spent per year in the United States is about 1.3 percent of gross domestic product (GDP).[17] One platform's gain (TikTok or the new Netflix ad platform) will be another platform's loss (Meta and Twitter). Musk can go thermonuclear on advertisers, and they will just smile.

If he had kept the strict content management rules in place, he might have been able to lure back the advertisers who had "paused" their ad buys in the wake of the antisemitism and N-word explosion, but his new right-wing fanboys and -girls would have unleashed the hounds of hell on him as a traitor to the cause. Instead, on Thanksgiving Day 2022, Musk announced a general amnesty for all users who had been banned for such offenses as violent threats, harassment, and misinformation. As his rationale he said that in a poll his right-wing fan base had voted to restore all the bad actors. Alejandra Caraballo, clinical instructor at Harvard Law's cyberlaw clinic, said, "What Musk is doing is existentially dangerous for various marginalized communities. It's like opening the gates of hell in terms of the havoc it will cause."[18] Certainly advertisers concerned for "brand safety" will continue to boycott Twitter. And since advertising is 90 percent of Twitter's revenue, it may turn out that Musk's acquisition of the company will be studied for years as the most disastrous business deal of our decade.

⌇

At this point, we have established that technology and inequality are inextricably linked. Which leads us to the question of politics. The legacy of the New Deal was that the government needed to alleviate inequality and provide basic services to the poor and that markets produced social ruin when left to their own devices. The libertarian revolution of the 1980s made these redistribution policies political poison. As 1987 economics Nobel laureate Robert Solow wrote, "If we know one thing, it's that redistributing income is not something we're very good at. And it's not about to happen." Solow believed that permanent growth is achievable only through technological progress. Writing in the 1980s, he thought he could confidently predict that the technological revolution would lift middle-class incomes. Except that turned out not to be true. The only people who benefited from the digital revolution were the stockholders of the Big Tech companies. Although the middle class did benefit from the wider ownership of stocks in retirement accounts, the charts all show a widening gap between the top 1 percent and everyone else.

An honest assessment of how we came to a point where Elon Musk and Jeff Bezos, the two richest men in the world, pay little or no income tax will pinpoint the Republican tax cuts for the wealthy passed by Ronald Reagan, George W. Bush, and Donald Trump. But much of the blame for the neoliberal regulatory climate that allowed the great tech monopolies to form must also be laid at the feet of Democratic presidents Jimmy Carter, Bill Clinton, and Barack Obama. And above all, we have to realize that in their budget priorities, both Republican and Democratic administrations have continued to feed the military-industrial complex, which robs the government of capital that might be used to invest in productivity-boosting infrastructure. All four Technocrats are intent on feeding at the military trough, even though many experts believe military spending is tremendously wasteful. As Col. Andrew Bacevich (US Army, Ret.) has written, "The Pentagon presently spends more in constant dollars than it did at any time during the Cold War—this despite the absence of anything remotely approximating what national security experts like to call a 'peer competitor.' " The United States spends 3.7 percent of its GDP on defense and security ($778 billion); China is estimated to spend about 1.7 percent of its GDP on defense and security (about $196 billion).[19] Elon Musk knows that if he is ever going to get close to Mars, he will need trillions of NASA's money. Although the *Washington Post* has reported on the growth of the private space industry, space tourism is mostly for millionaires to pay for an exclusive ride into orbit with Elon Musk or Jeff Bezos.[20] No one on Wall Street is ready to give SpaceX $10 trillion to go to Mars.

It comes down to this: as the Democratic Party fell in love with the high-tech future promised by Silicon Valley, it forgot about its traditional base: the working class. During Bill Clinton's first presidential campaign, the third-party candidate, Ross Perot (who got 19 percent of the popular vote), ran to Clinton's left on trade; ultimately Clinton won with only 43 percent of the popular vote. Perot's ability to peel off working-class voters angry about "the great sucking sound" of the North American Free Trade Agreement should have been a signal to the Democrats that their traditional base was at risk. But by the 1990s union membership (and thus union campaign financing) was in serious decline. Reagan's firing of all 11,300 union air traffic controllers in August 1981 signaled that the Republican government would actively try to cripple the unions (which had always supported Democrats). So the dominant voices inside the early Clinton cabinet were not those of labor-friendly progressives like Labor Secretary Robert Reich but rather those of the Wall Street wing, led by Treasury Secretary Robert Rubin, and the high-tech wing, led by Vice President Al Gore. Rubin had joined the Clinton administration from his post as cochairman of the investment banking giant Goldman Sachs. After he left the treasury secretary post, he became chairman of the board of Citigroup, the largest bank holding company in America.

Instead of championing the platform Clinton ran on—infrastructure-based fiscal stimulus policy and defense cuts—which would have enhanced Democratic prospects with the working class, Clinton and Rubin sought to appease the bond market vigilantes with an early version of austerity. Rubin's whole focus was on debt reduction instead of infrastructure fiscal stimulus, which would have financed good middle-class jobs. This was the beginning of the break between Democrats and the working class. Clinton decided to forget about the post–Cold War "peace dividend" of reduced defense spending he had promised in his campaign, and Vice President Al Gore pushed technology deregulation to speed the arrival of the "Information Super Highway." In 1993, when Clinton took office, the total federal deficit was $233 billion (3.7 percent of GDP). Rubin had argued that this was unsustainable and that the government would be at the mercy of its creditors. In 2021 the deficit was $2.7 trillion (12.1 percent of GDP).[21] The creditors have not shown up yet. And of course, we are paying for the fact that although Al Gore wanted to make massive investments in renewable energy in 1993, Rubin told him to forget about it. Deficit reduction came first.

For Big Tech, the Clinton era was a gold rush. Their lobbyists were able to insert a "Safe Harbor" liability shield into two Clinton administration bills (the Digital Millennium Copyright Act and the Telecommunications Act of 1996), which stated, "No provider or user of an interactive computer service shall be treated as the publisher or speaker of any information provided by another information content provider." This one sentence destroyed the music and newspaper businesses and allowed Facebook, Twitter, YouTube, and other social networks to create the modern disinformation economy. When the *New York Times* publishes an article, the article goes through fact checkers, who ensure all its claims are true. One reason for this precaution is the fact that anyone can sue the *Times* for defamation. The Safe Harbor legislation protects Facebook from such a fate. The site can publish the most outrageous lies and slander against an individual and never have to worry about being sued.

And beyond that, Safe Harbor relieves sites like YouTube from copyright violations for posting entertainment content without permission.

The disappointments for progressive Democrats in the latter half of the twentieth century were not limited to tech deregulation and defense spending. Reagan had managed to drastically cut the power and financial clout of labor unions, which had been a traditional source of Democratic campaign financing. The Democrats turned to Wall Street and Silicon Valley to finance their campaigns. By the end of the Clinton administration, the total embrace of Wall Street, driven by the party's desperate need for funds to reelect Clinton in 1996, led to the overturning of the Glass-Steagall Act. Signed by Franklin Roosevelt in the wake of the Great Depression, Glass-Steagall had separated commercial from investment banking. The notion that bank depositors' money should not be used for speculative investment was an obvious reaction to the near failure of the US banking system in 1932. The decision to kill Glass-Steagall, driven by Robert Rubin's future employer, Citibank, would come back to haunt the country during the recession of 2008, when Citibank received a grand total of $476.2 billion in cash and guarantees from the federal government to keep the bank solvent. Much as Democrats tried to put the blame for the bank bailout on the George W. Bush administration, it was obvious to many that the failure was rooted in the crony capitalism of the Clinton administration.

That both Rubin and his successor, Larry Summers, were huge supporters of bank deregulation and the repeal of Glass-Steagall aided their post-Clinton careers during the Bush administration. Summers, after a brief and controversial stint as president of Harvard, made $5 million a year advising the D. E. Shaw hedge fund and millions more on the business speaking circuit. Rubin led Citigroup to aggressively expand. But as Nassim Nicholas Taleb wrote, Rubin "collected more than $120 million in compensation from Citibank in the decade preceding the banking crash of 2008. When the bank, literally insolvent, was rescued by the taxpayer, he didn't write any check—he invoked uncertainty as an excuse."[22]

Antitrust policy also reflected the adherence of Democrats (as well as Republicans) to the neoliberal deregulation mantra. Major anticompetitive mergers were approved in media, telecommunications, technology, defense, and consumer products. In 1989, Warner Communications bought Time Inc., Standard Oil of California bought Gulf Oil, and Bristol Meyers bought Squibb. In the 1990s, Lockheed, the country's second-largest defense contractor, merged with Martin Marietta, the country's third-largest defense contractor. Pfizer bought Warner Lambert; Exxon bought Mobil; Citicorp bought Travelers Group. The list goes on and on.

Of course, by 2008, as the benefits of globalization and deregulation flowed to the 1 percent, that same money flowed from the Big Tech corporations and billionaires into Democratic National Committee coffers. So few complained. After the bailouts of the big banks in 2008, Wall Street was no longer a good source for campaign contributions. For Obama to take large contributions from banks that he had just bailed out to the tune of as much as $1 trillion was a bridge too far.[23] Obama turned to Silicon Valley, and Google's Eric Schmidt became the liaison between Big Tech and Obama. But Obama's fascination with the cool gadgets and seemingly progressive politics of the tech billionaires blinded him to the dangers social media posed to our democracy. At Stanford University in May 2022, he admitted this, saying, "What still nags at me is my failure to appreciate at the time just how susceptible we had become to lies and conspiracy theories...One of the biggest reasons for the weakening of democracy is the profound change that's taken place in how we communicate and consume information."[24]

The Great Recession of 2008 caused a rupture in the traditional alignment of US politics, with the pervasive sense that the Democrats had bailed out the ruling class leading to a strange split among their longtime allies. The fact that George W. Bush had initiated the bank bailouts was totally lost to the Tea Party faction that began to make its voice heard in the summer of 2009. In early 2010, the dependably leftist comedian George Carlin began to try out a new routine. It's a rant, but I'm going to quote it at length, because it shows the anger that was in the air—anger that has not disappeared.

> You know what they want? They want obedient workers. Obedient workers. People who are just smart enough to run the machines and do the paperwork, and just dumb enough to passively accept all these increasingly shittier jobs with the lower pay, the longer hours, the reduced benefits, the end of overtime and the vanishing pension that disappears the minute you go to collect it, and now they're coming for your Social Security money. They want your retirement money. They want it back so they can give it to their criminal friends on Wall Street, and you know something? They'll get it. They'll get it all from you, sooner or later, 'cause they own this fucking place. It's a big club, and you ain't in it.[25]

All of these failures—austerity, lack of defense cuts, and lax regulation—would come to haunt the Obama administration. On the defense side, Obama retained Bush defense secretary Robert Gates, thereby signaling to the military that their bloated budgets were secure. Then Obama chose Rubin allies Tim Geithner and Larry Summers to clean up the mess they had created by deregulating the banking industry at the end of the Clinton administration, when Summers was treasury secretary and Geithner was head of the Federal Reserve Bank of New York. Instead of hiring aggressive regulators who would have put Wall Street executives on trial for their extraordinary abuses of the mortgage market, the Democrats sought to sweep the problem under the rug. Writing in the *New York Times*, Gretchen Morgenson points to this issue as a major reason for Hillary Clinton's defeat in 2016: "There are many facets to the populist, anti-establishment anger that swept Donald J. Trump into the White House in Tuesday's election. A crucial element fueling the rage, in my view, was this: Not one high-ranking executive at a major financial firm was held to account for the crisis of 2008."[26]

Trump was able to harness that anger, though in four years he did nothing to really help the working class. He did, however, help the people in the club with a big tax cut. In the end, Trump was Thiel's agent of chaos. As Thiel's friend Michael Anton of the Claremont Institute wrote in an essay for the *Claremont Review of Books*, "2016 is the Flight 93 election: charge the cockpit or you die. You may die anyway. You—or the leader of your party—may make it into the cockpit and not know how to fly or land the plane. There are no guarantees. Except one: if you don't try, death is certain. To compound the metaphor: a Hillary Clinton presidency is Russian Roulette with a semi-auto. With Trump, at least you can spin the cylinder and take your chances."[27] Anton argued, essentially, that the election of a progressive woman to the presidency, especially Hillary Clinton, posed such a dire threat that it was preferable to let Donald Trump fly the ship of state into a mountain.

The presidential campaign of 2016 could have been an opportunity for the Democrats to distance themselves from Wall Street and the military-industrial complex. Obama had shown in two campaigns that it was possible to raise ample funds from small donor contributions; the traditional reliance on corporations and high-net-worth "bundlers" was a 1990s anachronism. Bernie Sanders understood this. But Hillary Clinton was still living in the 1990s. And more importantly, in the years since the end of the Clinton administration, the Clintons had gone from flying coach to taking private jets. Despite the good work the Clinton Foundation did, what Clinton crony Doug Band described as "Clinton Inc." was a reality. Both Hillary and Bill became multimillionaires due to the beneficence of the global corporate elite. This was the stink Hillary could never get rid of.

Of course, other factors were involved. For one, there is fairly good evidence that Trump had used Facebook effectively to suppress the Black vote with ads targeted at Black voters saying that Hillary Clinton called young Black men "super predators." Postelection polling showed a dramatic decline in the Black vote, from the 2012 election rate of 66 percent down to 59 percent in 2016.

In the face of Donald Trump's Facebook-fueled propaganda machine, Clinton could neither convince the white working class she was on their side nor inspire enough of what the Democracy Corps called the new American electorate (minorities, unmarried women, and millennials) to turn out. Ninety-six million eligible voters failed to show up at the polls. No amount of whining about James Comey, Vladimir Putin, or voter suppression could explain Clinton's deep failure in Rust Belt states like Pennsylvania, Michigan, and Wisconsin. These, of course, were the very states that put Joe Biden over the top in 2020.

᷍

When Trump lost in 2020, Peter Thiel doubled down, backing Trump-aligned candidates for the 2022 midterm elections. On the eve of the Russian invasion of Ukraine, J. D. Vance, the Ohio Republican Senate candidate Thiel financed to the tune of $15 million, stated, "I don't really care what happens to Ukraine one way or another." Thiel then convinced Trump and his son, Donald Jr., to endorse Vance and arranged multiple media appearances for Vance with Fox's Tucker Carlson. So the combination of Thiel's money (the most ever spent by a single donor on a candidate) and the public support of both Trump and Carlson was enough to give Vance the victory in the 2022 Republican primary.[28]

The fact that Vance got Trump's endorsement is pretty astonishing, given that Vance tweeted during the 2016 campaign, "I go back and forth between thinking Trump is a cynical asshole like Nixon who wouldn't be that bad or that he's America's Hitler. How's that for discouraging?" But Thiel brought Vance to Mar-a-Lago and made him kiss the ring. He promised his fealty to The Donald, and Trump gave his blessing, telling his followers, "J. D. Vance may have said some not so great things about me in the past, but he gets it now, and I have seen that in spades."

Trump's push was enough to propel Vance to a come-from-behind victory in the May 2022 Republican primary. Thiel also backed his coauthor of *Zero to One*, Blake Masters, for the Arizona Senate race, again with a $15 million donation.[29] Masters is notorious for stating that "one-third of the people outside the Capitol on January 6 were actual FBI agents." He also said in June 2022, "We need fresh and innovative thinking; maybe we should privatize Social Security. Get the government out of it." In a TV ad appearing next to Masters, Trump says, "I endorse Blake because he will protect our border, he stands for life, and he's strong on election fraud."

Having secured Trump's endorsement for his two top Senate candidates, Thiel had a third Senate candidate, Eric Schmitt, former attorney general of Missouri. After the election was over, both Vance and Schmitt had won, but Masters's ultra-MAGA pitch did not win the hearts of Arizona voters.

Thiel also became a major backer of the Rockbridge Network alongside Steve Bannon supporter Rebekah Mercer. In the pantheon of libertarian billionaires, the Mercer family ranks near the top. Robert Mercer and his daughter Rebekah helped finance not just Trump's campaign but also a right-wing media apparatus (Breitbart News, Cambridge Analytica) to support it. As one of Mercer's former partners at his Renaissance hedge fund, Nick Patterson, told the *New Yorker*'s Jane Mayer, "Trump wouldn't be President if not for Bob."[30]

One of Rockbridge's projects, according to the *Washington Post*, is a "lawfare and strategic litigation" fund "to hold bad actors, including the media, accountable." Thiel obviously believes that even the threat of suing another media business (like he did with Gawker) into bankruptcy may be effective. He and Bannon are guiding the Rockbridge strategy.

Elon Musk's takeover of Twitter, which will allow Trump's return to the platform, is only one sign of the growing power of the Technocrats. Their defenders say they are just playing the game by the rules the politicians have made, but their power ensures there will be no significant regulation of their businesses. In turn, income inequality will get worse, and disinformation will proliferate, degrading what's left of our democracy.

Let's project ourselves ten years into the future the Technocrats have in store for us. Let's assume that in the face of massive automation, they convince politicians to fund universal basic income to deal with the robot replacement issue. The Metaverse is filled with thirtysomethings with lots of time on their hands, giving us the problem of boredom. Erich Fromm, the sociologist whose writings, like *The Art of Loving*, were critical texts in the 1950s, said that just "satisfying our material needs leaves us with a feeling of intense boredom…[S]uicide and alcoholism are pathological ways of escape." The economists Anne Case and Angus Deaton have written about the startling rise in "deaths of despair since 2000," which include accidental drug overdoses, suicides, and alcohol-related deaths.[31] A Senate Joint Economic Committee report charts the scale of this increase—a doubling from 22.7 deaths of despair per 100,000 Americans in 2000 to 45.8 per 100,000 in 2017, easily eclipsing all prior records from the twentieth and twenty-first centuries. And a new study from Yale University researchers shows a clear link between these deaths of despair and Big Tech's automation: "The study, published Feb. 23, 2022 in the journal *Demography*, found evidence of a causal link between automation and increasing mortality, driven largely by increased 'deaths of despair,' such as suicides and drug overdoses. This is particularly true for males and females aged 45 to 54, according to the study."[32] At what point in the last twenty years was someone at the Centers for Disease Control and Prevention pounding on a desk, crying, "Opioid use is a national health crisis"? It appears this never happened. In 2021 opioid deaths topped one hundred thousand.

Boredom can lead to other odd behaviors. With live sports shut down by the pandemic, web personalities like Dave Portnoy, founder of the Barstool Sports website, turned their focus from sports betting to betting on stocks. Portnoy's huge online audience of young men followed him, opening "free" accounts on a relatively new online stock-trading app called Robinhood. Designed more like a slot machine, with lots of "rewards" in the form of automated bells and confetti whenever you made a trade, Robinhood took off, surpassing two million users in March 2020. At the same time, Portnoy touted a Reddit forum called Wall Street Bets, whose subscriber numbers rocketed to five million. A multimonth stock rally in the summer of 2020 seems to have been driven by retail traders on platforms like Robinhood, and in January 2021, all of this new demand turned its focus on one stock: GameStop. A retailer of video-games with many locations in strip malls, GameStop was like Blockbuster after Netflix launched—a deer in the headlights. Most video games were being downloaded online, and GameStop's stock had fallen to $2.57, under relentless pressure from short sellers who figured bankruptcy was right around the corner.

The bored twenty-eight-year-olds on Wall Street Bets (which relent-lessly touted GameStop), nostalgic for a company that meant a lot to them when they were fifteen, decided to gang up on the short sellers. There was no economic logic to their bet, but because there were so many borrowed shares on the books of the shorts, it didn't take much for the most incred-ible short squeeze in history to go down. In two days the stock went from $4.60 to $56.25. Five days later it fell back to $11.50. Chris Arnade, author of *Dignity: Seeking Respect in Back Row America*, analyzed the strange spirit that animates this behavior.[33] Here, he looks at how a "bunch of losers" tried to take on the big Wall Street short sellers around GameStop (and ultimately lost):

> Everyone is just playing games. Those at the top (the short sellers) get to dress up their game, even though it is destructive to everyone else, as legitimate, call playing it a career, and get rewarded mightily for it. Others, like them [the Game Stop losers], have to make it a hobby, and even though it is just harmless fun, get scolded for it.
>
> This will harden a cynicism that already exists in large parts of America. A cynicism that will convince more and more people to play all of their life, recklessly. To do what is known in gaming

circles, as Int-ing, or Intentionally dying. Running madly at the boss, unworried if they are going to lose, suffer, or die.

Because if you are not going to be allowed to win a rigged game, you might as well ruin it, and extract just a tiny moment of joy from that.

If the Wall Street Bets users' intention was to punish the shorts, it worked for a while. Then the inherent worthlessness of GameStop became too real, and the game ended. Most of the meme stock players lost their money. But as with buying crypto, the move to punish the Wall Street short sellers was more of a political act than a rational financial bet. If there are any lessons to be learned from this fiasco, they are not apparent to me—but it is perhaps a vision of things to come.

4

FANTASY CULTURE

The People who once upon a time handed out military command, high civil office, legions—everything, now restrains itself and anxiously hopes for just two things: bread and circuses.

—JUVENAL, AD 127

The rise of fantasy culture in America began with science fiction novels. As you will see, all of our Technocrats immersed themselves in science fiction reading during their somewhat awkward childhoods. But the foundational texts from our point of view are George Orwell's *1984* and Aldous Huxley's *Brave New World*. The notable media critic Neil Postman wrote about the difference between the two books:

In *1984*, people are controlled by inflicting pain. In *Brave New World*, they are controlled by inflicting pleasure.

What Orwell feared were those who would ban books. What Huxley feared was that there would be no reason to ban a book, for there would be no one who wanted to read one.

Orwell feared those who would deprive us of information. Huxley feared those who would give us so much that we would be reduced to passivity and egotism.[1]

The rise of social networks has proven that Huxley was right and Orwell was wrong. When I was working for Bob Dylan in the 1960s, the role of much of the pop culture was oppositional to the politics of the time. Musicians sang in support of the civil rights movement, and filmmakers made antiwar movies. Since the golden age of American cinema in the late 1930s and early 1940s, the studios have always made an occasional fantasy film. *The Wizard of Oz* and *King Kong* come to mind from that period. But starting in the late 1970s with *Star Wars* and *Superman*, the fantasy blockbuster began to dominate the movie business. And that success bled over into video games, music, and other forms of pop culture so that the ground was laid for the Metaverse, in which you could become a fantasy film character in your daily life. And as the fantasy/superhero genre came to dominate the movies and video games, pop culture's countercultural role faded away.

In creating his *Brave New World*, Huxley drew upon the ideas of the Roman poet Juvenal, who wrote about the decline of Roman politics in the first century AD. Juvenal believed that the Roman populous could be kept from revolting as long as the ruling class provided them sufficient food and lurid entertainments (lions eating Christians) to keep their minds off the sorry state of their lives. This is the role of contemporary fantasy culture, whether in movies, TV, music, video games, or gambling. And of course, with the rise of the Marvel Cinematic Universe, the victory of fantasy over realism is complete.

On the day in May 2012 when Marvel released *The Avengers*, *New York Times* critic A. O. Scott wrote a review praising some of the performances but complaining that Marvel was tending toward a kind of blockbuster conformity with its plots. "The secret of *The Avengers*," he wrote, "is that it is a snappy little dialogue comedy dressed up as something else, that something else being a giant A.T.M. for Marvel and its new studio overlords, the Walt Disney Company." The Marvel PR team enlisted one of the actors, Samuel L. Jackson, to go on Twitter and suggest to #Avengersfans that "A.O. Scott needs a new job! Let's help him find one! One he can ACTUALLY do!" Needless to say the #Avengersfans complied with the request in great numbers, heaping mostly unprintable suggestions upon the beleaguered Scott. Of course Scott knew that Marvel had long ago created the critic-proof movie formula; even suggesting their movies were not "cinema" was a fool's errand. But Jackson was unable to let it go. He tweeted, "If you say something that's fucked-up about a piece of bullshit pop culture that really is good," you essentially deserve all the online trolling. Here is the dilemma for a good actor like Samuel Jackson. He knows he's making a piece of "bullshit pop culture," but he's proud that it's well-crafted bullshit. But I wonder, watching *The Avengers* again, about the compromises fine actors like Mark Ruffalo or Jackson must be making as they shout long lines of exposition to the audience about closing the portal in the universe that has allowed aliens to invade and destroy New York City.

Hollywood has always been considered a bastion of progressive ideology, but the reality is that libertarians, who have dominated the written science fiction genre for decades, are now dominating the big-budget film business as well. As A. O. Scott wrote, "Mainstream American movies have, for decades, been in love with guns, suspicious of democracy, ambivalent about feminism, squeamish about divorce, allergic to abortion, all over the place on matters of sexuality and very nervous about anything to do with race."[2]

Libertarian ideology ruled science fiction as early as H. G. Wells's 1924 novel *Men Like Gods*, in which Wells imagined a parallel Earth with no need for a government; its citizens "spend their days enjoying their genetically engineered perfection and all the free love they can handle." Now the rise of the Marvel Cinematic Universe, complete with true believer libertarian heroes like Iron Man Tony Stark, has completed the libertarian takeover. Stan Lee, the creator of Iron Man, said that he invented Stark to piss off leftists in the 1960s:

It was the height of the Cold War. The readers—the young readers—
if there was one thing they hated it was war, it was the military, or,
as Eisenhower called it, the military-industrial complex. So I got a
hero who represented that to the hundredth degree. He was a weapons manufacturer. He was providing weapons for the army. He was
rich. He was an industrialist. But he was a good-looking guy and
he was courageous...I thought it would be fun to take the kind of
character that nobody would like—that none of our readers would
like—and shove him down their throats and make them like him.[3]

Box office gross alone would indicate that Lee succeeded. Writer
Junot Díaz has stated, "In a few short decades, the Marvel Universe
(in all its corporate manifestations) has rewired how millions, perhaps
even billions, of people imagine what is possible, what is heroic, what
is good."[4] The fact that a serious critic would make such an extravagant
claim seems ludicrous, and yet he may be right. But we must remember
that these heroes can fly and lift ten-ton trucks with their bare hands.
Their actions have nothing to do with the reality of the viewer's life. In an
ironic tribute to our Technocrats, *Iron Man* writer Jon Favreau identified
Elon Musk as the inspiration for the screen version of Tony Stark; Musk
even had a cameo in *Iron Man 2*. Imagining Elon Musk on a combat mission in Afghanistan stretches all credibility, but for Musk and his team
of Hollywood PR agents (he always hires the top firms), it was a way to
enhance his brand. No longer was he the PayPal nerd; he was Iron Man
incarnate. And in *The Avengers*, Tony Stark's nemesis, the Asgardian god
Loki, spouts a line that Musk would attribute to any "woke bureaucrat":
"Freedom is life's great lie. Once you accept that, in your heart, you will
know peace."

Of course Musk's personal jihad against woke culture is full of irony.
Musk tweets that his politics haven't really changed; rather, the "woke progressives" have moved further to the left. In a string of tweets announcing
his support for Republican candidates, Musk said he was abandoning the

Democrats who had been "(mostly) the kindness party" but were now the party of "division & hate." He continued in a paranoid vein, claiming, "Political attacks on me will escalate dramatically in coming months."

To combat these attacks, Musk pledged to spend $25 million supporting Republican politicians in the 2022 midterms. Like many of his pronouncements, this turned out be fiction, but there is no denying his move to the right. So between Peter Thiel and Musk, expenditures of $75 million in a midterm election were totally possible. But as Teddy Schleifer, who writes a daily column for the influential online magazine *Puck*, points out, "Silicon Valley may be somewhat culturally liberal, but its economic value system is as unmistakably conservative as Wall Street or Houston." The Technocrats want you to believe that the extreme economic inequality they represent is just a function of the natural world. And increasingly, anyone who doesn't believe this is cast as a woke, politically correct bullshit artist who can't stand the truth of America today.

This has been the magic trick of the Technocrats from the start. Their vocal embrace of cultural liberalism (gay rights, cannabis legalization, diversity in the workforce) has never interfered with their transgressive ability to use every tool in the capitalist arsenal to advance their businesses. In doing so, they continually bump up against the line of illegality. As Google's Eric Schmidt once admitted, "The Google policy on a lot of things is to get right up to the creepy line and not cross it." Obviously, Google's policies about your personal privacy are the most egregious examples, but there are many more. The whole point of surveillance capitalism is that the Technocrats will always know more than citizens, politicians, or regulators. Just as Musk has used his data to make sure Tesla is never unionized, Thiel has used his to land billion-dollar contracts with the CIA and the US Army for Palantir (see Chapter 9).

I produced two of Martin Scorsese's early movies (*Mean Streets* and *The Last Waltz*), and I have to agree with his comments about the Marvel Cinematic Universe: "That's not cinema. Honestly, the closest I can think of them…is theme parks. It isn't the cinema of human beings trying to convey emotional, psychological experiences to another human being."[5] Marty has hit upon the crux of the matter. People who can fly through the air, see through walls, and throw ten-ton trucks down the street are not human. Novelist Saul Bellow bemoans the dilemma of those of us interested in the humanities instead of computer science in *The Adventures of Augie March*: "The humanities would be called upon to choose a wallpaper for the crypt, as the end drew near."[6] Bellow's ironic assertion that poets, novelists, musicians, and painters will be relegated to picking out the velvet liner for their caskets would prove true in the age of science, technology, engineering, and math (STEM). To teach at a large university, as I did, is to know that most of the funding would go to STEM, and the humanities departments would starve. As Apple's Steve Jobs remarked at the launch of the iPad, "Technology alone is not enough…It's technology married with liberal arts, married with the humanities, that yields us the results that make our hearts sing."[7]

Certainly the Marvel Cinematic Universe represents the triumph of science (computer-generated special effects) over the humanities. It's clear that globalization favors the simpler storytelling of the Marvel formula, all spectacular set pieces strung together with small character quirks. And in general, the target audience gets younger (and some say dumber) every year. That's a classic "OK, boomer" statement, but let me try to give an example. In 1972, the top-grossing film in the United States was *The Godfather*. It won the Academy Award for Best Picture. In 2021, the top-grossing picture was *Spiderman: No Way Home*. It was not even nominated for best picture. Yet you can wander by a cinema today and see thirty-five-year-old couples lining up to see films targeting fifteen-year-old boys. Our ability to prolong cultural adolescence is quite extraordinary.

Which leads us to the question of exactly what magnetic pull these fantasy worlds exert. The simplest explanation I can come up with goes back to Max Weber's concept of the "disenchantment of the world." Weber believed that the rise of science in the late nineteenth century led us to believe that we could explain everything in rational terms. The world lost its mysteries, and the effect of that demystification was a world "leeched of mystery and richness—disenchanted." Fantasy culture re-enchants our lives. Marvel (and DC Comics) have been filling that need since the late 1940s in comic books, but only recently have they become a world-dominating cultural force, thanks to the magic of Hollywood special effects. Mark Zuckerberg named this as the value proposition of the Metaverse when he said, "It's an extremely magical sensation."

Most psychologists feel that those who spend hours a day in a fantasy universe (game players) are engaged in fairly primitive "escapism." And while no one doubts that obsessive video game play is escapism, researchers have identified both negative and positive modalities in such behavior. The negatives are depression, time wastage, negative mood, social anxiety, loneliness, and self-discrepancy. The positives are enjoyment, fun, and wishful thinking.

These same characteristics would apply to spending seven hours a day in the Metaverse. Leading a guild in battle for six hours a day in *World of Warcraft* is obviously more exciting than working the night shift at a 7-Eleven. But to take Weber's analogy further, one must acknowledge that there is also a quasi-religious component to fantasy films. An existential battle between the forces of good and evil is decided, more often than not, by the arrival of a savior with magical powers. George Lucas, for one, has acknowledged that Joseph Campbell's epic study of classical mythology, *The Hero's Journey*, formed the scaffolding on which the original *Star Wars* was built.

But the core philosophy of a film like *The Avengers* is transhumanism, the idea that humans can be made better with technological enhancements. All of our Technocrats fervently believe in this concept, and so do the people who run Marvel. Let's start with Tony Stark (aka Iron Man). Stark is a dissolute, arrogant playboy who transforms into a world-saving good guy once he dons his arc-powered exoskeletal war suit. Stark is not building this technology to help the disabled or the elderly—there is only one suit, and it's for Tony Stark. I don't need to go much further, but it's obvious that the other superheroes are transhuman as well: Thor, whom critic Kyle Munkittrick called "the Aryan wet dream," cast down to Earth from another planet because he is too arrogant; Captain America, the secret project of the military-industrial complex, built to keep the citizens safe as long as they pledge allegiance to America.

All of this underlying ideology suggests that the re-enchantment of the world presented by Marvel has a dark side. Joseph Campbell tells us that myths don't always have a happy ending; they are often warnings or laments. But Marvel is ultimately a Hollywood company, so most of its myths are not a guide to virtuous conduct. Rather, they are an entertainment spectacle that concludes with the superheroes on top. If they were myths in the Greek tradition, then a character like Mark Zuckerberg might end up tied to a rock like Prometheus, having his liver pecked out by an eagle for his hubris in giving Facebook to the world.

All of our Technocrats had troubled adolescent years, which led each of them to find solace in science fiction. Both Musk and Zuckerberg cite Iain Banks's nine-book Culture series as a seminal influence on their thinking. Marc Andreessen loves the hard science fiction (post-Singularity) of Charles Stross and Richard Morgan. And Peter Thiel cites *The Diamond Age* by Neal Stephenson as one of his favorite books. All four of them also claim The Lord of The Rings series had a profound influence on them. J. R. R. Tolkien's books are an attempt to construct new myths to help modern man deal with the moral chaos of our contemporary society. They are essentially very conservative pleas to "return the king" to his rightful throne. There is a sense that everyone has a place in this semifeudal society and should be content with that. The four men who sit on top of our neofeudal technological order, of course, share a desire to maintain their status quo.

The Iain Banks's Culture books Musk and Zuckerberg immersed themselves in during late puberty imagine a world based on Earth, populated with humanoid aliens living in a utopian, postscarcity society. Living to the age of 180 is normal. All work is done by a superadvanced set of artificial intelligences (AIs) called The Minds. All are provided a kind of universal basic income. To overcome boredom, citizens can choose from a panoply of drugs to alter their mood. Clearly Banks owes a debt to Aldous Huxley, but in Banks's brave new world, where every need is taken care of, the citizens define themselves through mastery of games, many of which involve combat in a virtual world. In that sense, everything in life can seem like a game, even political power. Here you can see the worldview of both Musk (everything is a game) and Zuckerberg (you won't have real work, so why not spend your time in a virtual world?).

Stephenson's *The Diamond Age*, so beloved by Thiel, is less well known than the author's *Snow Crash* (whence comes the original term *Metaverse*) and more utopian. Again, as in the Culture series, Stephenson imagines a world with free food and shelter for all; advanced AIs do most of the work and make stuff on demand using nanotechnology that is probably forty years ahead of the current state of the art. The polity in *The Diamond Age* is very tribal, a kind of replacement for the nation-state. In any given city are tribal groupings known as *phyles*. The three most powerful phyles are the Han (Han Chinese), the neo-Victorian New Atlantans (consisting largely of Anglo-Saxons but also accepting Indians, Africans, and other English-speaking cultures), and the Nippon (Japanese). I can see why *The Diamond Age* appealed to Thiel. Like Donald Trump, he believes that tribal loyalties are paramount and sees himself as a neo-Victorian. In his book *Zero to One*, he wrote, "The startup uniform encapsulates a simple but essential principle: everyone at your company should be different in the same way—a tribe of like-minded people fiercely devoted to the company's mission."

In *The Diamond Age*, technology has solved the basic challenges of humanity. Advanced AIs can solve all of our problems. There is no need to understand history. Your future is in good hands. For Thiel and the other Technocrats, this enchanting science fiction is a goal they want to reach in their lifetimes. They are also trying to re-enchant both their employees

and the consumers of their products by setting those "big hairy audacious goals" that may never be achieved. Musk's main BHAG is a colony
on Mars. Zuckerberg's is two billion people simultaneously occupying
the Metaverse. Thiel's is living to 160 years of age. And Andreessen's is
everyone's owning a secret "Swiss-like" account filled with crypto that the
government can never see. All these schemes are built around the idea of
freedom. But to assume that you have real agency in the Metaverse is to
misread the Technocrats who are building it. You will see only what Meta
and its advertisers want you to see.

More importantly, the Technocrats believe that if none of these
things ever occur, the aspirational effect of setting outrageous goals will
still spur their workforce to work harder and raise their stock price. In the
end it's a global hype machine for the benefit of its owners. You are being
asked to believe that you as a user will have some "ownership" (through
crypto). But that is a fantasy. For $20 million, you can buy 100,000 shares
(out of 2.2 billion) of Meta stock. The Metaverse will have nothing to do
with democracy.

॰॰

The story of the philosophical change in dramatic television is more complicated than the rise of Marvel's cinematic dominance. More than any
other factor, the nihilism that seems to dominate our culture flows from
television. And, of course, visions of traveling to Mars or escaping into
the Metaverse are the antidote the Technocrats prescribe for this condition. This dark trend starts with David Chase, creator and showrunner
of *The Sopranos*. Born in March 1945 to an Italian American hardware
store owner and a "drama queen" mother straight out of a Tennessee Williams play, Chase struggled through high school and college, plagued by
panic attacks and depression. He wound up in Hollywood, writing scripts
for episodic TV shows like *The Rockford Files* and *Northern Exposure*.
Despite his public disdain for network TV, it paid the bills. Chase said, "I

mean, that's the problem: the money. The money was attractive, particularly when you're raising a family. And I was lucky in that I was working with people who made shows that weren't disgusting to work on."[8]

Chase had grown up in the 1950s on film noir and 1930s-era mob films. His insight was that the United States was ready for an antihero like the ones he saw in those older films. When Bill Clinton gave his second inaugural address in January 1997, having survived impeachment and been reelected by a comfortable margin, Chase began pushing his idea of a gangster series with a protagonist, then called Don, who was in therapy. For Chase the idea that even the president could be forgiven opened a window into a Machiavellian character seeing a shrink. He tried to sell it to Fox and the other three big networks. They all passed. "I think they were afraid of it," Chase said later. "Because how could you like this guy?"[9] He also realized that his pilot script had broken all the rules of a mob drama: "It was a mob show but I didn't have anybody murdered. And I think that might've been one of the reasons why it didn't sell." Eventually the show found a home at HBO, and everything changed.

Since finishing *The Sopranos* fifteen years ago, Chase has had time to ponder why the networks were so wrong about Tony Soprano: "I could tell you a million reasons, but one of them, I'm pretty sure, is that Jim Gandolfini was a magnet…His eyes are sad. They're alive. His problems are our problems." And in the intervening years, Chase's dark pessimism about the direction America was heading now seems prescient. "I felt that things were going downhill," he told the *New York Times*' Willy Staley. "There was nothing but crap out there…I was beginning to feel that people's predictions about the dumbing-down of society had happened and were happening, and I started to see everything getting tawdry and cheap."[10]

While much of the film community was concentrating on the dystopian science fiction future, Chase was obsessed with a nihilistic present. There was no re-enchantment in *The Sopranos*. Tony tells his shrink, "Lately, I'm getting the feeling that I came in at the end. The best is over." As *Vanity Fair* critic James Wolcott writes, "*The Sopranos* is a choral litany of bitching and bemoaning rooted in bad faith: a refusal to take responsibility for their own actions and instead play the blame game. It's the Make America Great Again mentality in its dormancy, Trumpiness on training wheels."[11]

But the air of resignation and nostalgia caught on, and by the second season of the show, the antihero took over the serial drama on cable TV. The film noir nihilism of *The Sopranos* led to *Mad Men*, *Breaking Bad*, and many other shows of lesser import. Even as the creators depicted antiheroes Tony Soprano, Don Draper, and Walter White eventually getting karma-checked, many in the audience were what the *New Yorker*'s Emily Nussbaum called "bad fans"; they reveled in the bad behavior of these corrupt protagonists and "got irritated if other characters, fans or even the artists behind the shows suggested that they were anything other than awesome."[12]

In a sense, the antihero drama is a brief description of the mirror image of the Marvel fantasy. These shows depict the corruption of our hollow and banal present; the fantasy films seek to help us escape banality into a world of superhumans with magical powers. Neither *The Avengers* nor *The Sopranos* makes any attempt to depict a life that most of us could recognize. And like the actors in fantasy films, TV stars like James Gandolfini had to make compromises. On one hand he loved the part, but he also felt that he carried the gangster home with him every night, and it affected his family life.

Thanks to shows like *Succession* and *White Lotus*, the nihilistic culture show is not over, despite the success of optimistic comedies like *Ted Lasso*. Dominating all this media is a kind of fatalism, which belies the popular wisdom of Yuval Noah Harari, author of *Sapiens* and *21 Lessons for the 21st Century*, who argues that humans create optimistic myths to move society forward. Yet the characters in *Game of Thrones* and *The Sopranos* can never escape their fates. This constant reinforcement of fatalism bleeds into the consciousness of audience members, who increasingly come to believe that success in life is contingent on forces outside their control. The question culture makers in the period from

2008 to 2016 had to answer was this: To what extent did popular culture's consistent view that only corrupt liars survive in America lead to the assumption that we need a president like Tony Soprano, someone who can kick ass and take names? And this sense of fatalism is reinforced by the social networks that lead us to believe that corruption is the steady state of American politics. And for the Technocrats, deeply invested in the status quo, that's all good.

The music business has created its own fantasy universe, which lies much closer to *The Sopranos* than *The Avengers*. The rise of hip-hop as the dominant genre in pop music has been built around another kind of gangster mythology. It is hard for me to imagine HBO creating a contemporary gangster show like *The Sopranos* starring a Black drug kingpin and depicting his family life, his business associates, and the carnage of the gang wars. Yet, the story of Shawn Carter (aka Jay-Z) is told autobiographically in his lyrics for all to hear. In "Takeover," Jay-Z raps, "I was pushing weight back in '88." By all accounts this is not a gangsta boast but a reality. At nineteen, Carter was moving about a kilogram of cocaine and crack a week. He was the number two man in a large coke operation run by Emory Jones.[13]

Many years later, Jay-Z and Warren Buffet had lunch, and Buffet started talking about his luck in being born in Nebraska.[14] He noted that he was "wired for capital allocation," a trait that would have meant nothing if he had been born two hundred years earlier. Jay-Z told him how luck had played a role in his life too. He was making so much money in the drug business that when a friend got a record deal and headed to London to record, Jay asked if he could tag along. He told Buffet, "In those two months there was a sting operation and they took my friend I'm talking about [Emory Jones], for 13 years [to prison]. The only reason I wasn't there was because I was away doing this music stuff."

What role does the Black hip-hop superstar play in the larger Black culture? This is an existential question that will continually arise when we get to the role of the Black artist in promoting crypto currency as a way for anyone to change his or her fortunes. The role of fortune in a life like Carter's must weigh heavily on his conscience. On *The Black Album*, he raps, "I can't help the poor if I'm one of them, so I got rich and gave back, to me that's the win-win." Just how much Jay-Z gives back is open to interpretation, but the bitter irony is that the gangsta persona is baked into his identity as an artist, even as he cruises the Mediterranean in a two-hundred-foot yacht. As cultural critic Todd Boyd lays out in *The New H.N.I.C.*, the role of the Black musical artist in society has been contested since the birth of hip-hop: "There are generally two opposing camps…The gangsta camp, for instance, could be represented by figures like Jay-Z, Nas, Snoop, DMX, and Mobb Deep. These artists are often contrasted with a more overtly conscious political camp identified with artists like Common, Mos Def, The Roots, and Talib Kweli."[15]

For Common, the gangsta rappers' bragging about their riches (which hip-hop journal *XXL* put at around $150,000 to $15 million for just one song) was BS. He called out those artists, riding in the back of their Bentleys surrounded by bodyguards, still claiming to be men of the people. For many hip-hop artists, the thug life is a pose, but for a singer with a real rap sheet, the life can be hard to escape. As Pusha T raps, "The dope game destroyed my youth."

Todd Boyd argues that rap had to destroy the politeness and non-violence exemplified by the civil rights generation of Black heroes. He writes, "Hip hop, more accurately wants to provoke White people and 'bourgie ass niggas' to say something, while laughing all the way to the bank. This ultimate disregard for the approval of the mainstream is quite liberating." I find this argument unconvincing; I would posit that bragging about your Gulfstream G700 jet is actually seeking the mainstream's approval. Jay-Z wanted to have lunch with Warren Buffet for a reason. Hip-hop is mostly a first-person narrative medium—lots of use of *I*. As the Black filmmaker Blair McClendon writes, "That 'I' might get high, duck, dive, sling, get shot at and shoot back. But who is this 'I' who accumulates such an immense sum of money, he starts to see things from the other side while insisting we're still the same?"[16]

Jay-Z leads a life that most of his fans will never experience. For them, the gangsta rapper is a fantasy character, not so different from Tony Stark or Tony Soprano. But that doesn't stop them from wanting to emulate Jay-Z's lifestyle. FD Photo Studio in Los Angeles charges $64 an hour for young Instagram users to pose in the set of a private jet that is mostly used for hip-hop music videos.[17] The pretense of flying private, just like Kanye, is just the latest illusion posted on Instagram.

The artist may boast of riches and escaping assassination; is he playing a character like Tony, or is he living a dual life? That dichotomy was on the front page of the *New York Times* in May 2022, when the rap star Young Thug (whose real name is Jeffrey Williams) was arrested in Atlanta on suspicion of gang involvement and conspiracy to violate Georgia criminal racketeering law. As the *Times* wrote, "The indictment alleges that Mr. Williams is a founder of Young Slime Life, a criminal street gang that began in Atlanta in 2012 and is affiliated with the national Bloods gang. Mr. Williams's successful record label has been called YSL Records."[18] Among other crimes, Young Thug is alleged to have commissioned the murder of a rival gang leader in 2015. The *Times* notes, "The indictment claims that after the killing…Mr. Williams appeared in a video in which he stated that some people 'get killed bro, from me and YSL,' while using an expletive."

While Jay-Z and Beyoncé appear in formal wear for Tiffany ads, rap stars like Pusha T and Young Thug continue to push the gangsta persona. Their videos are full of guns; their social media profiles feature an endless stream of beefs with rival rappers. Is it art for art's sake, or, given that so many young people are under the tutelage of pop culture, does the hip-hop artist have a role in leading his community? The first issue to confront in answering this question is the shocking rise of gun violence among young Black men. A Johns Hopkins analysis found that Black men ages fifteen to thirty-four accounted for 38 percent of all gun homicide victims in 2020, though this group represented just 2 percent of the US population.[19] If Young Thug boasts of murder, what effect does that have on his millions of listeners? As McClendon writes, "The ghetto's music is starting to sound like prosperity gospel." Of course the prosperity gospel centered on the idea that if you were a righteous worshiper who prayed for wealth, it would be delivered to you. But in hip-hop the road to riches is not prayer but the thug life.

The role of the Black star was different in the spring of 1971, when I attended the Fight of the Century between Muhammad Ali and Joe Frazier at Madison Square Garden. With Ali returning to the ring after three years of forced exile following his opposition to the war in Vietnam, it was an event not to be missed. And the Harlem underworld elite emerged in regal splendor, like ten thousand people showing up to audition for the movie *Shaft*. I remember twins, who must have been six foot five, in matching yellow top hats and tails. Frank Sinatra was seated about ten rows in front of us. It was that kind of night. For those of us who wanted to see Ali triumph, it was a disappointment, but we couldn't complain because it was a good fight that went fifteen rounds.

It's hard to explain just how radical Ali's refusal to fight in Vietnam was. Like today, the establishment believed athletes and entertainers should not engage in politics. At the 1968 Olympics, Tommie Smith and John Carlos, who had won the gold and bronze medals in the two-hundred-meter sprint, raised their fists in the Black Power salute on the medal stand while "The Star-Spangled Banner" played. Politicians and sportswriters reacted with instantaneous outrage. Smith and Carlos's protest was not a spontaneous action. As they walked to the podium, they removed their shoes to protest poverty. They wore beads and a scarf to protest lynching. Carlos later wrote, "I looked at my feet in my high socks and thought about all the black poverty I'd seen from Harlem to East Texas. I fingered my beads and thought about the pictures I'd seen of the 'strange fruit' swinging from the poplar trees of the South." But Ali had gone even further, risking jail and giving up his title and his ability to earn a living. His courage was exemplary.

Since the rise of the Black Lives Matter movement, cultural leadership has passed from hip-hop artists to athletes. Certainly LeBron James did more for Black voters' rights in 2020 than Jay-Z, who seemed more interested in selling his champagne company for $1 billion. On June 10, 2020, James announced the formation of More Than a Vote, an organization that would work to get young people of color engaged in the voting process. "Yes, we want you to go out and vote, but we're also going to give you the tutorial," James said. "We're going to give you the background of how to vote and what they're trying to do, the other side, to stop you from voting." The reaction from Laura Ingraham and other Fox News commentators was essentially, "Shut up and dribble, LeBron."

The notion that some Fox News pundit should tell LeBron James he has nothing to contribute to the national conversation on race is absurd on its face. But from Richard Nixon onward, Republican politicians have learned how to weaponize patriotism. (Of course, Nixon himself learned this technique from Joe McCarthy and McCarthy's strategist Roy Cohn.) By railing against Colin Kaepernick, Donald Trump was just echoing the tactics of his mentor, Cohn. Like the ancient Roman dictators he admired, Trump wanted athletes and entertainers to be passive participants in the sort of "bread and circuses" entertainments used since time immemorial to distract citizens from political problems.

Whether the political strain of hip-hop will return in force is up for grabs. Certainly the rap artist Questlove is trying, but the younger generation seems more intent on acquiring a Lamborghini than exercising political power. In an earlier time, Public Enemy took an overtly political stance with "Fight the Power." The group's leader, Chuck D, told *Spin* magazine in 1988, "Rap is black America's TV station. The only thing that gives the straight-up facts on how the black youth feels is a rap record."

In 2008, Tricia Rose, who describes herself as "a pro-black, biracial, ex-working-class, New York–based feminist, left cultural critic," wrote

The Hip Hop Wars: What We Talk About When We Talk About Hip Hop—and Why It Matters.[20] She called for hip-hop artists to abandon much of their "raging sexism" and adopt a more socially conscious style, even though she admitted it might hurt their sales: "From this sober perspective on consciousness, gangstas appear to be the only ones having fun." Responding to the call for more socially conscious hip-hop, *New Yorker* music critic Kelefa Sanneh wrote, "I sometimes think of many of my own favorite rappers as making 'unconscious' hip-hop instead: reckless, rather than responsible; dreamlike, rather than logical; suggestive, rather than conclusive." So perhaps both the artists and the audience would rather remain in the unconscious fantasy world—to escape into the beats. As I write in May 2022, the number one song on the Billboard charts is a rap by Future called "Wait for U." Cowritten with Drake and six other contributors, it features a call-and-response between the rapper and his girlfriend. Future's highly processed vocals have a certain bleary, drugged-out desperation as he raps, "When I'm loaded, I keep it real." This might be the song to put in the 2022 time capsule.

I would argue that if people like Elon Musk have become new cultural heroes, then we might have to look back to musical artists or even sports stars to raise the issues of equality, justice, fairness, and democracy. That would mean that artists like Jay-Z will have to "check their privilege" and return to the community roots from which they rose. If fame is just a measure of net worth, then no one is going to outshine Elon Musk for a while. But he clearly does not care about equality or justice. But what *does* Elon stand for? A multiplanet world? Does Jay-Z still know what he stands for? It appears that maybe LeBron James can answer that question. But the rise of fantasy culture in the music world is setting an unreal example for the larger society. Given the political situation of Black America, are the hip-hop artists just providing the circuses for our brave new world? Certainly Kanye West's turn to reactionary and anti-Semitic ideology, together with his embrace of Trump and the Black-owned white supremacy of Candace Owens, is disturbing. But not to worry for West. After he was kicked off Instagram for his anti-Semitic rants, Elon Musk tweeted, "Welcome back to Twitter, my friend."

⌇

Just as the hip-hop genre has historically been drawn to the mythology of the drug lord, the video game genre has had similar success reveling in imagined crime—take *Grand Theft Auto III*, in which players can pay for the services of prostitutes to restore their health and, if they wish, kill them to get some of their money back. The entire Grand Theft Auto franchise has, in total, sold over 370 million units priced at $60 apiece. That $2.2 billion haul can match almost any movie franchise in history. And the video game business continues to grow (spurred on by the pandemic); gross revenues rose from $34 billion in 2015 to $85 billion in 2021.

Video games clearly plowed the earth for the seeds that Zuckerberg is planting in the Metaverse. They showed that people are willing to sit in front of a monitor for six hours in a fantasy universe killing people. Just what effect all of this virtual violence is having on the generation of kids who are nearing addiction levels of game play is a matter of debate. According to the American Psychological Association, "Scientific research has demonstrated an association between violent video game use and both increases in aggressive behavior, aggressive affect, aggressive cognitions and decreases in prosocial behavior, empathy, and moral engagement."[21] Video game defenders have replied that this is just the most recent moral panic of the sort that periodically gets trotted out to explain teenagers' antisocial behavior—akin to the targeting of comic books and rock and roll in the 1950s, pot smoking in the 1960s, and heavy metal music in the 1980s.

Whatever the conclusions, we are now at a point when you can make a living sitting at home playing video games and charging others to watch you, just like in the Culture series so beloved by Musk and Zuckerberg. Could the number of people making media (including influencers) surpass the number of people who are just consumers? At the time of writing, there are seventy million tracks on Spotify. Sixty thousand new tunes are uploaded to the platform each day. Five hundred hours of video are uploaded to YouTube every minute worldwide. According to Mediakix.com, there could be as many as thirty-seven million influencers online globally. This is a half-serious question, but how much of this content passes the "who cares" test? Daniel Ek of Spotify boasts that there "will be 50 million creators" on his platform by 2025. George Orwell, in *Confessions of a Book Reviewer*, was probably closer to the mark when he wrote, "In much more than nine cases out of ten the only objectively truthful criticism would be, 'This book is worthless.'" Or perhaps the famous Sturgeon's law—that "ninety percent of everything is crap"—applies. It seems almost cruel for the proprietors of Meta, YouTube, TikTok, Spotify, and Twitch to hold out the fantasy that a person can make a great living being a content creator on their platforms. Technology does not increase the distribution of genius in society. Nor does it make access to viewership more even.

Take Tyler Steinkamp, a mixed-race video game player who spends ten hours a day on Twitch, the Amazon game-streaming platform. He has the body of a weightlifter, even though he spends his days in front of a computer screen. He makes a decent living from ad revenue and sponsorships from Doritos, but it comes at a cost. Every two hours he gets a three-minute bathroom or food break while Twitch streams commercials on his feed. He plays the battle game *League of Legends* while an average of twenty-eight thousand fans around the world watch his stream and type (often racist) abuse or encouragement into his chat box. As the *Washington Post* reported, "Tyler, whose father is Black, has endured years of personal insults and sometimes explicitly racist abuse. And as his online world has grown, his real one has shrunk dramatically. Tyler has millions of fans but no friends; before spending a recent day with a *Post* reporter, no one besides his girlfriend and family had visited his house in several years."[22] Steinkamp earns a lot more than most Twitch streamers, but, as the *Post* reported, "though more than 7 million people stream on

Twitch every month, only the top 3,000—less than 0.1 percent—made more than the typical American household earning $67,000 a year. The vast majority earned next to nothing, streaming to empty chat rooms, waiting for a single person to come watch."

To stay in that top 0.1 percent of content creators, Steinkamp cannot take any time off. "If you take one day off, they're like, 'Where were you, bro? How could you?'" he said. "So I don't miss days. Ever." He takes daily doses of Adderall, an amphetamine, to stay "pumped" for his ten-hour sessions. In 2017 he was banned from *League of Legends* for "extreme abusive behavior." One of the players he abused wrote on Discord that Steinkamp would die "from a coke overdose or testicular cancer from all the steroids." When the ban was lifted, he returned to his top-ranked spot, saying that he was a reformed man.

In making the decision to go all in on the Metaverse, Mark Zuckerberg has clearly been observing game platforms like Twitch and Roblox. In his view, if people will spend ten hours a day watching some guy play video games, getting them to spend seven hours a day in the Metaverse should be easy. Again, we return to the pervasive notion that everyone can earn a decent living as a "creator." Spotify boasts of a potential fifty million creators, but like Twitch, only the top 0.1 percent are making serious money from the platform. This, of course, is the underlying fallacy of social media: the claim that if you make the tools of creativity available to everyone, a Bob Dylan or Kendrick Lamar will emerge from nowhere. Where is the Francis Ford Coppola of YouTube? Yes, Lil Nas X emerged from TikTok, but check back with me in ten years and tell me he was one for the ages.

I cannot leave the world of fantasy entertainment without acknowledging the growth of the greatest fantasy of all—that you can beat the house in gambling. Online gambling is opening up in most states, and the increase of sports betting is due in large part to the launch of legal wagering in thirteen states and more than $1 billion invested in marketing and advertising by some of the country's largest sportsbooks, like FanDuel, DraftKings, Caesars, and MGM. Online gambling revenues amounted to $61.5 billion in 2021 and are forecasted to rise to $114.4 billion by 2028. In keeping with the marketing hook of heroin dealers ("the first one is free"), the sportsbooks are spending millions in incentives to get users addicted. Writing in *The Atlantic*, Stephen Marche argues that gambling is a way to escape the insecurity of the Precariat: "Gambling expresses, through entertainment, the basic truth of the moment: Everything—every little thing—can be converted into a marketplace with winners and losers, and the house always wins. The only vice left is being broke."[23] University of Illinois economist Earl Grinols has estimated that the cost of gambling addiction (crime, lost work time, bankruptcy, and family hardship) is more than $54 billion a year.[24] The small print at the bottom of sportsbook ads on TV direct you to gambling-addiction sites. I doubt they will be of use to the millions holding on to the fantasy that one bet will make them rich and secure.

The toll taken by this easy access to gambling from your phone can be seen in the case of a college kid named Mike (he wouldn't reveal his last name), who downloaded the FanDuel app two days after Connecticut legalized sports betting. Within weeks, he had blown through all the money his parents had given him to pay for housing and food at college. When he called the state gambling helpline, he told the addiction counselor, "I can't tell my parents about any of this. I can't talk to anybody about it. What do I do?" The North American Foundation for Gambling Addiction estimates that at least ten million Americans have a gambling addiction.[25] And gambling is linked to other addictions. Duane (no last name), another recovered gambler who also had a heroin addiction, noted, "When you have an addictive personality, it's just like doing drugs. You're getting in debt, maxing out your cards, doing the same thing and getting the same results, every time."

Professional athletes are also beginning to get addicted to sports betting. In 2012, NFL commissioner Roger Goodell laid down the law: "It's a very strongly held view in the N.F.L.—it has been for decades—that the threat that gambling could occur in the N.F.L. or fixing of games or that any outcome could be influenced by the outside could be very damaging to the N.F.L. and very difficult to ever recover from." But the lure of money from sharing gaming revenues with the sportsbooks, as well as the incredible amount of advertising the sportsbooks would bring to NFL broadcasts, changed Goodell's mind. In the fall of 2021 he announced that seven sports books (FanDuel, Caesars, DraftKings, MGM, Fox, PointsBet, and Wynn) would have exclusive deals with the league. The press release noted, "No sportsbooks outside of these seven operators will be permitted to purchase this select NFL advertising and media inventory."[26] Just how much the sports books paid for this exclusivity was not disclosed.

Because sports betting has been going on in Europe for years, a look across the pond is instructive. Tony Adams, the former Arsenal soccer captain, has called gambling among professional players "an epidemic." The *Toronto Star* recently noted, "A quick scan of the British soccer headlines over the past few years has often brought with it the story of another ex–Premier League star who has lost millions to the bookmakers who've long been a fixture in that sporting culture."[27] Sports-betting expert Declan Hill notes, "You can't have your athletes gambling. It's like running a nunnery out of a brothel."

For forty-five years (since *Star Wars*) the fantasy genre has dominated the entertainment industry. We have lived our lives in these fantasy worlds in increments—two hours in a dark theater watching *Black Panther*, three hours at a computer playing *World of Warcraft*, two hours at the roulette wheel in Vegas. But now we are entering an era when fantasy is 24/7. Fifty million Republicans are living the fantasy of a stolen election. And early adopters are spending six hours wearing a virtual reality headset trying to navigate the Metaverse. All the tools for creating alternate realities are here (even if they are crude), and even Musk's computer visualizations of life on Mars or Thiel's imagining of eternal life seem a bit more plausible, thanks to the years of fantasy culture.

5

PEOPLE OF THE LIE

Falsehood flies, and truth comes limping after it, so that when men come to be undeceived, it is too late.

—Jonathan Swift

I n 1983, eminent psychiatrist Dr. M. Scott Peck published a book about malignant narcissism titled *People of the Lie*. Peck would recognize the QAnon Shaman in a headdress, who invaded the US Congress on January 6, 2020, as a classic malignant narcissist. His name is Jake Angeli, and he spent most of the two years before the January 6 insurrection acting as a counterprotestor at Black Lives Matter rallies or demonstrating against Covid-19 lockdowns in Arizona. He would carry a sign saying, "Q sent me." Obviously QAnon and the other great conspiracies of our time (the "Trump won" big lie; antivaccine hysteria) are built on falsehoods, but the question still arises: Why does a free individual commit to a cult like MAGA or QAnon?

Here I come back to Erich Fromm, who was trying to understand the appeal of fascism in his 1941 book *Escape from Freedom*. Fromm wrote that the modern man who is always crying for "negative liberty" (freedom from external restraint, i.e., government) finds himself unable to grasp "positive liberty"—having the power and resources to fulfill his own potential. In this alienated state, we see a "readiness to accept any ideology and any leader, if only he promises excitement and offers a political structure and symbols which allegedly give meaning and order to an individual's life."[1] This was the role Adolf Hitler played. Clearly Donald Trump's MAGA movement is built on the same premise. The chairman of the Joint Chiefs of Staff, Gen. Mark Milley, understood how close Trump had come to fascism when he wrote a letter of resignation (it was never sent) after Trump, in June 2020, told him to shoot the Black Lives Matter protestors outside the White House in the legs. Milley wrote that Trump didn't understand the purpose of having fought World War II.

> Between 1914 and 1945, 150 million people were slaughtered in the conduct of war. They were slaughtered because of tyrannies and dictatorships. That generation, like every generation, has fought against that, has fought against fascism, has fought against Nazism, has fought against extremism. It's now obvious to me that you don't understand that world order. You don't understand what the war was all about. In fact, you subscribe to many of the principles that we fought against. And I cannot be a party to that. It is with deep regret that I hereby submit my letter of resignation.[2]

Both Nazism and Trumpism were built on a lie, a fact that the Germans had to reckon with in 1945. Our reckoning is still to come.

At both the elite and the mass levels, American society has devolved into a sort of permanent adolescence, characterized by rage, relentless social media self-promotion, a lack of impulse control, and delusional fantasies about how the world actually works.[3] In 2008, Andrew Price-Smith published *Contagion and Chaos*, which looked at the 1918 Spanish flu pandemic, HIV/AIDS in sub-Saharan Africa, SARS, and mad cow disease.[4] Price-Smith argued that epidemic disease represents a direct threat to the power of a state, eroding prosperity and destabilizing its internal politics. I would argue that the Covid-19 pandemic did not just destabilize the internal politics of the United States but unhinged the country's collective social dialogue from reality.

The cult nature of phenomena like the crypto craze, MAGA, and QAnon has created a kind of "cognitive dissonance." Psychologist Leon Festinger first promulgated this concept in 1956 after he observed a UFO doomsday cult, whose leader, Marian Keech, had prophesied that the world would end on December 21 of that year. The members of the cult appeared at Keech's house to be borne off to space by aliens just before Earth perished. When the prophecy failed to come true and the anxious cult members started to break down, Keech delivered a new message, telling them that their collective energy had convinced God to spare the planet. Festinger theorized that the failed message induced a state of cognitive dissonance in the believers, which he equated to a state of uncomfortable anxiety. The only way to lessen the anxiety was to accept the new (false) prophecy that their actions had saved Earth. After many other experiments, Festinger concluded that "human beings when asked to lie without being given sufficient justification will convince themselves that the lie they are asked to tell is the truth." The revelation that the Stop the Steal fundraising was basically a $250 million grift for the benefit of Trump and his family clearly induced cognitive dissonance among MAGA cultists.[5] As Alan Simpson, a former Republican leader and Wyoming senator, said, "This is not a Republican Party anymore. It's a cult."

Two Duke University researchers, in a paper published in April 2021, have located the personality type that accounts for the majority of the disinformation spread online. "We found that it's not conservatives in general who tend to promote false information," they wrote, "but rather a smaller subset of them who also share two psychological traits: low levels of conscientiousness and an appetite for chaos."[6] The quality of conscientiousness is seen as "the tendency to regulate one's own behavior by being less impulsive and more orderly, diligent and prudent." Truly distinguishing purveyors of false information is the "desire for chaos—that is, a motivation to disregard, disrupt, and take down existing social and political institutions as a means of asserting the dominance and superiority of one's own group." Critics might argue that the Duke research is outdated, in that so many members of Congress continue to spread the lie that the 2020 election was stolen.

The Covid-19 pandemic brought the spread of QAnon disinformation to a boil. Between March and June 2020, QAnon activity nearly tripled on Facebook and nearly doubled on Instagram and Twitter, according to Agence France-Presse.[7] The irony, given my discussion of fantasy culture in the previous chapter, is that both Trump and QAnon are products of Hollywood. The businessman Donald Trump played on *The Apprentice* bore no resemblance to Trump himself, an epic bankrupt. Trump Atlantic City Casino companies filed four bankruptcies between 1991 and 2009. And while he was seeking bankruptcy protection, he still pulled over $1 million a year in salary from the failing companies, while stiffing local contractors. He even went so far as to sue the banks that were trying to collect on the loans they gave him, claiming that they should have known not to lend him the money.[8] The Trump who starred in *The Apprentice* was a completely fictional construct.

The same applies to QAnon. An extraordinary piece by *Los Angeles Times* columnist Anita Chabria, titled, "Lizard People, Deadly Orgies and JFK: How QAnon Hijacked Hollywood to Spread Conspiracies," lays out how QAnon has appropriated the tropes of fantasy culture to enhance its allure: "In August, a Santa Barbara man drove his 2-year-old son and infant daughter to Mexico, where he killed them with a spearfishing gun. A federal indictment said he confessed to the killings and to being influenced by QAnon, believing that his wife 'possessed serpent DNA and had passed it on to his children' and that he was 'saving the world from monsters.'"[9] Here we see in action the American Far Right's ability to use the tools of social media to label its opponents as inhuman—one of the essential tools of the fascist.

The algorithms driving QAnon followers further down conspiracy rabbit holes threaten to eviscerate the humanism that has been the basis of our society since Thomas Jefferson wrote the words "life, liberty and the pursuit of happiness." The political point of conspiracy theories on the right is to delegitimize the other side. The Democrats are not just misguided; they are evil. If you lost an election to an evil cabal, would you concede? Ultimately, we need to acknowledge that Facebook and Twitter are responsible for much of the spread of these conspiracies. *NBC News* reported, "An internal investigation by Facebook has uncovered thousands of groups and pages, with millions of members and followers, that support the QAnon conspiracy theory, according to internal company documents reviewed by NBC News."[10] As former major Facebook investor Roger McNamee wrote, "This suggests that Facebook is responsible for 2 million of these people being pushed to QAnon from Facebook's recommendation engine."[11]

The results of this algorithmic herding are stark. In February 2021, a poll by the American Enterprise Institute found that 29 percent of Republicans believe the central claim of QAnon: that Donald Trump has been secretly fighting a group of child sex traffickers that include prominent Democrats and Hollywood elites. For the QAnon faithful, "distinctions between believable and unbelievable, true and false, are not relevant for people who have found that taking up outrageous and disprovable ideas is instead an admission ticket to a community or an identity."[12] In the spring of 2022, Facebook began to crack down on some of the most outrageous QAnon groups. They quickly moved over to Donald Trump's Truth Social platform, which openly welcomed them.[13]

An in-depth look at a woman who quit QAnon in 2021 reveals how social media leads to these kinds of pathologies. Identifying herself only by the pseudonym "Megan," she described falling down the QAnon rabbit hole to *Politico*'s Anastasiia Carrier.[14] In June 2020, Megan had been cooped up in her house for days and was going stir crazy.

Tired of staring at the ceiling, I decided to watch the "Fall Cabal" YouTube series a friend of mine had told me about. "It's really weird.

I'd love to get your opinion on it," she messaged me a few days before along with a link. The 10 episodes wove together a narrative about "The Cabal," supposedly a secret and satanic pedophile ring run by members of the liberal elite, and Trump's secret fight to overthrow them. I didn't sleep at all that night. Instead, I found dozens of articles and videos confirming my new political views. By the morning, I was a true believer.

I think the fact that I was already a big supporter of Bernie Sanders primed me for the transformation—a process people call being red-pilled. One thing QAnon and Bernie have in common is the belief that there is a group of corrupt elites that makes it hard for everyone else in the country and the world to stay afloat. I hadn't trusted the government entirely before 2016—for example, I didn't find the explanations of 9/11 or the assassination of John F. Kennedy to be satisfactory.

The famous investor Charles Munger, who is Warren Buffet's partner in Berkshire Hathaway, has for years written about the psychology of crowds and cults—two phenomena that effect every investor's portfolio. In a long essay on behavioral psychology, Munger wrote, "Pure curiosity…made me wonder how and why destructive cults were often able, over a single long weekend, to turn many tolerably normal people into brainwashed zombies and thereafter keep them in that state indefinitely."[15] In seeking an explanation, he cites what psychologists call the social-proof tendency, the automatic propensity of a person to think and act as he sees others around him thinking and acting. The classic experiment places ten lab assistants in an elevator, all facing toward the back. A stranger entering the elevator will often turn around and do the same.

The application of this theory to Megan's case seems critical. As Munger wrote, "Because stress intensifies Social-Proof Tendency, disreputable sales organizations, engaged, for instance, in such action as selling swampland to schoolteachers, manipulate targets into situations combining isolation and stress. The isolation strengthens the social proof provided by both the knaves and the people who buy first, and the stress, often increased by fatigue, augments the targets' susceptibility to the social proof." Clearly the stress of the pandemic drove many otherwise sane people into the QAnon house of mirrors. Psychologists have found that obsessive social media use is tied to both narcissism and reward sensitivity (i.e., behavior motivated by the prospect of access to a reward). And the right-wing promoters who are profiting off these weaknesses know it.

Recently, various QAnon factions have begun to spar over access to the money to be earned from promulgating conspiracy theories. Many of them make paid public appearances or run subscription websites.[16] Of course Trump himself was the biggest beneficiary of this disinformation. His Election Defense Fund, which collected $250 million after the November 2020 election, went not to Trump's dysfunctional legal team but rather into the Trump Political Action Committee, which then doled out the money to Mark Meadows's charity, to a conservative organization employing former Trump staffers, and to the Trump Hotel Collection.[17]

⌇

Megan was able to rescue herself from the paranoia fostered by QAnon with the help of a very patient boyfriend. When the promised Storm (i.e., the arrest and execution of Hillary Clinton and Barack Obama by Trump) never arrived and JFK Jr. didn't return from the dead ready to run as Trump's vice president in the run-up to the 2024 election, she gave up. But she is in the minority. Another reformed QAnon adherent told *Politico*, "I think it's inevitable that more real-world violence will occur in the future. Eventually, Anons will get tired of waiting for the Storm. Then, they will take the bringing of the martial law into their own hands."

Robert Pape, who directs the University of Chicago Project on Security and Threats, agrees. In researching the January 6 insurrectionists,

Pape was struck by the fact that most of those arrested had decent jobs. As he told the *Atlantic*'s Bart Gellman, "The last time America saw middle-class whites involved in violence was the expansion of the second KKK in the 1920s...This really is a new, politically violent mass movement."[18] Surely anyone paying attention to the sway of Trumpism over contemporary Republican politics knows how fear of crossing Trump's base—including fear for their families' physical safety—drives otherwise rational Republicans to fall in line. Even after the January 6, 2021, Capitol insurrection, the majority of House Republicans voted against accepting the results of the 2020 election. This was clearly the result of the kind of authoritarian intimidation we mostly associate with third world dictatorships. In viewing the behavior of a politician like Ted Cruz or Kevin McCarthy toward Donald Trump, I return again to Fromm's *Escape from Freedom*: "Is there not also, perhaps, besides an innate desire for freedom, an instinctive wish for submission? If there is not, how can we account for the attraction which submission to a leader has for so many today?"

It's one thing to have an eccentric billionaire like Elon Musk indulge his fantasy of going to Mars. To have 30 percent of the country living in a violent fantasyland is another—and it's deeply dangerous. How did millions of people come to believe that the Covid vaccines were a plot by Bill Gates to implant a microchip in their bodies? How did 66 percent of the Republican Party come to believe that the 2020 election was stolen? How did we get to the point at which William Barr, Trump's attorney general, could say of the former president, "He's become detached from reality"?

What changed was the arrival of Facebook, Twitter, and YouTube. Though we marveled at the utility of the newly invented iPhone and Facebook News Feed in 2007, social scientists almost immediately began to notice strange, unintended consequences. By 2012, rates of teenage depression, loneliness, self-harm, and suicide had begun to rise sharply. By 2019, just before the pandemic, rates of depression among adolescents had nearly doubled. As Facebook whistleblower Frances Haugen told Congress, Facebook's own data on Instagram use by young girls backed up these findings. Yet the company did nothing about it. As psychologists Jonathan Haidt and Jean Twenge recently wrote,

> We both came to suspect the same culprits: smartphones in general and social media in particular…In 2009, Facebook added the like button, Twitter added the retweet button and, over the next few years, users' feeds became algorithmicized based on "engagement," which mostly meant a post's ability to trigger emotions. By 2012, as the world now knows, the major platforms had created an outrage machine that made life online far uglier, faster, more polarized and more likely to incite performative shaming.[19]

For Facebook, this "performative shaming" was a source of endless profits. Starting in 2017, Facebook gave users the ability to react to posts with more than just a like button—with angry and sad emojis, for example—and counted emoji reactions as five times more valuable on the algorithm than a like. By May 2022, a *Wall Street Journal*–NORC poll showed that 64 percent of the respondents believed platforms such as Facebook and Twitter "are harmful for society because they emphasize differences between people."[20] Notably, Pew Research shows that political polarization in America changed very little between 1994 and 2004 but radically increased between 2004 and 2014. Two events clearly account for much of this change: the election of Barack Obama and the rise of Facebook.

The great irony is that in times of social unrest, amid status anxiety and the loneliness described by Jonathan Haidt (*The Coddling of the American Mind*) and Jean M. Twenge (*The Narcissism Epidemic*), the alienated individual has only two ways to seek status. The first is to acquire some sort of fame, hence the dream that a post might go viral. The second is through intimidation.

Facebook provides a tool set for both routes. Danish political scientist Michael Bang Petersen has written, "Individuals who are high in the pursuit of dominance play a central role in political destabilization. They are more likely to commit political violence, to engage in hateful online interactions and to be motivated to share misinformation."[21] In *The Shame Machine: Who Profits in the New Age of Humiliation*, Cathy O'Neil argues that Facebook profits by sowing discord, which keeps the keyboard warriors glued to the platform. Even though various factions of the neofascist movement are fighting over the financial spoils of the conspiracy industry, ultimately the people really getting rich off of all this discord are Mark Zuckerberg, Elon Musk, and their shareholders (like Marc Andreessen and Peter Thiel).

The disruptive power of social media was why Thiel so valued his position as Facebook's senior board member. Steve Bannon, who worked with Thiel on the Trump transition team in 2016, said, "Peter's idea of disrupting government is out there. People thought Trump was a disrupter. They had no earthly idea what was being pitched by Thiel."[22] For instance, both candidates he identified to run the Food and Drug Administration— his Silicon Valley associates Jim O'Neill and Balaji Srinivasan—argued that the agency should dump its requirement that drugs be proven effective before reaching the market.

Bannon and Thiel instrumentalized Facebook for Trump's regime by using a new form of propaganda. Bannon said, "The Democrats don't matter. The real opposition is the media. And the way to deal with them is to flood the zone with shit."[23] The idea was not to convince people of a specific policy point but to overwhelm them with disinformation to such an extent that they became disoriented and reality lost all meaning. For many citizens it was not a matter of denying the truth but rather a deep weariness that the truth was even knowable. And, of course, the new AI-driven ChatGPT will make it even easier to flood the zone. The *New York Times'* Ezra Klein notes, "And what unnerved me a bit about ChatGPT was the sense that we are going to drive the cost of bullshit to zero when we have not driven the cost of truthful or accurate or knowledge advancing information lower at all."[24]

Of course, Bannon didn't invent this strategy. Dictators, starting with Adolf Hitler and Benito Mussolini, have refined it over the years. But Thiel realized (with Bannon's help) that it was no longer sufficient to proclaim "liberty" as your movement's North Star. You needed coercive state power to achieve your goals on immigration, banning abortion and pornography, and stopping the woke revolution around Black and LGBTQ social justice reform. But as British historian Geoff Eley (*Nazism as Fascism*) points out, the fascism of 2022 "no longer relies as much on street fighting, pitched confrontations, imposing displays of paramilitary strength, and the spectacle of uniformed massed force. It operates, rather, by verbal onslaughts, internet trolling, instantly produced and transmitted visual incitements, and all the other virtual means of displaced but no less brutal assault."[25] This is Bannon and Thiel's specialty, aided of course by Zuckerberg's Facebook and Musk's Twitter.

John Ganz, an American writer for the *New Statesman*, says Thiel is "probably the most clearly fascist prominent figure in the U.S. today, including Trump."[26] Thiel has always had an apocalyptic vision—one that assumed getting people to come over to his view of the future would take a backlash against globalization and a financial catastrophe. As the global economy began to melt down in 2008, he wrote, "The entire human order could unravel in a relentless escalation of violence—famine, disease, war, and death." For the next eight years, Thiel railed against the Obama administration; by 2015, he grasped that Trump could be the vehicle to bring on the end times he so desired. And he realized that Facebook could be an ideal megaphone for Trump's "American Carnage" vision. Curtis Yarvin, one of Peter Thiel's favorite bloggers, wrote that some people are "more suited to slavery" than others. Yarvin leads the Neoreactionary movement, whose adherents believe that American democracy is a failed experiment and should be replaced by a monarchy, with the ruler similar to the CEO of a corporation.[27] Though Thiel might not be willing to go that far publicly, Yarvin believed he had convinced Thiel that libertarianism was a doomed project without the inclusion of authoritarianism. He argued, "We should get over our dictator-phobia." After Thiel said that Republican members of Congress who voted for Trump's impeachment after the January 6 attacks were "traitorous," Yarvin noted of Thiel, "He's fully enlightened, but just plays it very carefully."[28] Looking forward to the 2024 election, Yarvin believes the Republican candidate (Trump or a Trump clone) should campaign on a specific mandate: "If I'm elected, I'm gonna assume absolute power in Washington and rebuild the government." Once that's done, Yarvin believes elite institutions like Harvard and the *New York Times* need to be closed down. And then we nationalize all local police and National Guard troops. Yarvin's law-and-order prescriptions are simple:

> A trivial database query can identify the set of humans in the country who are either (a) productively employed, (b) independently wealthy, or (c) a well-supervised dependent of (a) or (b). Everyone else, including all minors, gets the tag. This inconspicuous device fits on your ankle and continuously reports your position to the authorities. If no crimes are committed near your location, you have nothing to worry about.
>
> Saddled with a large number of residents who are effectively dependents of the state—for example, those who receive housing subsidies. These people need to be reprocessed to determine whether they can become members of productive society, and during this time there is no reason to leave them where they are. Therefore, we can expect to establish secure relocation centers, in which the 20th century's artificially decivilized subpopulations will receive social services in a controlled environment while they are reintroduced to civilized society.[29]

To me this is fascism, full stop.

In 2019, Trump's use of Facebook ads as a key propaganda tool began to push the envelope of acceptable fabrications. At the same time, Thiel fought hard to keep Trump on the platform. He urged Zuckerberg to resist pressure from "woke" Facebook employees and board members to remove him.[30] In the midst of these internal deliberations, Thiel flew Zuckerberg to Washington in October 2019 to meet secretly with Trump and Trump's son-in-law, Jared Kushner. Out of that dinner came the understanding that Facebook would not fact-check Trump's pronouncements on the platform, under the aforementioned and newly created "newsworthiness" standard. In return, Kushner promised, "the Trump administration would lay off on any heavy-handed regulations."[31] Facebook subsequently contested reports of the Trump-Zuckerberg dinner.

Those of us old enough to remember the epic battle between the *Washington Post* and the Richard Nixon administration during the Watergate scandal still believe that a free press is our last defense against a criminal presidency. And yet today, according to a recent Pew Research poll, 36 percent of Americans get their news from Facebook, a readership that dwarfs that of papers like the *Washington Post*.[32] But Facebook has no ethical core or journalistic mission to put the truth in front of the millions of users that believe they are getting "the news" from social media.

Throughout the battle over Trump's ads, Thiel cited internal Facebook research that proved right-wing content was more popular than left-wing. As his biographer Max Chafkin wrote, "Facebook wasn't biased against conservative media; it *was* conservative media…[T]he company's news feed was essentially a popularity contest, and inside of Facebook, the Trump ideology, which combined white identity politics and economic populism, was more popular than anything else."[33]

Only after the attempted coup of January 6, 2021, did the rest of the board overrule Thiel's defense of Trump and ban the ex-president from Facebook. Soon after, Thiel resigned from the board. By this time, Trump had entered his own Metaverse, where he could create a fiction that he had won the 2020 election and continue to rule American politics by personally selecting candidates to run in the 2022 midterms. Astoundingly, 53 percent of Republicans chose to enter into this fantasy world with him. As *Washington Post* columnist Paul Waldman noted, Trump's appeal was to shared hatred: "There are people you hate—immigrants, racial minorities, uppity women, gays, liberals of all kinds—and I hate them, too. I will be your weapon against them."[34]

The temporary ban of Donald Trump from Facebook seems unlikely to cool the hot rhetoric of hate that flows into news feeds on millions of Americans' phones and computers. Short of facing legal liability for publishing falsehoods (through removal of its Safe Harbor shield), Facebook has no economic incentive to moderate its content. The company knows that anger keeps people glued to its site and that time spent on the service translates directly into increased ad revenues. That is all that matters to Mark Zuckerberg.

In the spring of 2022, Elon Musk decided to join Thiel, Andreessen, and Zuckerberg and invest in social media. In deciding to buy Twitter, Musk declared, "Free speech is the bedrock of a functioning democracy, and Twitter is the digital town square where matters vital to the future of humanity are debated." Marc Andreessen's firm agreed to put up $400 million to support Musk's bid. The headline of Steven Pearlstein's *Washington Post* column on the deal says it all: "An overleveraged billionaire's bid for an overvalued company may signal the last gasp in an age of magical thinking about markets."[35] Apple employees used to talk about Steve Jobs's ability to deploy a "reality distortion field" when he wanted to do something his colleagues didn't think made sense. Musk's own reality distortion powers are amplified by his ostensive one hundred million Twitter followers. However, the *Wall Street Journal* has reported, "One estimate says spam, fake or inactive accounts make up the vast majority of his followers."[36]

Almost immediately Musk got a case of buyer's remorse and tried to back out of a signed deal. Twitter immediately sued to enforce the contract. Why did Musk need to own Twitter? He was already one of its most successful power users. Perhaps his libertarian ideology led him to believe that he could change politics by controlling the platform. Conservative commentators started to make the case that Musk could actually create a "light touch" form of content moderation that both liberals and conservatives could respect.[37] But by inviting Trump back on Twitter, Musk undermined whatever goodwill his supporters ascribed to him.

But Musk didn't care. He had become, in the words of the *New York Times*, "a geopolitical chaos agent." In October 2022, after the judge overseeing Twitter's lawsuit to force Musk to close the deal made some rulings favoring Twitter, Musk asserted he would buy Twitter after all. He then exhibited what *Politico*'s Jack Shafer called "histrionic personality disorder... associated with narcissism, attention seeking behaviors and manipulation."[38] He began by proposing on Twitter a peace plan for Ukraine that could have been written by Vladimir Putin. This was just the beginning of the week, as the *Washington Post* reported, "The person most likely to own Twitter next month has proposed solving the war in Ukraine by letting Russia keep territory, won praise from a top Chinese diplomat for suggesting China take control of Taiwan, and welcomed a widely followed celebrity [Kanye West] back to Twitter who had just had his Instagram account suspended for threatening Jews."[39] Ian Bremmer, of the Eurasia Group, wrote privately to his clients that Musk had told him at a conference in Aspen that he had spoken directly to Putin about his proposed peace plan, which would presumably be a violation of the Logan Act. Musk later denied that he had said that to Bremmer. Whether he talked to Putin directly or to one of Putin's staff, being contacted by important people feeds the ego needs of an insecure arriviste like Musk or Trump. Musk is acting as a messenger for Putin, serving as what in the Cold War was known as "a useful idiot."[40]

Then Musk's romance with Putin deepened. On October 7, 2022, after Ukraine's ambassador to Germany had responded to Musk's "peace plan" with the tweet "F— off is my very diplomatic reply to you @elonmusk," SpaceX wrote the US State Department saying it could no longer fund the deployment of its Starlink internet system, which had been providing critical communications for the Ukrainian army. He then tweeted in response to the ambassador's tweet, "We're just following his recommendation." Musk had been praised for providing the Starlink terminals to Ukraine, but according to the SpaceX letter, the vast majority was partially or fully funded by other parties, including the US government, the United Kingdom, and Poland. Histrionic personality disorder may seem like a fake disease, but it's real, recognized by psychologists as "a pattern of exaggerated emotionality and attention-seeking behaviors." Musk believed he could muscle the Pentagon for $400 million to cover the next twelve months of the critical service for the Ukrainian army. Already Ukrainian forces were complaining that thirteen hundred Starlink terminals went offline in the two weeks after Musk's demand letter. Two observers believe that Musk had "geofenced" the service so it was not available in the regions Russia had annexed. As CNN reported, "Musk's control of the signal gives him significant sway over the battlefield at a time when he has come under heavy criticism for arguing that Ukraine should sue for peace and give up some of its territory."[41] Historian Timothy Snyder tweeted, "What Musk means by freedom of speech is his freedom to suppress your speech while you are risking your life for everyone's freedom."

This was not the first time Musk had dabbled at playing Henry Kissinger. When a cabal of lithium miners (lithium is a key component of Tesla batteries) appeared to be trying to overthrow the Bolivian government of Evo Morales, Musk (signaling support for the coup plotters) tweeted, "We will coup whoever we want, deal with it."[42] For Musk, access to cheap lithium tops any human rights concerns. It's the old banana republic diplomacy.

As Josh Marshall of *Talking Points Memo* wrote about Musk, "Many of our would-be oligarchs in the United States seem quite attracted to the

Russian strongman/oligarch model. It's not just the authoritarianism but the way oligarchs operate within it. It's part of the broader anti-democratic, authoritarian turn within a large swathe of the tech industry."[43] Like Thiel, Musk has a somewhat apocalyptic view of our economy and fully embraces this notion of the strongman leader. In May 2022, he tweeted that he welcomed a global recession so money would stop "raining" down on "fools." Of course, he neglected to tweet that his companies were the beneficiaries of the rain, as they (according to the *Los Angeles Times*) have received some $5 billion in government support in the last four years.[44]

Here is the squeeze Musk found himself in after he made the offer for Twitter. He had already pledged about half of his 173 million shares of Tesla stock to fund other ventures and activities like the Boring Company (the notorious Hyperloop adventure). He then said he would pledge an additional 40 percent of his Tesla stock to secure the new loans to buy Twitter. That left only 10 percent of his Tesla shares available as collateral. Tesla's corporate policies allowed major shareholders to borrow only 25 percent of the value of each share. This would suggest that Elon had about $5 billion left to play with. And here is the real problem. Musk took out some of the margin loans on his Tesla shares when the stock was above $1,200 (before the three-to-one stock split). The day the Twitter deal was announced, Tesla shares started to tank. Within ten days the stock had fallen to $700. As of July 1, 2022, the shares were trading at $673 (on August 24, 2022, the stock split three to one). If they went much lower, Musk would face a margin call requiring him to put up more stock or more cash—and he is short on both fronts.

Musk's decision to try to own Twitter at first seemed to be a grift—what we used to call a self-fulfilling prophecy. Mike Milken, the main financier of 1980s corporate raiders, invented this financial concept. Milken ran the junk bond department at the investment banking firm Drexel Burnham. As a partner at a rival firm (Merrill Lynch), I could only gasp at Milken's audacity and his chicanery. He eventually went to prison for insider trading and paid a fine of $600 million to the government.

But Milken's formula for success was simple. Essentially, a raider quietly buys 5 percent of an undervalued stock, then files a Schedule 13D with the Securities and Exchange Commission (SEC), saying he is "seeking to enhance shareholder value" and may buy more. The stock immediately goes up in anticipation of a takeover, meaning the raider has already made a huge profit (i.e., a self-fulfilling prophecy). Even if he doesn't succeed in taking over the company, he makes a killing, because the target company usually buys back the raider's shares. That tactic was labeled "greenmail" in the 1980s. But Musk didn't even play by the buccaneer rules of the 1980s, because he failed to notify investors when he had passed the 5 percent threshold. As the *Wall Street Journal* reported, "Federal regulators are investigating Elon Musk's late disclosure last month of his sizable stake in Twitter Inc., according to people familiar with the matter, a lag that allowed him to buy more stock without alerting other shareholders to his ownership."[45] Of course the problem for Musk in executing the self-fulfilling prophecy was that the price he offered was too high to attract any competing bids (especially in the face of the tech sector crash a week after his bid). And of course, unlike the targets of many corporate raids of the 1980s, Twitter didn't have the cash to "greenmail" Musk by buying back his shares. So in the end, he had no choice but to buy Twitter at a wildly inflated price.

Look, Musk obviously has had an eye for talent. He recognized that the Tesla electric car built by Martin Eberhard and Marc Tarpenning could be a breakthrough product, and he invested enough money into their company to take control and force them out. He also recognized the rocket designer Tom Mueller was the key to starting SpaceX. Without Mueller there would have been no SpaceX. But as with Trump, Musk's greatest talent is promotion. He told an interviewer the week after the Twitter deal closed (when the company was losing $4 million a day) that it could one day be the most valuable company in the world. So as a hype artist, he is unparalleled, but he also has played fast and loose with the SEC for years, even going so far as to blackball a lawyer in private practice because he once worked for the SEC (and never on a case involving Musk).[46] But con men like Musk and Trump manage to wiggle out of most sticky situations they find themselves in. They hire the best lawyers. On May 20, 2022, in the midst of the Twitter battle, Musk tweeted, "Tesla is building a hardcore litigation department where we directly initiate & execute lawsuits. The team will report directly to me." He was turning himself into a Trump clone, assuming he could sue his way out of danger.

For a long time in American history, one had to get a license from the Federal Communications Commission (FCC) to own a broadcaster. To get that license, you had to prove that you were an upstanding public citizen and that you hadn't been sued by the SEC (and settled). You also had to pledge to operate the broadcast station "in the public interest." These rules don't apply to the internet, but it still seems clear to me that Elon Musk plans to operate Twitter solely in the interests of Elon Musk. As he tweeted that he voted for Mayra Flores, the QAnon-loving Republican congressional candidate in Texas, and that he was leaning toward backing Florida governor Ron DeSantis for president, there can be no doubt about Musk's new right-wing political temperament. Given the way he operates his other businesses, who would stop him from trying to use Twitter to help his side win the 2024 election? Just before the 2022 midterms he tweeted to his 110 million followers that they should vote the Republicans into power.

It should be obvious that the rise in the vast fortunes of the Technocrats has afforded them extraordinary influence over our nation's communication system. They not only control the information flow over social media but also are inventing new ways to penetrate your home with disinformation.[47] The Technocrats' defenders say we are living in a "post-truth age" and just have to get used to it. Case in point is some research done at Dartmouth.

A pair of political scientists had given 130 students a mocked-up news report on a speech about the invasion of Iraq that described the country as "a place where terrorists might get weapons of mass destruction." Half the subjects then read a correction to that news report, noting that the CIA had found no evidence of such weapons in Iraq. For students who were politically conservative, the correction didn't work the way it should have; instead of making them more suspicious of the idea that Saddam Hussein had been hiding WMDs, it *doubled* their belief in it.[48]

This is what Karl Rove meant when he told the *New York Times'* Ron Suskind, "We create our own reality."[49] This is also what Andreessen means when he says that "reality is woefully lacking" for many Americans and so the Metaverse can help them create their own reality. But what he and the other Technocrats are really proposing is a formal end of the Enlightenment—that age championing the use and celebration of reason and truth.

‿

On a quiet Saturday in May 2022, at a supermarket in Buffalo, New York, an eighteen-year-old white man named Payton Gendron, clad in full body armor and carrying an assault rifle, killed ten people and injured three more, almost all of them Black. As the *New York Times* noted, "Shortly after Mr. Gendron was captured, a manifesto believed to have been posted online by the gunman emerged, riddled with racist, anti-immigrant views that claimed white Americans were at risk of being replaced by people of color. In the video that appeared to have been captured by the camera affixed to his helmet, an anti-Black racial slur can be seen on the barrel of his weapon."[50]

Astonishingly, for thirty minutes before he murdered ten people, Gendron invited a number of people into a private chat to discuss detailed plans for his massacre on the Discord platform, used by video game players to communicate with each other. A spokeswoman for Discord said, "A private, invite-only server was created by the suspect to serve as a personal diary chat log. Approximately 30 minutes prior to the attack, however, a small group of people were invited to and joined the server." Why not a single one of them reported this to the police is a mystery. Here was a young man publicizing his violent, fascist plans for mass murder, and no one responded.

Gendron then decided to live stream the mass murder on Twitch. "Live streaming this attack gives me some motivation in the way that I know that some people will be cheering for me," the shooter said after he made his first kill. Strikingly, most school shooters in the United States are boys under the age of twenty-one, a group that psychologists say is reckless and prone to violence. Tellingly, the leading causes of death for men aged fifteen to twenty-one include fights, shootings, accidents, driving too fast, and other impulsive behaviors.[51] Being able to broadcast their acts of mass murder to their peers on Facebook, Twitch, TikTok, or YouTube sometimes becomes a major motive for the act.

Frank Robertz, director of the Institute for Violence Prevention and Applied Criminology in Berlin, told the *Washington Post*, "A common thread among shooters is the connection between a disturbed adolescence and escapes into a fantasy world."[52] Given the violent results of such escapes, Meta's desire to provide more opportunities for these young men to flee into a fantasy world seems extraordinarily destructive. Gendron described being transformed over a couple of months of pandemic lockdown into a white supremacist. How does this happen?

One element came to light a week before the Buffalo shooting, when the *New York Times* published a three-part investigation into Tucker Carlson, the Fox News personality who has done more than anyone in America to popularize the "great replacement" theory, which has become increasingly important in white nationalist circles. It holds that people of color, primarily immigrants, are coming to the United States illegally with the intent of rendering the white population a political minority within the country. Clearly the August 2017 Unite the Right Rally in

Charlottesville, Virginia, with the torch-carrying parade of young men shouting, "Jews will not replace us," was an early harbinger of this movement. It's clear from reporting in the *New York Times* and other media that white fear of losing status is the main driver behind the move to return Trump to power.[53]

It is not coincidental that Gendron wrote in his manifesto, "Why is diversity said to be our greatest strength? Does anyone even ask why? It is spoken like a mantra and repeated ad infinitum?" In late 2018, Carlson spoke these words on his program: "How, precisely, is diversity our strength? Since you've made this our new national motto, please be specific as you explain it." Defending himself two days after the mass murder, Carlson said, "What is hate speech? Well, it's speech that our leaders hate." As the *New York Times* reported, on the following evening, "Mr. Carlson first professed ignorance of the [great replacement] conspiracy theory, then said it was true, then insisted, 'The great replacement theory is coming from the left.' "[54] Whether Gendron was a viewer of Tucker Carlson's program is not the issue—Fox makes sure that clips of Carlson are distributed widely on YouTube and Facebook. So if Gendron saw Carlson say this (and repeated it in his manifesto), it was probably on Gendron's Facebook feed. Media Matters reported that between 2020 and 2022 its researchers found at least fifty ads on Facebook promoting aspects of the "great replacement" theory and related themes.

Carlson's attempts to deflect blame rang hollow to Michael Edison Hayden, a senior investigative reporter at the Southern Poverty Law Center. "As long as very wealthy people are willing to exploit these feelings of anger in the country, this is going to keep happening," Hayden said. "The reality is, they know what they're doing when they bring up [the] Great Replacement Theory on the air. They know what they're doing when they dehumanize immigrants. They know what kind of effect it's going to have on people who are already predisposed to being mistrustful and frightened."[55]

In 1994, the CIA began organizing a Political Instability Task Force, made up of analysts and academics who study civil unrest around the world. They looked at all the civil wars in the last half century and found a couple of key similarities. First, instability gets serious in a middle ground between democracy and autocracy. Full democracies almost never have civil wars, and full autocracies rarely have them. It's when institutions begin to weaken that armed insurgents begin to wreak havoc. The second factor, as Barbara Walters, author of *How Civil Wars Start: And How to Stop Them*, has shown, is when parties stop identifying around ideology and start identifying "almost exclusively around identity: ethnic, religious or racial identity."[56] Walters thinks the organized militias in America are a real sign of trouble. She told the *Washington Post*, "What we're heading toward is an insurgency, which is a form of a civil war...An insurgency tends to be much more decentralized, often fought by multiple groups."

How do these militias organize and recruit? Even after the January 6 insurrection, more than two hundred militia pages and groups were on Facebook, according to a report by the Tech Transparency Project.[57] So for Walters, a lot of disturbing signs are present. We have weakening institutions and distrust of government. We have a Republican Party built around white identity. And we have a media system that can both inspire and organize an armed insurgency.

⌒

To understand how Tucker Carlson could have built what the *New York Times* called "the most racist show in the history of cable news" on a major network, we need to return to the Ronald Reagan era, during which the last barrier to hyperpartisan news broadcasting—the fairness doctrine—was destroyed.

In 1974, Rupert Murdoch moved to New York from Australia, where his News Corp had been headquartered since his father had died in 1952 and left him a failing newspaper company with a single viable asset: the *News*, Adelaide's only newspaper. Murdoch revived the *News*, then set out on a campaign of acquisition that eventually included England's two most popular tabloids, the *News of The World* and the *Sun*. He told Larry Lamb, his newly appointed editor at the *Sun*, "I want a tear away paper with lots of tits in it." That's what he got.

After moving to New York, he acquired the *New York Post*, another tabloid. America was too puritanical for Murdoch to put bare-breasted women on page three, but he did fill the *Post* with gossip, scandal, and murder. The acquisition was well timed to take advantage of the Son of Sam serial killings (eight murders by David Berkowitz in the summer and fall of 1976) and the rise of real estate braggart Donald Trump, who became a daily feature in the *Post*'s Page Six gossip column. A delighted Trump went so far as to pretend he was a PR man, phoning in items to the *Post*. He didn't even try to disguise his voice. As Princeton historian Sean Wilentz wrote in a *Washington Post* review of Maggie Haberman's 2022 book on Trump, *Confidence Man*, "The dynamics that defined New York City in the 1980s, Haberman observes, 'stayed with Trump for decades; he often seemed frozen there.' Zombielike, he swaggers and struts and cons on the world's largest stage, much as he did when gossip columnists fawned over him as The Donald."[58]

But the individual who benefited most from Murdoch's emergence as an American media baron was Ronald Reagan. Murdoch had hired Trump's friend Roy Cohn, despite Cohn's being a totally shady character. Since his time as Joe McCarthy's chief counsel, hunting communists in the government, Cohn had taken to representing various Mafia dons and dabbled in stock swindles and perjury convictions—with four indictments in the late 1960s and early 1970s.[59] Cohn's job was to make sure that Murdoch's political connections were secure in Washington, DC. The first important introduction he made for Murdoch, in late 1979, was to Roger Stone, then head of presidential candidate Ronald Reagan's New York operations. From Murdoch's very conservative political position, Reagan was the ideal candidate, and he delivered daily support for Reagan's campaign in the *Post*. As the *New York Times* reported in February 1981 after Reagan's inauguration, "Representative Jack Kemp, a New York Republican, said, 'Rupert Murdoch used the editorial page, the front page and every other page necessary to elect Ronald Reagan President.'" Perhaps Kemp, trying to curry favor with Murdoch, was overstating the power of a New York tabloid, but within a few years Murdoch owned both the *Wall Street Journal* and Fox News, and so his political power continued to grow.

Murdoch famously expects repayment of any favor; in the spring of 1986, he called in his chit. He had decided he needed to expand into television. Mike Milken, the junk bond king, had told him that because of the very loose Australian accounting standards, Milken could arrange financing for Murdoch to acquire the six Metromedia Television stations in a transaction that would be almost completely debt financed. This would allow Murdoch to maintain majority control while vastly expanding his empire. He had already bought 20th Century Fox Studios, and the combination of TV production and TV station ownership was critical to the launch of Fox Broadcasting.

There were a few hurdles. First, only a US citizen could control a US broadcasting license. Second, existing laws prevented a single company from owning both a TV station and a newspaper in the same market. Murdoch, Cohn, and Stone went to work on Reagan. Within months, Murdoch was given US citizenship. Soon afterward the cross-ownership rules were relaxed.

But Murdoch wanted more than just hit shows like *The Simpsons* on his network. Since the 1940s, the FCC had held that when broadcasters are "licensed to operate in a public domain, the licensee has assumed the obligation of presenting all sides of important public questions fairly, objectively and without bias." This fairness doctrine had been challenged in 1969 (*Red Lion Broadcasting v. Federal Communications Commission*), but that year the Supreme Court unanimously upheld its constitutionality. Justice Byron White wrote the opinion: "It is the purpose of the First Amendment to preserve an uninhibited marketplace of ideas in which truth will ultimately prevail, rather than to countenance monopolization of the market, whether it be by the government itself or a private licensee."

In August 1987, Reagan's FCC eliminated the fairness doctrine, stating that "because of the many media voices in the marketplace, the doctrine

[is] unconstitutional. The intrusion by government into the content of programming occasioned by the enforcement of [the fairness doctrine] restricts the journalistic freedom of broadcasters." Exactly what role Murdoch, Cohn, and Stone played in this decision is unclear. Perhaps it was payback for Murdoch's political support of Reagan. Regardless, the effect on the content of the media was almost immediate. Within six months, *The Rush Limbaugh Show* was being offered to AM stations for free (with four minutes of ads per hour reserved for Limbaugh's production company to sell to national advertisers). Within three years Limbaugh was on five hundred stations.

Rush Limbaugh changed the nature of American political dialogue. Soon after Reagan left the White House, he wrote Limbaugh a letter naming him as his spiritual heir.[60] Limbaugh's show would feature such segments as a daily "AIDS update" underscored by Dionne Warwick's "I'll Never Love This Way Again." Trump picked up on the way Limbaugh's kind of cruelty played so well with his audience. It became part of his public style when he ran for president.

By 1996, Murdoch had created Fox News. Even though it was a cable channel (and not subject to FCC regulation), the popularity of Limbaugh had set the template and proved that advertisers would back conservative content. All of the technology needed to bring us to our present partisan crisis was in place. Fox News could use "Fair and Balanced" as a marketing slogan, but it was just an inside joke. There was no longer a need to cover all sides of an issue. Murdoch shifted the whole media narrative toward a populist wave. And even if two of his children (James and Elisabeth) hated Fox News, Murdoch didn't care. The profits were too big to let go of the hard-right message.[61]

Ironically, Tucker Carlson understood better than anyone the power of the media instrument Murdoch had unleashed around the world. Carlson tried to talk about propaganda and liberalism in the fall of 2021, but he was really just patting himself on the back. "Propaganda tends to bewilder people, to confuse them when they first hear it," he said. "It is so completely and obviously untrue, 'What is this?' you think. And yet for that very reason, because it's so ridiculous, so absurd, propaganda tends to be effective."[62]

At the end of World War II, US intelligence operatives discovered the personal diary of Dr. Joseph Goebbels, Hitler's propaganda minister. In it, Goebbels laid out the five core principles of propaganda:

- Avoid abstract ideas—appeal to the emotions.
- Constantly repeat just a few ideas. Use stereotyped phrases.
- Give only one side of the argument.
- Continuously criticize your opponents.
- Pick out one special "enemy" for special vilification.

The diary list could have been used as a production guide for *Tucker Carlson Tonight*. And so we must be clear: Carlson is following a long tradition that stems from the rhetoric of Germany in 1933. As Jason Stanley, Yale philosophy professor and author of *How Fascism Works*, wrote after the Buffalo massacre, "As Gendron's manifesto makes clear, white replacement theory is not just an attack on minorities. It is a weapon directed by fascists at American democracy itself."

That fascist propaganda has been an enormously profitable business for Rupert Murdoch and Tucker Carlson cannot be denied. From custom-built $2 million studios in one of his three homes (Maine, Florida, and New York), Carlson structured nearly every topic on his show as a "ruling-class plot" against "you." In that sense he is no different from Peter Thiel, Elon Musk, Marc Andreessen, or Mark Zuckerberg. There are millions of dollars to be made from exploiting chaos and alienation. And for the tech monopolists as well as people like Rupert Murdoch, extremes of partisanship guarantee that no meaningful media regulation will ever pass Congress.

PART III
The Future

6

WELCOME TO THE METAVERSE

Being in this metaverse will be a bigger part of our lives than being in the outside world.

—Augmented reality designer Louis Rosenberg

In October 2021, in an eighty-minute video, Mark Zuckerberg unveiled the future he hopes we will live in by the end of this decade. He calls it the Metaverse, and he believes so fervently in this vision that he has renamed his company Meta. The Metaverse is an immersive virtual world users will access in two modes: virtual reality (VR), with a VR headset and avatar, and augmented reality (AR), with AR glasses. In 1981, French sociologist Jean Baudrillard published *Simulacra and Simulation*, in which he prophesied that we were moving toward a world of *hyperreality*, where reality and fantasy are seamlessly blended, so that there is no clear distinction between them. For Baudrillard, this was the harbinger of looming dystopia; for Zuckerberg, it is a future to be embraced. Users could experience the fantasy world of both entertainment and politics 24/7 in a virtual world. If we worried about how online exposure to hours of first-person shooter games or violent alt-right Reddit threads might be warping young minds, we might heed the old Al Jolson line from the first talking movie, *The Jazz Singer* (1927): "You ain't seen nothin' yet."

As he told technology analyst Ben Thompson, who edits the *Stra-techery* online magazine, Zuckerberg's business case is that you will spend most of your waking hours in the Metaverse.[1] The time you currently spend using your smartphone will become augmented reality time, and, in his telling, the seven hours a day you spend in front of a screen (TV or computer) will instead be spent in virtual reality in a vast world Meta has named Horizon. You will purchase your custom designed avatar and outfit it regularly with new digital clothing from Gucci and other high-end brands. You won't need to buy pants because your avatar won't have legs. You will enjoy the Jay-Z/Beyoncé concert in your home, though you will feel (if you've paid enough) like you are in the front row of a fifty-thousand-seat stadium. And when you don't have the headset on, you will still be able to bring part of your fantasy world into your office or hotel room by putting on your Meta AR glasses. While you are in the Metaverse, you can also shop for nonfungible tokens (NFTs), which are essentially virtual art pieces constructed by artificial intelligence (AI). You have prob-ably seen a "Bored Apes" NFT on the web somewhere. At one point they were selling for thousands of dollars. Now you can't give them away.

If Zuckerberg is right in believing he can get people to exist in the Metaverse for seven hours a day—"immersive, all-day experiences will require a lot of novel technologies"—then we need to examine the health problems associated with such long-term use of VR. The problems with the technology are legion.

Many people report headaches, eye strain, dizziness and nausea after using the headsets. Such symptoms are triggered by the VR illusion, which makes the eyes focus on objects apparently in the distance that are actually on a screen just centimetres away. Known as vergence-accommodation conflict, this is now under investiga-tion for its long-term effects, especially among children. A recent study by researchers at Leeds University found that just 20 min-utes exposure to VR could affect the ability of some children to discern the distance to objects. There are also concerns that regular use of VR could accelerate the global epidemic of myopia—short-sightedness—which [was] predicted to affect one in three of the world's population by 2020.[2]

These drawbacks have obviously limited the appeal of VR, which Zuckerberg has been pushing ever since he acquired Oculus in 2014 for $2 billion and merged it into Facebook. Currently, Meta is heavily marketing the Meta Quest 2 headset for $300 on TV sports shows (they make no profit on the headset) and has sold a little more than ten million units. Tech analyst Benedict Evans notes that the Quest 2 sales numbers are "certainly not nothing, but [the headset] appears to have high abandonment rates and it's not clear that it's really cut through yet." Internal memos show that "most visitors to Horizon generally don't return to the app after the first month, and the user base has steadily declined since the spring, according to the documents, which include internal memos from employees…According to internal statistics, only 9% of worlds built by creators are ever visited by at least 50 people. Most are never visited at all."[3]

But the problems of getting customers to adopt Meta's headset are mirrored inside the company, where Horizon is described as notoriously buggy. On September 15, 2022, Meta's vice president of the Metaverse, Vishal Shah, wrote a memo to his team: "For many of us, we don't spend that much time in Horizon and our dogfooding dashboards show this pretty clearly. Why is that? Why don't we love the product we've built so much that we use it all the time? The simple truth is, if we don't love it, how can we expect our users to love it?" Meta's October 2022 earnings release showed that only two hundred thousand people enter Horizon each month, far below the company's projections.[4]

Evans believed Meta would have to go to a much more expensive headset ($1,000 or more) to "shift perceptions with a dramatic jump forward in experience, showing people what's possible, and wait for the price to catch up." But when Meta released a new $1,500 headset on October 10, 2022, *Stratechery*'s Ben Thompson wrote that "the presentation was a cringe, and seemed to lack any compelling demos of virtual reality." For now, Meta is marketing the Quest 2 as a fitness appliance. The ads never show users wearing the helmet.

But ultimately Zuckerberg's vision of millions of people simultaneously interacting in virtual reality may be the biggest fantasy of all. As Raja Kaduri, a senior vice president at Intel, has written,

> Consider what is required to put two individuals in a social setting in an entirely virtual environment: convincing and detailed avatars with realistic clothing, hair and skin tones—all rendered in real time and based on sensor data capturing real world 3D objects, gestures, audio and much more; data transfer at super high bandwidths and extremely low latencies; and a persistent model of the environment, which may contain both real and simulated elements. Now, imagine solving this problem at scale—for hundreds of millions of users simultaneously—and you will quickly realize that our computing, storage and networking infrastructure today is simply not enough to enable this vision.[5]

Zuckerberg is fighting a—so far—losing battle for VR adoption. Jony Ive, Apple's famed design chief, who has argued against VR, zeroes in on the challenge Zuckerberg faces. Ive, whom Queen Elizabeth II knighted for his design expertise, designed the Apple Mac computers and the iPhone. He said, "VR alienated users from other people by cutting them off from the outside world, made users look unfashionable and lacked practical uses." Ive was also "unconvinced that consumers would be willing to wear headsets for long periods of time."[6]

‿

Meta's struggles in marketing VR to the masses would not be surprising to anyone who has studied the history of virtual reality. In 1838, English scientist Charles Wheatstone realized that the brain processes the different two-dimensional images from each eye into a single object of three dimensions. His subsequent invention of the stereoscope became popular after Queen Victoria publicly praised it at the Great Exposition of 1851 in London. The term 3-*D* came into common use, and eventually an American company produced the View-Master, a cheap 3-D device with a rotating cardboard disk containing image pairs. Producing hundreds of disks of exotic locations, the View-Master was marketed as a "virtual tourism" device. It enjoyed a brief burst of popularity in the late 1950s among adults and then was relegated to being a child's toy.

In the 1930s and 1940s, the military developed several flight simulators to train pilots on the ground. None of these used a head-mounted display; rather, they projected film onto the three windows of the simulator. Then Morton Heilig, one of the men who had worked on the flight simulators, decided to take it to the next level. Heilig patented the Sensorama in 1962. Meant to go in arcades, it featured a wrap-around cabinet with stereo speakers, a stereoscopic 3-D display, fans, smell generators, and a vibrating chair. Heilig created short films in which the viewer was operating a motorcycle, dune buggy, or helicopter. It never took off, however, and Sensorama folded.

The real birth of what we now know as VR occurred in 1985, when Jaron Lanier and Thomas Zimmerman formed VPL Research and produced both a head-mounted display and a set of gloves for the first real VR experience. But VPL's gear was very expensive: VR goggles: $9,400 to $49,000; gloves: $9,000. There was a brief flurry of hype around Jaron Lanier, who looked like a cross between Jerry Garcia and Bob Marley, but again, VR never caught on.

In 1993, at the Consumer Electronics Show, Sega made a major announcement: a VR headset for the Sega Genesis console. But despite millions in marketing dollars and a consumer-friendly $200 price point, the device was a total flop. In 2012, however, Palmer Luckey raised $2.5 million on Kickstarter for the Oculus Rift head-mounted display. Within two years, he was able to sell the company to Facebook for $2 billion. The VR enthusiasts who had witnessed so many false starts believed that they had finally found a champion in Mark Zuckerberg—someone so deeply invested he wouldn't give up, despite continued consumer resistance.

I have tried almost every version of VR since Jaron Lanier introduced his first headset. I have always had nausea problems, but I still believe that certain kinds of virtual reality applications can be helpful in training and therapy. When I was running the Annenberg Innovation Lab at the University of Southern California, my colleagues at the Institute for Creative Technologies invented some VR applications to treat post-traumatic stress disorder in veterans returning from Iraq. The technology showed promise, but the VR sessions had to be limited to forty minutes or less.

My friend documentary filmmaker Doug Pray (*The Defiant Ones*) wrote me that some films are "shot in 360°. It's not VR, but you can change the angles and look around wherever you want and it's kind of cool when applied to sports, or design, or tours through an interesting space, where multiple perspectives are dynamic. But it doesn't enhance the art of storytelling, any more than a rear-view video camera on your car enhances the destination you're driving to."

But therapy or architectural tours are not what Zuckerberg's Metaverse is about. The goal is to make billions off advertising and e-commerce. In addition to developing the VR headset, Meta is spending millions on technology to read your mind. Meta suggests that the new VR headset will give us the ability to control digital devices—from keyboards to augmented reality glasses—using just our thoughts. This new access to our brain data, Meta executives suggest, will provide new opportunities for "personalized" advertising and experiences.[7] The very act of visualizing something in a Metaverse shopping environment would trigger brain activity that would let Meta know you desire that jacket before you even know it yourself.

Cultural critic Julian Sanchez makes the good point that "you sort of have to wonder if mass entertainment hasn't tilled the soil for the current explosion of [fantasy and] conspiracy theories. For decades Hollywood has fed us the appealing fantasy that YOU—seemingly average viewer—may secretly be the World's Most Special Boy (or, less often, Girl)."[8]

And it is here that the coming Metaverse will feed the fantasy culture described in Chapter 4. No longer will you be just an *Avengers* fan. You can *be* Tony Stark. With enough crypto tokens at your disposal, you can live in his awesome house, put on his Iron Man suit, and fly off to Paris with Gwyneth Paltrow's avatar, which you have rented for the night from the Meta Celebrity Avatar Service.

How you design your avatar will have an effect not only on your life in the Metaverse but on your self-representation in the real world. Stanford Communications School researchers Nick Yee and Jeremy Bailenson wrote a seminal paper titled "The Proteus Effect: The Effect of Transformed Self-Representation on Behavior."[9] The abstract reveals their findings.

In 2 experimental studies, we explore the hypothesis that an individual's behavior conforms to their digital self-representation independent of how others perceive them—a process we term the Proteus Effect. In the first study, participants assigned to more attractive avatars in immersive virtual environments were more intimate with confederates in a self-disclosure and interpersonal distance task than participants assigned to less attractive avatars. In our second study, participants assigned taller avatars behaved more confidently in a negotiation task than participants assigned shorter avatars.

The more attractive your avatar, the more intimate your behavior with strangers in the virtual world. The taller your avatar, the more aggressively you'll act.

But most surprisingly, these changed behaviors continued outside the virtual world. As Yee and Bailenson wrote, "In addition to causing a behavioral difference within the virtual environment, we found that participants given taller avatars negotiated more aggressively in subsequent face-to-face interactions." As discussed earlier, psychologists have long known that behavior learned inside first-person shooter video games often has real-world implications. Maybe one implication of the Stanford study is that the Metaverse will be populated only with tall, thin, attractive people. Fans of the Metaverse argue that surely people will find other ways to stand out in a virtual crowd. Obviously expensive virtual clothing will be one way. Perhaps purple hair will also be in vogue?

Regardless, as you browse the Ready Player Me site, which advertises itself as "your one stop shop for all your avatar needs," you will find no fat people—all the girls look like Kim Kardashian, all the guys like Chris Hemsworth.[10] Mark Zuckerberg is well aware of the implications of the Stanford research. At the outset, Meta used a selfie to create a user's avatar, but it turned out people didn't want to look like themselves. When Zuckerberg released a picture of his own avatar, one commentator tweeted, "This looks like a 2002 Nintendo GameCube release called World Baby." The avatar was so crudely cartoonish that the company went into a ten-day full sprint to produce a better avatar for the boss.

In a recent interview, Zuckerberg said, "Part of it is, we're building out this avatar system that is going to get increasingly expressive on the one hand, and then if you want, also increasingly realistic. Although I think not everyone wants to be exactly realistic all the time, so you want to kind of offer both expressive and realistic."[11] His use of the word *expressive* to mean "make me look like Kim Kardashian" is quaint. I can see the avatar creators and the plastic surgeons having a symbiotic relationship in the 2030s. Research has already proven that couples who meet in VR are reluctant to meet in person. Clearly they want to be represented by their "expressive" avatars rather than their "realistic" selves.

But that does not resolve the inevitable effect of looking in the mirror after seven hours in the Metaverse and realizing you don't look like Kendall Jenner after all. Even now on Instagram, the use of the FaceTune tool to change your selfies has led to what *New Yorker* writer Jia Tolentino called "the gradual emergence, among professionally beautiful women, of a single, cyborgian face."[12] Is the average overweight schlub really going to walk up to the most beautiful girl in his high school class and ask for a date? Highly doubtful. More likely, his "date" will be renting the avatar of a Kardashian to take to the Metaverse prom.

Soon we will also have to confront the problem of "digital blackface," which is already plaguing TikTok. Digital blackface is when a white person dances and/or lip syncs to a Black person's voice or music. "In order to put on the voice of a Black woman, they feel like they also have to put on an entire performance as well, which is often quite offensive," said Alexis Williams, a Black TikTok creator with two hundred thousand followers.[13] As the Metaverse's user base expands, there will almost certainly be questions about young, white hip-hop singers creating Black avatars to give them the final bit of cred.

≈

Even the most optimistic promoters of the Metaverse do not believe it will arrive in this decade. Matthew Ball, the most visible promoter of the Metaverse who runs a fund ($META) that invests in Metaverse-related stocks, including Meta, has come out with a book titled *The Metaverse*. Zuckerberg has said that his talks with Ball have focused his thinking, but Jamie Burke of Outlier Ventures (a firm pushing for a truly open Metaverse) has asked, "So it is reasonable to say there is history between Zuck and Matthew and it would probably be helpful to understand if Matthew has ever engaged in paid consultancy with Facebook (in any capacity over the last several years) as a point of clarification. If for nothing but to rule it out."[14] No matter how conflicted Ball may be, he is clear that the near future of VR is just gaming. He told the *Washington Post* "how weird it seems that the next generation of the Internet is being pioneered by a relatively small portion of the leisure economy—gaming."[15]

Clearly debate is fierce over how the Metaverse will be governed and who will control it. The Deloitte consulting firm has charted out three potential scenarios.[16]

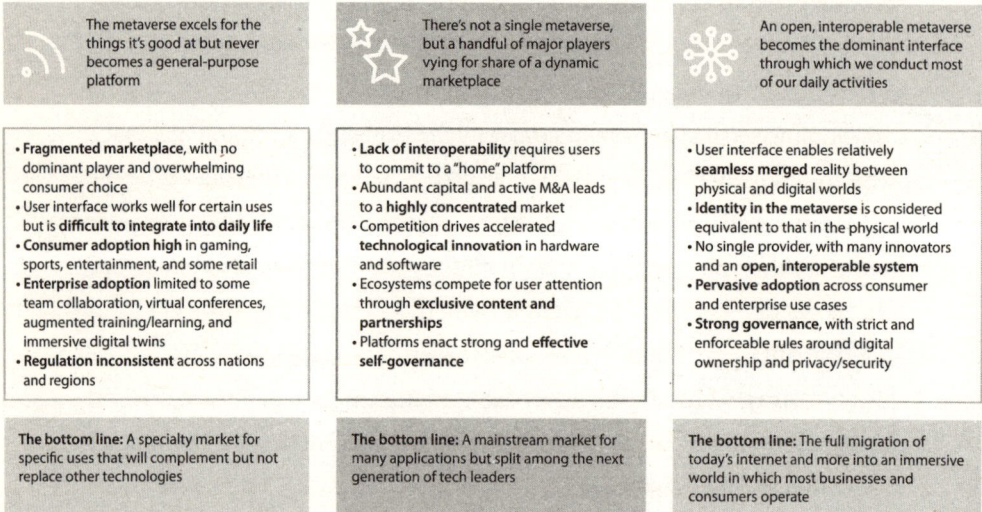

The metaverse excels for the things it's good at but never becomes a general-purpose platform	There's not a single metaverse, but a handful of major players vying for share of a dynamic marketplace	An open, interoperable metaverse becomes the dominant interface through which we conduct most of our daily activities
• **Fragmented marketplace**, with no dominant player and overwhelming consumer choice • User interface works well for certain uses but is **difficult to integrate into daily life** • **Consumer adoption high** in gaming, sports, entertainment, and some retail • **Enterprise adoption** limited to some team collaboration, virtual conferences, augmented training/learning, and immersive digital twins • **Regulation inconsistent** across nations and regions	• **Lack of interoperability** requires users to commit to a "home" platform • Abundant capital and active M&A leads to a **highly concentrated** market • Competition drives accelerated **technological innovation** in hardware and software • Ecosystems compete for user attention through **exclusive content and partnerships** • Platforms enact strong and **effective self-governance**	• User interface enables relatively **seamless merged** reality between physical and digital worlds • **Identity in the metaverse** is considered equivalent to that in the physical world • No single provider, with many innovators and an **open, interoperable system** • **Pervasive adoption** across consumer and enterprise use cases • **Strong governance**, with strict and enforceable rules around digital ownership and privacy/security
The bottom line: A specialty market for specific uses that will complement but not replace other technologies	**The bottom line:** A mainstream market for many applications but split among the next generation of tech leaders	**The bottom line:** The full migration of today's internet and more into an immersive world in which most businesses and consumers operate

In my assessment, by 2030 we will be in Deloitte's "Low Orbit" scenario (a fragmented marketplace concentrating mostly on games), despite the investment of billions by Zuckerberg and Marc Andreessen in technology and marketing. It strains credulity to believe we end up in the "Big Bang" scenario (multiple corporate Metaverse sites seamlessly integrated and interoperable), which would involve companies like Meta, Google, and Apple surrendering their intellectual property and operating systems to some third-party consortium.

And here, Meta encounters an even deeper problem, in that it doesn't have a widely used operating system like Apple or Google. Ironically, three partners in Andreessen Horowitz, the firm that is the most aggressive investor in the consolidation of Web3, have made an almost socialist argument for the "Big Bang" scenario: "In a metaverse, all stakeholders should have a say, proportionally to their involvement, in the governance of the system. People should not just have to abide by the edicts passed down by a group of product managers at a tech company. If any one entity owns or controls this virtual world, then much like Disney World, it may offer a certain form of contained escapism but will never live up to its true potential."[17]

In Wall Street talk, the Andreessen Horowitz partners are "talking their book." In the midst of an epic meltdown in the crypto and NFT space, they are pretending that they want a new, decentralized web at the very moment when their NFT platform, OpenSea, controls 80 percent of the internet's current NFT content. Twitter founder and former CEO Jack Dorsey's tweet on this is much closer to reality: "You don't own web3. The VC's do. It will never escape their incentives. It's ultimately a centralized entity with a different label." Though I referenced this earlier, I think it's important to underscore that this is the critical factor. The VCs, or venture capitalists, Dorsey is referring to, of course, are the partners at Andreessen Horowitz. Andreessen is pitching Web3 as a response to the general perception that the current internet is controlled by a few monopolies and that somehow Web3 will "democratize" the web. He and Zuckerberg are pushing this narrative while simultaneously aiming to control most of the central platforms of Web3.

Dorsey is right: the history of the internet tends always toward monopoly. Google has a 90 percent market share in search advertising; Meta owns four of the five most-used social media platforms. I have worked in the media business for more than fifty years and have watched an endless series of consolidations. Based on that experience, I have no doubt that the Metaverse hype machine will force media companies like Walt Disney to investigate making programming for virtual reality. And while VR is suitable for first-person shooter games, almost every important film director I have talked to thinks that it is a horrible medium for traditional narrative fiction movies. As one director put it, "I spend hours composing a scene with a series of cuts that builds the drama. I don't want the audience to look in the opposite direction." Doug Pray was even more insistent that the Metaverse is the wrong artistic tool.

Our entire craft is built around the art of carefully manipulating sounds and images to coalesce into a strong emotion or epiphany. You're taking your audience on a meaningful journey. Just as a writer collects and arranges words, sentences and paragraphs to make a specific point.

To take that end goal—the very purpose of an artist's work—and toss it out the window in favor of "whatever or wherever the viewer wants" makes the entire exchange meaningless. It might be entertaining, but it's not entertainment. It might be virtual, but it's not virtuous.

If there is a killer app for the Metaverse (beyond first-person shooter games), it's probably the virtual mall. Here, the tech wizards at Meta can maximize the monetization of every minute you spend walking down their virtual Rodeo Drive. There will be personalized billboards you can't avoid; every object that you touch in the virtual Gucci store will be available for both your avatar and you (because Meta will already have your sizes in their database). Stephane Kasriel, head of commerce and financial technologies at Meta, outlines his vision of the future as follows: "Imagine a world where entertainers or athletes can sell NFTs that fans purchase to display in their virtual Horizon homes. Or imagine all of this coming together when your favorite artist is playing a concert in the Metaverse and shares an NFT you can buy to get a backstage pass for after the show."[18]

So let's parse this out. In the first scenario, I wander into a virtual NFT art gallery, select a "virtual painting," and pay for it with Meta tokens. I can then take it to my virtual Horizon home, which I have also purchased from Meta (for a lot more Meta tokens). Of course, if I wanted to take my Meta painting into my Roblox (the immersive kids game platform) house, no luck: Meta NFTs would only work inside Meta virtual houses.

In the second scenario, after paying a lot of Meta tokens to go to the virtual Beyoncé concert, I can then (for a lot more Meta tokens) purchase a virtual backstage pass so I can pretend to hang out with a virtual Beyoncé. Really?

Marc Andreessen, who is on the Meta board, is convinced that a lot of lonely people will love this fantasy. He thinks Zuckerberg's coming Metaverse is just the solution for our current cultural despair. "We should build—and we are building—online worlds that make life and work and love wonderful for everyone, no matter what *level of reality deprivation* they find themselves in."[19] In the same interview Andreessen went on to say that only "a small percent of people live in a real-world environment that is rich, even overflowing, with glorious substance, beautiful settings, plentiful stimulation, and many fascinating people to talk to, and to work with, and to date." So the rest of the population will be anxious to live for most of the day in a fantasy world—the Metaverse.

Others distrust Zuckerberg's vision of an alternative virtual reality where you can't skip the ads. As Rob Horning, editor of *Real Life* magazine (which covers living with technology) noted, "Facebook would also like to secure the ability to prevent people from any right to absence… The Metaverse is fundamentally a place you will be forced to be."

I want to investigate Andreessen's notion of "reality deprivation," because only in such a condition might we consent to strap on Zuckerberg's headset for seven hours a day. The most obvious real-world deprivation that will be commercially available in the Metaverse will be sex. As with videocassettes and streaming media, porn will likely drive adoption. An earlier attempt at the Metaverse called Second Life dissolved into a cesspool of kinky virtual sex before it expired. In thinking about this scenario, it is instructive to study men's rights activists who claim they are in a "beta rebellion." In their parlance, a beta male is a young man who can't find a sexual partner because all the beautiful women are too busy mating with so-called alpha males. But MRAs don't blame the alphas; they are mad at the women, who, thanks to the advances of feminism, have the power to choose their partners. In the Metaverse, that dynamic will be reversed—with enough crypto, all users will have the sex they desire immediately available.

Rob Brooks, an evolutionary biologist based at the University of New South Wales in Sydney, writes about the future of virtual sex in *Artificial*

Intimacy: Digital Lovers, Virtual Friends and Algorithmic Matchmakers.
Here, he muses about the future of sex in the Metaverse:

> VR offers users the chance to move through a virtual scene, inter-
> acting—socially and sexually—with other characters. For now, those
> characters are porn performers. Users don headsets to view scenes
> filmed as if the viewer were either a third-party observer or a partici-
> pant. The next leap will involve the generation of scenes where a user
> can interact freely with the characters. Once users can take the scene
> in original directions, and characters can respond, moving, making
> sounds and conveying touch, VR porn will cross over into VR sex.[20]

Religious conservatives like *New York Times* columnist Ross Douthat
believe the Metaverse could trigger a huge moral backlash. In *The Decadent
Society*, Douthat writes, "You wouldn't necessarily need the huge AI or bio-
tech leap: even a refinement of existing virtual reality, one that draws more
people more fully into the violence and pornography of unreal playgrounds,
would seem to demand a religious response, even a dramatic one."[21]

Ironically, in 2002, in *Ashcroft v. Free Speech Coalition*, the Supreme
Court struck down a federal law barring the creation of virtual child pornography, ruling that computer-generated child porn was free speech
"that records no crime and creates no victims by its production." This
ultimate libertarian ruling neglects one critical point, as Harvard constitutional scholar Adrian Vermeule (author of *Common Good Consti-
tutionalism*) observes: "The law is a teacher of virtue, and it should not
teach that animated or simulated child porn is somehow a victimless
crime."[22] It should be noted that the Silicon Valley–funded Electronic
Frontier Foundation has been on the front lines, defending the rights of
pornographers to use the internet without interference.[23]

We can get a glimpse of what this virtual sex work will look like via
the e-pimps of OnlyFans. For those who have spent the last two years on
a desert island, OnlyFans is a website that allows anyone to earn money

from users who subscribe to their content—the "fans." The majority of the content is "exclusive" porn (straight and gay). The problem with the business is that it rests on the illusion of personal intimacy between the "performer" and the fan, conveyed mostly through text messaging. Needless to say, for a popular performer, this doesn't scale well. Enter the e-pimps, who provide a posse of virtual impersonators known as chatters. While the porn star strips for the clients online, the chatters, each pretending to be the star, coax the marks into buying expensive pay-per-view videos recorded "just for them." Using this methodology, an Only-Fans performer can service a large audience, all of whom believe they are having an intimate one-to-one relationship with him or her. An e-pimp (most are based in Miami, America's crypto capital) can run a string of two hundred performers from his bedroom.

This is our current reality. Our Technocrats are looking to a near-term future in which the chatting won't even be done by humans. The GPT-3 AI writing tool is already so good that you can give it a topic and a tone, and it can write an infinite number of messages or essays, instantly responding to prompts or questions.[24]

But like real-world sex, virtual sex may also involve virtual rape. *Business Insider* described how a female researcher's avatar was raped at a private party in Meta's Horizon world:

> The researcher "was led into a private room at a party where she was raped by a user who kept telling her to turn around so he could do it from behind while users outside the window could see—all while another user in the room watched and passed around a vodka bottle," per the report.
>
> Even though it happened in virtual reality, the incident left the researcher "disoriented," she said in the report. The researcher noted her controller vibrated when the male avatars touched her, resulting in a physical sensation that was a result of what she was experiencing online.

"One part of my brain was like WTF is happening, the other part was like this isn't a real body, and another part was like, this is important research," she said in the report.[25]

Meta has assured the world that the deeply embedded AI in its Metaverse will make it a safe place to work and play, but there is no evidence that this is happening. Imagine, if you will, that, as in *World of Warcraft*, in the Metaverse you will be able to purchase extraordinary powers: amazing strength, the ability to fly. Would not some people use those powers to take advantage of their fellow citizens in the virtual world? The advocacy group Sum of Us (a community of people committed to curbing the growing power of corporations) reported, "Chanelle Siggens was approached by another player, who then 'simulated groping and ejaculating onto her avatar.' Another player named Mari DeGrazia reported witnessing harassment more than three times per week. DeGrazia also experienced abuse while wearing a haptic vest, when 'another player groped her avatar's chest.'"

In March 2021, Andrew Bosworth, Meta's chief technology officer, wrote in an employee memo that moderating what people say and how they act in the Metaverse "at any meaningful scale is practically impossible."[26] The experience of the founders of Second Life ten years ago might be instructive. Over the course of two weeks, the house one young woman had built by the shore of a virtual lake was blown up by virtual vandals. In another bizarre incident, an avatar flew over the welcome area in a spaceship. Other avatars were tractor-beamed up through an open pod door into the ship, which then flew away with them.[27]

Despite Meta's hype about using AI to protect people in the Metaverse, its real purpose is to increase ad revenue. A newly filed Meta patent claims Meta will have the technology to alter the user's experience according to what generates more engagement. "To increase user interaction with the virtual world, objects and locations presented in the virtual world may be customized for individual users of the online system." Advertisers will be able to bid in real time for the right to make their products one of the "objects or locations" customized for the user. This is why Andreessen is so confident that you will never be reality deprived once you put on the helmet.

But I want to consider another, more desperate reality deprivation. What about the Facebook employees' concern that the Metaverse will become a new opiate for the masses? The *New York Times* reported a major pushback inside the company against Zuckerberg's obsession with the Metaverse, noting, "One senior leader complain[ed] that the amount of money the company had spent on unproven projects made him 'sick to my stomach.'"[28]

The one hundred thousand Americans who died from opioid over-doses last year were certainly "reality deprived." Do the people at Meta have any idea what a tool for addiction they are trying to build? Frances Haugen researched the addictive qualities of VR before she resigned. She noted that in *Snow Crash*, the 1992 sci-fi novel that coined the phrase Metaverse, "it was a thing that people used to numb themselves when their lives were horrible." She went on to tell the Associated Press, "So beyond the fact that these immersive environments are extremely addic-tive and they encourage people to unplug from the reality we actually live, I'm also worried about it on the level of—the Metaverse will require us to put many, many more sensors in our homes and our workplaces," forcing users to relinquish more of their data and their privacy.[29]

⌇

Perhaps the only way to understand what Mark Zuckerberg really sees in the Metaverse is to look at his marketing. Evan Selinger, a professor of philosophy at Rochester Institute of Technology, writes, "What's sur-prising about Meta's branding is that it revolves around a religious theme of transcendence—an end to injustice and unhappiness and the begin-ning of complete personal freedom."[30] Meta's 2022 Super Bowl ad for the Metaverse featured an animatronic dog that played in a band, went through a series of humiliations, and hit rock bottom; finally, after someone put the Meta Quest 2 headset on the dog, he reunited with his old friends (virtually) and was able to play music again.

What are we to make of this? Meta is saying that your real life is a series of unmitigated disasters, but if you can enter the magical world of the Metaverse, all will be well, and your true desires will be realized. This is what Meta employees feared when they asked if the Metaverse was just a virtual opioid for Gen Z. In that sense, the Metaverse bears a striking resemblance to Aldous Huxley's fictional *Brave New World*. Unlike George Orwell's in *1984*, Huxley's dystopian view of the future saw people pacified through drugs (Soma, distributed to everyone) and entertainment (the Feelies—a predecessor of the Metaverse). This brings me to the heart of my objection to the Metaverse. As Yale's Jason Stanley, a political scientist, has written, "The fascist politician possesses specific techniques to destroy information spaces and break down reality."[31] To date, social media has held primacy in this effort. Now the Metaverse proposes complete elimination of the boundaries between truth and fiction, between the real and unreal.

AI inventor Chris Hamilton suggested that early in the development of the Metaverse, we might witness "Avatar Trump," a personalized, AI-driven avatar of the former president that would show up as you walked down the street in the Metaverse.

His image, voice and political essence will be crammed into a matrix. Avatar Trump will hand out political endorsements, respond to the news and talk with real people, in ways barely discernible from Real Trump…But the MAGA public might be able to influence the Trump avatar, which will monitor engagement quality. Do people prefer Regular Trump or Superman Trump? Boorish Trump or Polite Trump? Avatar Trump could also be personalized to appeal to individual audience members, much as Google and Facebook target users.[32]

Hamilton goes so far as to suggest that Avatar Trump could hang around long after the real Donald died. The Trump family could sell appearances to what will surely be Proud Boys conventions in our future Metaverse. Whole new generations of young neofascists can feel what a Trump rally was like.

I am aware that using the term *fascism* to describe the crisis we face may seem hyperbolic. But I am dead serious. Yale historian Timothy Snyder, citing the rise of authoritarianism in Russia, Turkey, the United States, Brazil, India, and Saudi Arabia, recently wrote, "We err in limiting our fears of fascism to a certain image of Hitler and the Holocaust. Fascism was Italian in origin, popular in Romania—where fascists were Orthodox Christians who dreamed of cleansing violence—and had adherents throughout Europe (and America). In all its varieties, it was about the triumph of will over reason."[33] Studying history tells us that the authoritarians of the twentieth century rose to power using communications technology to spread propaganda. What radio was to Adolf Hitler and Benito Mussolini, social media is to Donald Trump.

I'm not saying that Mark Zuckerberg, Marc Andreessen, and Elon Musk are fascists (though, as noted earlier, Peter Thiel has written, "I no longer believe that freedom and democracy are compatible"). I'm saying that they are providing the tools "to destroy information spaces and break down reality." And if our children do spend seven hours a day in the Metaverse in 2035, the secession from reality will be complete. We will have realized Huxley's dystopian vision of a passive, blissed-out citizen, addicted to the Feelies, getting by on the dole. Writing after World War I, in a time of technological optimism very similar to our current era, Huxley did not believe that the solutions to war, disease, and poverty lay in the new inventions of radio and commercial air travel. He was watching Hitler and Joseph Goebbels use the newly ascendant radio as a primary tool of the daily propaganda that was moving Germany to become a fascist state. Huxley knew there were ways to keep citizens in line without the threat of the firing squad.

The Technocrats have risen to levels of previously unimagined wealth while providing tools to autocrats around the world. If, as I stated at the outset of this book, the two biggest problems facing our country are economic inequality and the survival of our democracy, then the Technocrats have to choose which side they are on: democracy or autocracy. That likely means deciding if they are going to wear the VR helmet for seven hours a day or choose to remain in the real world. Marc Andreessen thinks the "snobs" who choose not to enter the Metaverse will have "reality privilege." He wrote, "The vast majority of humanity, lacks Reality Privilege—their online world is, or will be, immeasurably richer and more fulfilling than most of the physical and social environment around them in the quote-unquote real world." Is Andreessen saying that *reality* is broken? That instead of using our collective resources to improve the world we inhabit (reality), he and the other Technocrats need to spend trillions to build new worlds (on Mars) and new realities (in the Metaverse). It seems insane. But this is very much their plan.

〜

Mark Zuckerberg's pitch to Wall Street is that the Metaverse will be Facebook's way of recapturing Gen Z, which has abandoned his platform for TikTok, Twitch, and Snapchat. After the 60 percent fall in Meta's stock price in 2022, Zuckerberg desperately needs the Metaverse to happen. President Joe Biden's Federal Trade Commission has sued Facebook in an attempt to force it to sell Instagram and WhatsApp, the two growing parts of the Facebook empire. There is a better than 50 percent chance they will succeed. Zuckerberg would then be the CEO of a dying business. Certainly Zuckerberg is pulling every lever available to him to make the Metaverse seem important. But I doubt that Microsoft's integrating the Excel spreadsheet program inside the Metaverse conference room, as announced in October 2022 at the big unveiling of the new $1,500 VR helmet, is the killer app that will attract millions of new users.

Recent ads for the Metaverse, aimed at Gen Z, help reveal that this is a desperate attempt to bring young people back to Facebook. And perhaps living in a fantasy world where you can create your own identity and buy digital versions of all the clothing you see on celebrities but can't actually afford is the perfect antidote for the Gen Z ennui that fills social media. The dark sense that "humans were a mistake," which seems to pervade a lot of Gen Z social media, is perhaps telling us that some sort of escape through technology or psychedelic drugs is the future for that generation.[34]

We need to ask ourselves if investing trillions in virtual reality or going to Mars will add to the collective wealth of society through real, productive growth. I believe the answer is no. As William & Mary behavioral economist Peter Atwater wrote in a private newsletter in January 2021,

> That today's most popular investments tie to themes like space travel and futurism speaks to our insatiable appetite for the psychologically distant—the anti real, as it were. Strangers in a strange land are the new limitless opportunity. And here is what I don't think the crowd fully appreciates: extreme abstraction will quickly revert to extreme realism. Rather than Mars, we will focus on what is next door. Physical cash and gold—or whatever else the crowd decides represents real money/value—will replace all those intangible (cyber) monetary instruments.

The 60 percent decline of Bitcoin from November 2021 to June 2022 shows he was right, because a lot of people fled the fantasy of easy cyber wealth.

If the Metaverse and all of Web3 are to succeed, the Technocrats will need the same protection the government has afforded them since Bill Clinton's Digital Millennium Copyright Act of 1998. Of course, if the crypto craze is experiencing an apocalyptic crash, Peter Thiel will be able to weather angry mobs of citizens, searching the high-income neighborhoods of Beverly Hills for crypto touts like Kim Kardashian, Matt Damon, and LeBron James. Kardashian has already paid a $1.26 million fine for her paid shilling of Bitcoin. But Thiel is smart enough never to go on Instagram and "talk his book." I wouldn't be surprised if we find out that Thiel dumped all his coins at the market top; in his Miami penthouse, he will pull from a drawer his 2007 essay "Politics and the Apocalypse," in which he muses, "The destiny of the postmodern world would be either the limitless violence of runaway mimesis, or the peace of the kingdom of God."[35]

Ultimately, these views led Thiel to conclude that Trump was the perfect candidate for a moment when, for many, the apocalypse was seemingly right over the horizon, in the form of marauding immigrant caravans. When the final story of Trump's rise is told, I believe Thiel's guidance, especially in getting Trump to use Facebook as his premier advertising vehicle, will be seen as immensely impactful. I would also observe that Zuckerberg, Musk, and Andreessen were perfectly happy with Thiel and Trump's close relationship. When Zuckerberg needed to get off the hook from the right-wing backlash, Thiel arranged the dinner with Trump. Thiel introduced Musk to the Trump family and got him on President Trump's business council. Trump said at the time that Musk was "one of our great geniuses, and we have to protect our genius." And that is why all of them would be happy to see the Republicans return to power. As Mike Allen of *Axios* wrote, "If Republicans win control, their natural antipathy toward new market restrictions could prove to be an even bigger barrier to tech regulation."

For the past twenty years—Google was getting big even in 2002—maintaining the political power to grow and keep their monopolies intact has been the Technocrats' primary objective. They have gotten help from both Democrats and Republicans. But in order to maintain their rule, Big Tech needs political gridlock. As David Chavern, president of the News Media Alliance, noted, "Hyperpartisanship is the most powerful force supporting the status quo, and the big tech platforms work hard to fan the flames."[36]

In the fall of 2021, as regulatory scrutiny was increasing, Facebook looked to divide Congress along party lines, precluding any bipartisan attempt to better regulate social media platforms. Facebook's Washington team called Republican lawmakers to push the story that whistleblower Frances Haugen was trying to help Democrats; at the same time, they called Democrats to alert them that Republicans were focused on Facebook's decision to ban statements of support for Kyle Rittenhouse, who was charged with killing two people during the 2020 civil unrest in Wisconsin.

From fighting unions to paying almost no income taxes and financing politicians who will fight attempts to regulate their businesses—the reality of the Technocrats' worldview is very different from the gauzy PR ad campaigns their companies pump out. Liberals like President Barack Obama and California governor Gavin Newsom have fallen in love with Big Tech's promise to remake society. In 2013 Newsom wrote, "Technology has rendered our current system of government irrelevant, so now government must turn to technology to fix itself."[37] He probably would think differently now. But again, in allying themselves with the coastal tech elites, these liberal luminaries have abandoned the noncollege working class, for which Big Tech has neither use nor understanding. This served the monopolists; the trade-off for being culturally liberal while not having to pay taxes or be regulated was a no-brainer. As The Who once sang, "Meet the new boss / Same as the old boss."

While I've been suspicious of the term *late capitalism*, which has been bandied about in leftist circles over the past few years, I have come to believe that a certain decadence is in fact flowing into our economic and cultural world. Cultural historian Jacques Barzun wrote, "The forms of art as of life seem exhausted, the stages of development have been run through. Institutions function painfully. Repetition and frustration are the intolerable result." Barzun's epic history of Western cultural retreat, *From Dawn to Decadence*, probably should be required reading for every Big Tech executive as well as every incoming college freshman. Unlike the narratives of the Technocrats, Barzun shows that periods of cultural creativity wax and wane. They often don't last very long and only come about amid a curious mix of competition and collaboration among artists, scientists, or other inventors.

Could it be that the Technocrats have surrendered their optimism and believe the most salable service in the future will be escape, both literal (Mars) and virtual (the Metaverse)? Or is this a very expensive example of shiny object syndrome (SOS), in which a man like Zuckerberg, facing society's collective wrath for his company's egregious conduct, decides to avert our attention to a shiny new object—the Metaverse?

In 2019, the Business Roundtable issued a call to abandon the libertarian belief that the only purpose of a corporation was to make a profit for its shareholders. The statement begins with the sentence "Americans deserve an economy that allows each person to succeed through hard work and creativity and to *lead a life of meaning* and dignity."[38] But part of the problem for leaders like Musk and Zuckerberg is that their employees do not often feel they are leading this kind of life. Does the Black Tesla worker, constantly assigned to the most menial task on "The Plantation," feel any dignity? Does the female Instagram employee feel any sense of meaning, knowing that her bosses refuse to do anything about the highly reported self-harm the platform is pushing on young teenage girls? The Business Roundtable suggested that a business has many "stakeholders," which is different from the classic notion that only the shareholders count. As I will discuss in the concluding chapters, another vision of capitalism, called "regenerative economics," is on offer. It is one that the Technocrats reject, but it deserves our consideration.

Ultimately, the Technocrats have to answer one question: Even if a Mars mission or the Metaverse is not some expensive SOS maneuver, what human problem are you trying to solve with these projects?

I have yet to get an answer.

7

THE CRYPTO CON

*Bitcoin has no reason to exist. It delivers no meaningful benefit
for society. It is a form of gambling, propelled by naked greed
and generating vast quantities of CO_2 emissions.*

— Fabio Panetta, European Central Bank

Bitcoin and the whole realm of crypto currencies represent the ultimate triumph of libertarian magical thinking over reason. As Bitcoin inventor Satoshi Nakamoto wrote in his original white paper, "With
e-currency based on cryptographic proof, without the need to trust a third
party middleman, money can be secure and transactions effortless." But
this is a lie. As Nassim Nicholas Taleb, author of *Black Swan*, wrote, "Owing
to the absence of any explicit yield benefiting the holder of bitcoin, if we
expect that at any point in the future the value will be zero when miners
are extinct, the technology becomes obsolete, or future generations get into
other such 'assets' and bitcoin loses its appeal for them, then the value must
be zero now."[1] Taleb is arguing that Bitcoin is a virtual currency and that,
like many of the other topics in this book, it is both unreal and perhaps
worthless. In early July 2022, when the Celsius Network crypto exchange
closed down and prevented its customers from withdrawing their money,

the real-world effects of the many fraudulent crypto exchanges became visible. Alla Driksne, a thirty-four-year-old woman with an online cooking course business, had placed all her life's savings in Celsius. She told a journalist, "Since it is such a huge company and there are so many people that trusted them, somewhere in the back of my head, I'm hoping maybe there's a small, small chance of not losing everything."[2] It was not to be. Many young investors had been persuaded about the crypto con by arguments made by, among others, Peter Thiel, who argued that Bitcoin's rise "is telling us that the central banks are bankrupt, that we are at the end of the fiat money regime." Gold enthusiasts have been making this argument for the last ninety years, since the early Federal Reserve interventions during the Great Depression. The Fed would inflate away its debts, and the dollar and government bonds would be worthless. You would only survive the crash if you held gold. The number of books written on this thesis could fill a decent-sized library. But of course, it never happened. Thiel's advice to preserve capital by putting it in Bitcoin turned out to be similarly worthless.

The very idea that crypto is a way to combat a big government "fiat money regime" is comical, in that Bitcoin and all other crypto currencies use an algorithm invented and patented by the US National Security Agency (NSA) and released to the public under a royalty-free license. Here we return to the theme of libertarians railing against government control while availing themselves of infrastructures like the internet and NSA's Secure Hash Algorithm 2, both invented and paid for by the government. Crypto acolytes claim the movement is all about freedom and decentralization, but in practice, the crypto ecology is centralized and authoritarian. Early backers (including Thiel, Elon Musk, and Marc Andreessen) of all the major crypto currencies and tokens are called "whales"; they are large crypto asset holders whose individual holdings can move markets like a whale makes waves.

The invention of Bitcoin is shrouded in mystery. Late in the evening of January 3, 2009, a person calling themself Satoshi Nakamoto released thirty-one thousand lines of code that created what they claimed was a new currency: Bitcoin. Nakamoto is surely a pseudonym, and the reasons for its use are obvious. It was not clear that someone could legally create a currency out of thin air, so at the start the fact that no one could find the creator was helpful. Since that time, reporters all over the world have tried unsuccessfully to reveal Nakamoto's real identity. One, the *New Yorker*'s Joshua Davis, described the brilliance of creating the artificial scarcity behind Nakamoto's ultimate goal of twenty-one million Bitcoins: "Every ten minutes or so, coins would be distributed through a process that resembled a lottery. Miners—people seeking the coins—would play the lottery again and again; the fastest computer would win the most money."[3]

This project was not an altruistic endeavor on Nakamoto's part. They reportedly took one million Bitcoins for themselves, which are currently worth $20 billion. In 2010, Nakamoto transferred the source code repository and the network alert key to a Massachusetts programmer named Gavin Andresen and disappeared. Subsequent reportorial efforts to find or even identify Nakamoto have rivaled the search for Deep Throat, of Watergate fame. For those of you too young to have lived through the Watergate scandal, Deep Throat was *Washington Post* reporter Bob Woodward's anonymous source (revealed twenty years later as FBI official Mark Felt), who helped force Richard Nixon's resignation.

Bitcoin's original libertarian objective was to protect citizens from what Nakamoto suggested was the state's power to debase its currency by printing more of it. The suggestion was that Bitcoin would be a hedge against this inevitable inflationary spiral. But while inflation did arrive in 2021, neither the dollar nor Bitcoin reacted the way Nakamoto or Thiel had predicted. In October 2021, Thiel touted Bitcoin as an inflation hedge and said that the dollar was finished. Since that statement, Bitcoin has fallen 30 percent against the dollar. As of this writing, the total value of crypto currencies has fallen 70 percent since November 2021. The market value of the entire crypto economy has been reduced in less than eight months from nearly $3 trillion in November 2021 to $945 billion, according to CoinMarketCap.

But before the fall, a young man with tousled hair and slacker clothing named Sam Bankman-Fried was the face of the crypto industry. SBF, as he was called by one and all, ran both FTX, the largest American crypto exchange, and Alameda Research, a crypto trading hedge fund. Celebrities like Tom Brady, Bill Clinton, and Katy Perry would show up at his Bahamas headquarters for his yearly crypto conference. He was featured on the covers of *Forbes* and *Fortune* magazines as the face of an industry that was ready to challenge the established banking system. Starting in late October 2021, FTX (along with allied exchanges like Crypto.com) started advertising on network television. They employed stars like Matt Damon, Steph Curry, LeBron James, Tom Brady, and Larry David to appear in elaborate commercials and bought so many spots on the Super Bowl telecast that *Fortune* magazine called the event "the Crypto Bowl." But if you had responded to the ad push by Thanksgiving 2021 and made a big bet on Bitcoin at $60,000 per coin, you would have been hurting badly by the fall of 2022, when Bitcoin hovered around $19,000 per coin. Much of the problem is the kind of predatory marketing to a working-class audience—acting as if crypto were a safe investment—that the big exchanges are involved in.[4] A Harris poll in 2021 found that 23 percent of Black Americans own crypto currency, compared with only 11 percent of white Americans; this suggests that the marketing by Black sports stars such as LeBron James and Steph Curry, who implied that crypto was a safe path to wealth, was an incredibly cynical but effective way to relieve ordinary people of their money. A reporter from *Politico* did a Google Maps search for Bitcoin ATMs in Los Angeles. When she clicked on the photos of the locations, she found "vape stores, check-cashing spots and gas stations in down-at-heel, cracked-plaster strip malls" in the poorest neighborhoods.[5]

In one Crypto.com commercial, a contemporary LeBron James tells a computer graphics version of his younger self to buy crypto and "make history." In a November 2021 ad for Crypto.com, which aired during the Super Bowl, actor Matt Damon asserted, "Fortune favors the brave." The financial site Finbold noted that if you purchased $1,000 worth of Bitcoin when that commercial came out, it'd now be worth $375.

But even the fall of crypto into the summer of 2022 did nothing to tarnish SBF's reputation. In the 2022 midterms he donated over $30 million to (mostly) Democratic candidates. He appeared regularly with lobbyists and the Congress members tasked with writing crypto regulation. And then in one week it all collapsed. It started with a tweet from Changpen Zhao, the Chinese owner of Binance, the world's largest crypto exchange, who had helped finance FTX and still held a large amount of FTX tokens (FTT): "Liquidating our FTT is just post-exit risk management, learning from LUNA. We gave support before, but we won't pretend to make love after divorce. We are not against anyone. But we won't support people who lobby against other industry players behind their backs. Onwards."

Zhao was angry that SBF had been working with US legislators on regulations that Binance didn't support. Zhao's tweet started a run on FTX, with $5 billion in withdrawals in the first twenty-four hours. The value of FTT plunged, which then caused a huge problem for Alameda, which had made many risky investments collateralized by its holdings of FTT. Within a week FTX and Alameda had declared bankruptcy, leaving hundreds of thousands of customers to lose all of their crypto. SBF will now be prosecuted for fraud, but the repercussions of FTX's fall will take months to play out.

The average crypto currency trader is under forty and does not have a college degree, according to the National Opinion Research Center. In a research note, the center added, "Investors get their information about cryptocurrency investing mostly through the crypto exchanges themselves (26 percent), general trading platforms like Fidelity or Robinhood (25 percent), or social media (24 percent)." Billionaire Mike Novogratz, who runs Global Digital Holdings, a very large crypto holder, has continued to tout investing in crypto since October 2021, even as Global Digital was quietly unloading most of its crypto holdings onto the unsuspecting public.[6] This tactic of the crypto whales to take advantage of the FOMO (fear of missing out) crowd is playing itself out across the world. The *Wall*

Street Journal also noted, "Four top Coinbase officials have collectively pocketed more than $1 billion by selling shares since the cryptocurrency exchange's public listing in Spring 2021."

Other problems of privacy are also tied up in the supposedly open nature of the blockchain ledger. One of the selling points of crypto was that every transaction would be listed in a public ledger on blockchain for all to see. As Molly White pointed out, say you go on a Tinder first date; when you get home, you Venmo your half of the bill to your date in Bitcoin. What you've really done is give a random stranger access to all your transactions. You have enabled a potential economic stalker. As the Federal Trade Commission reported in June 2022, the losses in crypto scams were sixty times what they were in 2018.

There is a certain fiendish logic behind crypto marketing. The average middle-class worker has likely figured out French economist Thomas Piketty's famous formula in his book *Capital in the Twenty-First Century*, $r > g$: the return on capital is higher than the growth rate of wages. In other words, the chances of changing your station in life by working for wages is slim at best. Of course this doesn't apply to the men and women in the C-suites of major corporations, but working-class Americans generally know they will never get rich off of their paychecks. They follow people like Elon Musk tweeting from a yacht in the South of France and understand that the investing class is the leisure class; if you want to join the leisure class, you need to find some investment that is going to give you a giant payout (what venture capital investors call a 20X return). Needless to say, if you had bought Bitcoin at less than a dollar in 2009, you would have had not a 20X but at least a 100X payout, assuming you sold out at the top. It seemed for a while that anyone could buy a winning lottery ticket. Those suspicious of crypto were dismissed with acronyms like HFSP (have fun staying poor). But the easy route to the leisure class turned out to be a mirage, and it was really the Bitcoin whales like Mike Novogratz who made out well.

Most people only learn about the supposed easy road to wealth near the end of the pyramid scheme. The FOMO crowd, driven by $250 million

in TV ads, piled into crypto as the 2021 football season wound down, buying from the whales who had all the tokens. Now they have lost two-thirds
of their capital, and Reddit forums like Wall Street Bets (which had been
behind the aforementioned GameStop fiasco) have turned dark. "I lost
over 450k usd, I cannot pay the bank. I will lose my home soon. I'll become
homeless. Suicide is the only way out for me," one member posted.

The largest crypto lender, Celsius Network, was paying 18.63 percent
interest on crypto deposits in early June 2022. If that seems too good to be
true, it was. On June 13, 2022, Celsius simply turned off the sell button on
its website, announcing a halt to all withdrawals. It released a statement:
"We are taking this necessary action for the benefit of our entire community in order to stabilize liquidity and operations while we take steps
to preserve and protect assets." Traders immediately saw the contagion
spreading to all parts of the crypto ecosystem and predicted a "crypto
winter." Most of the big exchanges started laying off personnel, and by the
end of the week, thousands of jobs had been eliminated. As of the fall of
2022, Celsius has not paid back any investors.

In January 2022, FTX (one of the largest crypto exchanges) began
running a multiplatform (TV, print, and digital) ad campaign featuring
Tom Brady and his wife, Gisele Bündchen, using the tag line, "Are you
in?" This is a classic multilevel marketing (MLM) pitch.[7] If you get in, you
know your doing so increases the value of the stakes of those who were
in before you, but you assume that those coming in behind you will raise
the value of your stake in turn. The success of any influential idea, be it
a religion or mass movement, is dependent on consistently enticing new
supporters who subscribe to the movement's core tenets.

As the pyramid base widens, more money flows up from the bottom
of the pyramid to the top. The very top of an MLM is the place you want
to be. That's where the crypto whales, such as FTX founder and CEO Sam
Bankman-Fried, live. The pyramid operates not to "expand the pie" but to
reward the early believers at the expense of the FOMO crowd. It's obvious
that right now, at least, Andreessen, Musk, and Thiel are at the top of the

pyramid. But they were not the suckers. For instance, Tesla sold 75 percent of its Bitcoin, which was worth about $2 billion at the end of 2021, just before Bitcoin started to crash. They will have reaped large rewards, but if the house of cards is now collapsing, will they not share part of the blame? My cynical response is probably not.

⌇

The lie of crypto gets worse. It turns out that blockchain does not offer "secure and effortless transactions." Bitcoin can only process about seven transactions per second, as opposed to Visa, which can handle two thousand per second. Each transaction is basically a lottery to see which miner's high-end computers can solve the crypto puzzle. The result is both a human and bandwidth resource problem. As Stephen Diehl, one of the most experienced cryptographers in the world, notes, "Blockchain solutions are vastly more expensive to maintain than centralized solutions (such as a Mastercard transaction), and centralization always wins purely from its ability to physically serve data over a network to customers more efficiently." A single transaction on the Bitcoin blockchain currently requires 232 kWh, equivalent to the power consumption of the average US home over seven days.

The proof that Bitcoin will never become a usable currency is already in. In September 2021, El Salvador made Bitcoin legal tender for all transactions in that country and heavily subsidized the adoption of Bitcoin ATMs and other technologies. In the twelve months following, Bitcoin usage plunged, with only 20 percent of the companies in El Salvador willing to accept Bitcoin as payment and less than 5 percent of all retail sales done with Bitcoin. The reason is obvious: with the crypto currency's value falling or rising by as much as 15 percent in a day, it is hardly a stable currency. In a recent poll 77 percent of Salvadorians said that Bitcoin was a bad idea.[8] The poor, it turns out, don't need a new currency; they need cheaper ways to use the old one.[9] In that sense, Bitcoin fails abysmally.

ATM fees can reach 20 percent of the total amount withdrawn, and trans-action charges can go as high as $62 for a small transaction that can often take half a day to clear.

What would happen if Bitcoin ever became widely used? Columbia University economic historian Adam Tooze, author of *Crashed: How a Decade of Financial Crises Changed the World*, has the answer.

> Whereas the gold standard promised, roughly, that the value of money would remain stable, bitcoin, were it actually to enter wide-spread use as a stable currency, would be more or less guaranteed to appreciate over the longer term. And no, that is not a good thing. An appreciating currency is not better than a stable or mildly inflat-ing currency. It is far worse. A growing economy denominated in bitcoin would deflate. That would be crippling for debtors and busi-ness. The macroeconomic costs would dwarf any conceivable effi-ciency gains from a decentralized crypto currency.[10]

So aside from the fact that a wide-scale adoption of Bitcoin could lead to a global financial disaster, the biggest present problem is that libertar-ians ignore the externalities of crypto. Bitcoin currently uses as much electricity as the Netherlands. It also generates as much e-waste (from the disposal of worn-out mining computers) as that country and enables a $15 billion per year ransomware industry.

It turns out the only people who really need Bitcoin are criminals. Willem H. Buiter, professor of international and public affairs at Colum-bia University, has argued for an outright ban on crypto currencies, writ-ing, "The anonymity afforded to cryptocurrency holders raises serious concerns about illegal uses of funds, including tax evasion, money laun-dering, hiding proceeds from ransomware attacks and other cybercrimes, and financing of terrorism. The issue has become urgent—and regula-tion may not be enough."[11] The fact that Bitcoin was introduced only a month before the arrival of the infamous Silk Road dark web market for heroin, cocaine, and fentanyl led one reporter to suggest that Nakamoto was really Ross Ulbricht, Silk Road's founder. At the time, Silk Road only accepted payment for its contraband goods in Bitcoin.

Marc Andreessen, who is leading the forces that oppose government regulation of crypto currencies, has noted, "Crypto potentially represents the creation of a whole new category of technology, quite literally right wing tech that is far more aggressively decentralized." But this is a lie. Control of Bitcoin is extremely centralized. Rice University data scientist Alyssa Blackburn concluded that at any given time only five or six whales were controlling the Bitcoin price, and in many instances only one or two miners held most of the power.[12] In 2021 crypto was responsible for about $15 billion in crypto fraud and almost $18 billion in ransomware. Global credit card fraud amounted to about $24 billion. As an example, in March 2021, insurance giant CNA Financial sustained a ransomware attack on its critical systems. Within four days it paid a ransom in Bitcoin of $40 million.[13]

The more you study crypto, the more it looks like a Carl Hiaasen novel full of colorful grifters staying one step ahead of the authorities. Case in point would be Tether, a so-called Stablecoin, which is supposedly pegged to the dollar and therefore less volatile. Although you may not have heard of Tether, in 2018 it surpassed Bitcoin in trading volume, with the highest daily and monthly volumes of any crypto currency on the market. Actor Brock Pierce, whose main claim to fame was a role as a child in Disney's 1992 film *The Mighty Ducks*, founded Tether. After failing to graduate into adult acting roles, Pierce became involved in the Digital Entertainment Network (DEN), which was about to go public before the dot-com crash in 2000; the IPO was withdrawn in the wake of lurid sexual allegations about Pierce and his partners. Three employees sued Pierce and his copresident, Marc Collins-Rector, saying they were plied with drugs and pressured for sex. Collins-Rector was convicted, but the plaintiffs later dismissed their claims against Pierce.

Pierce disputes the allegation that he engaged in any sexual predation, but when he tried to join the board of the Bitcoin Foundation, over a dozen members of the board resigned in protest.[14] DEN declared bankruptcy and shut down. Pierce moved into crypto in 2012 and created an initial coin offering for a token, which eventually became Tether. Its distinction was that it was supposedly backed by US dollars, one to one, although when the New York attorney general sued Bitfinex (the company that acquired Tether), it appeared to have only twenty-nine cents of cash for each token, with the rest held in the volatile commercial paper markets. (Tether and entities later agreed to cease trading activity with New Yorkers, paying $18.5 million in penalties.)

Bitfinex, registered in the British Virgin Islands, is run by another character, named Giancarlo Devasini. A former Milan plastic surgeon, Devasini went into selling computer hardware with a company that he claimed was grossing €100 million a year. A *Financial Times* investigation put the revenue figures at closer to €12 million. (Tether insisted that Devasini "portrayed the facts entirely accurately".) The investigation unveiled a series of other fraud suits, including counterfeit software charges from Microsoft and fraudulent tax losses on a memory chip business.[15] After these failures, Devasini ended up at Bitfinex, a crypto exchange banned in the United States but very popular in Asia and Russia. For years Bitfinex was unable to have a legitimate banking operation, but it did hold enough Bitcoin to buy Tether. Devasini ran both companies but kept them separate. Bitfinex was the exchange, and Tether was the coin that it printed with abandon.

Lacking a place to stash all their cash in 2018, Devasini placed $850 million worth of Tether's Bitcoin in the Crypto Capital Corp (CCC), a shadow bank fronted in Panama by a former minor league football player named Reggie Fowler. Fowler billed himself as "an NFL investor," but the *Minnesota Star Tribune* reported that he lost his stake in the Vikings in 2014 after failing to make payments because of problems with his other businesses. Fowler would later plead guilty to charges of bank fraud, wire fraud and conspiracy. But first, Interpol arrested CCC founder Ivan Manuel Molina Lee in Poland (he remains in custody at the time of writing) for laundering millions for drug cartels. Soon after, authorities seized the $850 million that Fowler had convinced Bitfinex to deposit with Crypto Capital. Desperate to deal with the shortfall, Devasini had Tether lend Bitfinex $625 million.

For a year, Bitfinex hid the losses. As the *Financial Times* reported, "Messages revealed by [New York attorney general Letitia] James's office showed Devasini, under the alias 'Merlin,' pleading for months with a CCC individual called 'Oz' for the return of their cash. 'Please understand all this could be extremely dangerous for everybody, the entire crypto community. [Bitcoin] could tank to below 1k if we don't act quickly.'"[16]

Subsequent investigations by University of Texas finance professor John Griffin purported to show why Devasini was so concerned. Bitfinex had been using Tether to manipulate the price of Bitcoin whenever it fell. Griffin reported that Tether "was creating price support for bitcoin, and over the period that we examined, had huge price effects. Our research would indicate that there are sophisticated people harnessing investor interest for their benefit."[17] In the worst-case scenario, Tether could start a 1930s-style bank run: if all the holders of Tether tried to exchange their coins for dollars, Tether would collapse, and billions of dollars would be lost, with potential contagion in other markets. (Tether responded that "Tether and its affiliates have never used Tether tokens or issuances to manipulate the cryptocurrency market or token pricing.")

When I started thinking about this book in the late summer of 2021, the crypto frenzy was just beginning to build. The more smart software engineers I talked to, the more I became convinced that billions of dollars were going to be lost in a crypto crash. Yet I had some smart friends who were convinced that Nakamoto's design of artificial scarcity for Bitcoin would make it incredibly valuable. I remember reminding one crypto fan that there was a time between 1995 and 1999 when the Beanie Babies craze, modeled on the same sense of artificial scarcity, created what many call the "world's first Internet sensation." Individual plush toys were being traded online for thousands of dollars each. And then the fad just ended.

People with hundreds of Beanie Babies put away for their retirement couldn't give them away.

∽

As with Facebook and YouTube, there is no effective regulation of the crypto industry—a phenomenon that can be seen in Elon Musk's manipulating the value of Dogecoin with a single tweet. As Gary Gensler, the Securities and Exchange Commission (SEC) chairman, told a *Wall Street Journal* CEO Summit, "There are gaps in our system." Gensler urged all of the major crypto exchanges to register with the SEC, saying it is highly likely that they are offering securities on their platforms. US courts (all the way up to the Supreme Court) have applied a test of what qualifies as a "security" (the Howey Test), summarized as follows: "A security requires an investment in a common enterprise with expectations of profit via efforts by others."[18] Common sense would argue that crypto could meet this requirement, but as of this writing, none of the crypto exchanges have taken Gensler up on his offer to register with the SEC. Coinbase went so far as to say that it only trades assets "for which we determine there are reasonably strong arguments to conclude that the crypto asset is not a security." This may seem like a distinction without a difference, but for the people controlling crypto, it is an existential issue. They do not want the regulatory scrutiny of the SEC controlling their business. The whole ability to own Bitcoin in a pseudonymous account could be destroyed, because the SEC does not allow you to own stock without disclosure.

In the middle of the spring 2022 "crypto winter," Peter Thiel went to a crypto conference in Miami to call out the real villains. These were not crypto scam artists. No, Thiel put up a slide of Warren Buffet, next to Buffet's quote calling Bitcoin "rat poison." Buffet, "the sociopathic grandpa from Omaha," was number one on Thiel's enemies list. Number two and three were JP Morgan CEO Jamie Dimon and BlackRock CEO Larry Fink. As each picture came up, the crypto crowd booed raucously. Thiel said, "When they choose not to allocate to Bitcoin, that is a deeply political choice, and we need to be pushing back against them ... It's a political question whether this movement is going to succeed or whether the enemies of the movement are going to succeed in stopping us."[19] The political threat from the Trumpists on behalf of crypto seems clear. Within weeks of Thiel's speech, some big asset managers like Fidelity said they were exploring letting their customers own crypto in their retirement accounts. Of course, six weeks after Thiel's speech, a crypto lender he backed, Vauld, froze operations after users pulled out almost $200 million over the three previous weeks.

And the crypto winter has not been kind to Andreessen Horowitz. Having announced a $4.5 billion crypto fund, the firm saw the value of its flagship fund fall 40 percent in the first half of 2022. One of its largest crypto investments, Solana, has lost 80 percent of its value since January 2022. Andreessen also lost $2.9 billion in its main crypto exchange, Coinbase.[20]

Thiel, Andreessen, and the other Technocrats aren't leaving it to chance that they will succeed in keeping crypto unregulated. Politicians of both parties are being recruited to support "financial freedom and innovation" and make sure no serious regulation is passed. Crypto advocates have already hired former SEC chairman Jay Clayton and former SEC counsel Elad Roisman as lobbyists. And Ro Khanna, a reliably progressive Democratic congressman from Silicon Valley, is advancing a bill asserting that cryptocurrencies are not a security and therefore are ineligible for regulation by the SEC.

Marc Andreessen is determined to exploit the regulatory gaps in the crypto market, as the *New York Times* reported: "At a moment when technology companies have a bad odor in Washington and as the fast-evolving crypto industry is drawing increasing scrutiny from lawmakers and regulators, Andreessen Horowitz is pursuing a particularly audacious plan: to both own big chunks of the emerging world of digital currencies and have a hand in writing the rules for how it will operate."[21] Andreessen's biggest advantage when he lobbies lawmakers is crypto's inherent complexity. If senators at a hearing in April 2018 with Facebook CEO Mark Zuckerberg had a hard time understanding how Facebook made money if they gave the product away for free ("It's advertising, Senator Hatch," said Zuckerberg),[22] imagine their confusion trying to understand crypto and blockchain. For Andreessen, the bug ("It's complicated, Senator") is a feature.

Consider Wyoming senator Cynthia Lummis, who has been courting Andreessen and the crypto lobbyists for two years. She has taken control of writing the crypto regulation bill; an early leaked draft seemed like more of a vehicle for skirting securities laws and ducking taxes than any real attempt at regulation. The bill classifies crypto as a commodity like corn or oil, thus placing it under the guidance of the Commodities Futures Trading Commission, which has a much smaller enforcement staff than the SEC. Former SEC official Ty Gellasch noted, "The industry effort doesn't seem focused on getting clarity, but rather getting loopholes."

The deeper one looks, the more obvious it is that Web3—the combination of the Metaverse and crypto—is an attempt to market crypto as a natural extension of earlier internet inventions. But an invention uses technology to solve a specific problem. There is no problem that crypto currencies are solving. As economist Paul Krugman recently wrote, "It sounds extreme and implausible to suggest that an asset class that has become so large, whose promoters have acquired so much political influence, could lack any real value—that it is a house built not on sand, but on nothing at all. But I remember the housing bubble and the subprime crisis. And if you ask me, it looks as if we've gone from the Big Short to the Big Scam."[23]

As Andreessen knows better than most, the internet does not disperse economic power; rather, it centralizes it. This is why Google, Facebook, and Amazon are monopolies. There is nothing to indicate that Web3 will be any different. In fact, the only really useful deployed versions of blockchain have nothing to do with crypto currencies; known as private enterprise blockchains, they are used to track supply chains around the world. A good example is TradeLens, a private blockchain developed by IBM and the shipping giant Maersk, which allows all the stakeholders across a supply chain, such as ocean carriers, an importer, and financial service providers, to track the status and global position of a single shipment. Former IBM executive Irving Wladawsky-Berger told me, "The cyber blockchain community views these private enterprise blockchains as just distributed databases, rather than true permissionless blockchains like the ones used for cybercurrencies and NFTs. But that's like saying that the Internet is just a network, and Linux is just an operating system."

Like the last man who bought a tulip in 1637, when it was the most expensive object in the world, many will find their crypto tokens worthless. Already the crypto winter has affected the treasuries of two important American companies. Tesla reported in June 2022 losses of more than $650 million on its Bitcoin holdings. Far more seriously, data intelligence company MicroStrategy in September 2022 reported losses of more than $1.5 billion on its Bitcoin holdings.

The ultimate crypto crash might be brought on by a real invention. Perhaps Andreessen is not paying attention to the huge gains in quantum computing being made at US and Chinese labs. Quantum computers perform calculations based on the probability of an object's state before it is measured, which means they have the potential to process exponentially more data exponentially faster than classical computers. In a national security briefing I attended in 2020, one thing was made clear: a working quantum computer could theoretically break the internet's most secure cryptography, thereby destroying the whole crypto currency industry. This also means that much of the encryption in the traditional banking industry is at risk. Like artificial intelligence, quantum computing could cause more problems than it solves, but we are in a quantum arms race with the Chinese, so there may be no way to stop it.

A total crypto meltdown might not even require quantum computing. Jon Cunliffe, the Bank of England's deputy governor for financial stability, said in an October 2021 speech that crypto currencies could spark a global financial crisis. He noted that the price of Bitcoin has fallen by more than 10 percent on a single day thirty times in the last five years.[24] It fell 40 percent in a single day in March 2020. The International Monetary Fund is also concerned, saying, "Amid greater adoption, the correlation of crypto assets with traditional holdings like stocks has increased significantly, which limits their perceived risk diversification benefits and raises the risk of contagion across financial markets."[25]

⌒

Bitcoin has also spawned the ultimate fantasy culture, nonfungible tokens (NFTs), the greatest art scam in history. Bill Gates has remarked that the whole NFT economy is "100% based on the greater fool theory" (the notion that there will always be a greater fool to come along and buy your worthless "Bored Ape" NFT). A remarkable example was the announcement on December 3, 2021, that an NFT collector had spent $450,000 to own a plot of virtual land in the Snoopverse, a virtual environment being developed by the rapper Snoop Dog. The old scam of selling swampland in Florida to unsuspecting rubes still thrives in the Metaverse.

NFTs initially attracted attention when a digital "artist" named Beeple put together a large collage of ordinary images (none of which he had permission to use for commercial purposes), called it an NFT, and sold it for the Ethereum equivalent of $69 million. This attracted a great deal of press and a desire by many fringe players in the art market to get in on the NFT game. But it turned out that the buyer of Beeple's collage had another motive. He was using the NFT as the foundation for a new fractionalized investment coin called B20. So an overvalued NFT became the collateral for a new crypto coin, and because of the mythology around the original NFT, people bought into B20. Then reality set in. Over four days of hype in March 2021, B20 went from fifteen cents to $28. By May 15, 2021, the price was back to zero.

Part of the thesis of my last book, *Move Fast and Break Things*, was that Silicon Valley used the content of the world's creative artists to build businesses, with no concern for the rights of the musicians, photographers, filmmakers, or artists. And now Marc Andreessen and Peter Thiel on their jointly owned NFT platform, OpenSea, are taking this disdain to a whole new level. OpenSea recently admitted that more than 80 percent of the NFTs created using its software "were plagiarized works, fake collections, and spam."[26] Former CEO of the Walt Disney Company Bob Iger told Kara Swisher in a *New York Times* podcast that there were hundreds of thousands of unauthorized Disney, Marvel, Pixar, and *Star Wars* NFTs on the web. Just Google "Black Panther NFT" and OpenSea will come up at the top with hundreds of pirated pictures. Nor has the fact that the NFT market is a vast sea of piracy stopped major brands from trying to jump into the NFT space. Recently I came across a Virtual Nike sneaker on OpenSea, which sells for 1.29 ETH (Ethereum's token), then about equivalent to $1,800. That it would cost more to clothe yourself in virtual reality than in real life is rather absurd.

A perfect example of the convergence of piracy and grifting in NFT culture is the "Squid Game Token." Capitalizing on the popularity of the Netflix series, a group of anonymous developers set up a website for a "play to earn" crypto currency called Squid. The idea was that you could use this token to play in the "forthcoming Squid Video Game." Squid tokens couldn't be traded without a separate accompanying "marble" token. On October 28, 2021, Squid was trading at one cent. In less than a week, its price jumped to over $2,856. In the next week, fans purchased $3.38 million in Squid tokens. And then the rug pull: neither the game nor the marble token was actually released, so you couldn't sell your Squid tokens, which went to zero by November 5, 2021. Within a week the website had vanished, along with $3.38 million in cash.

This and other NFT scams have put a damper on the market. In May 2022, the NFT market collapsed, with sales showing a 92 percent decline from their peak in the fall of 2021.[27] FOMO disappeared. In a few years NFTs will seem like a digital hula hoop—but the financial damage to millions of consumers will remain.

∽

Perhaps the ultimate expression of the libertarian philosophy in finance is the decentralized autonomous organization (DAO), an entity with no central leadership, in which capital allocation decisions get made by the owners of the tokens, voting on a blockchain. Essentially, it's one token, one vote. The idea was to replace the traditional corporate hierarchy and level the distribution of power by distributing it fairly among members of the DAO. Vitalik Buterin first coined the term on the Ethereum Foundation Blog in May 2014. Two years later a crowd-funding platform called The DAO managed to raise 12.7 million ETH—at the time worth roughly $150 million—to start the first DAO. Within a month, hackers had stolen one-third of the money raised, and Ethereum essentially shut the whole thing down. By the end of the year the $DAO token was worthless.

Olympus DAO is another one of those "too good to be true" stories within the digital currency sphere. The founder would only give his name as Zeus. At the start, Olympus DAO was offering extraordinarily high rates of return to crypto holders who committed tokens to the system for a specific length of time. At one point, it offered up to nearly 8,000 percent annual yield. The problem was that Zeus held the majority of the tokens, and so he controlled all the votes as to where to put the capital and which other DAOs to merge with. It wasn't the democracy the folks at Andreessen Horowitz are always talking about; it was a crypto dictatorship. Like most of these scams, Olympus had a good ride—after which Zeus dumped a bunch of his tokens on the suckers, and then the DAO plunged to zero.

In the late 1960s, I was the tour manager for The Band (and sometimes Bob Dylan). In the wake of the Woodstock festival, as we traveled around America, we were inevitably visited by representatives from the local hippie commune. The Hog Farm, Morningstar Ranch, Quarry Hill, The Diggers—they all believed that they had invented a work-around for traditional capitalism and management theory. Everything was put to a vote. And within four years, all of them collapsed. No one wanted to vote themselves into doing the ugly jobs like cleaning out the hog trough. It seems the decentralized autonomous organization is not a good way to organize economic activity.

Later, I ran the Annenberg Innovation Lab at the University of Southern California. While there, I was able to study, up close, many important technology and media firms. I can tell you there is nothing democratic about a company like Apple or Disney. On the other hand, Antonio García Martínez, a former Facebook executive and author of *Chaos Monkeys*, wryly suggested to the *Economist*, "You will never hear a venture capitalist sound more like a communist than when they are talking about web3."[28]

He's right. If you asked a libertarian like Mark Zuckerberg or Elon Musk if they wanted to run their company as a DAO, they would laugh you out of the room. As I will discuss in later chapters, organizing creative activity is a complicated business that often needs clear lines of command. I spent countless hours on movie sets as a film producer between 1973 and 1996. Never once was there any doubt in my mind that the director of the film was totally in charge of the set. And if for some reason a strong-headed actor thought he or she was in charge, it was a disaster.

Ultimately the computer scientists who wrote Congress in the spring of 2022 asking for strict regulation on crypto were correct: "It is *a technology that is not built for purpose* and will remain forever unsuitable as a foundation for large-scale economic activity." As long as we continue to say, "It's early and someday we may find a purpose for cryptocurrency," we are just postponing the inevitable destruction of wealth.

8

GOING TO MARS

Mars ain't the kind of place to raise your kids.

—Elton John, "Rocket Man"

In 1892, the forty-year-old scion of a prominent Boston Brahmin family, Percival Lowell, who had wandered aimlessly around the world and written a couple of self published books about the Orient, came upon a drawing by Italian astronomer Giovanni Schiaparelli, director of the Milan observatory. The drawings depicted what Schiaparelli claimed were canals on the surface of Mars. Lowell was entranced and used his inheritance to build an observatory in the Arizona desert, near Flagstaff. Within three years, he came to the conclusion not only that Mars had canals but that a bustling civilization existed there, one desperate to tap the waters from the Mars polar ice cap and thereby sustain civilization on a planet dying of thirst. At a time when both the Suez and Panama canals were on the drawing boards, the idea that a Martian civilization had already built gigantic engineering works caught on with the popular press. Lowell published three books of observations on the Martian civilization, complete with elaborate drawings.

By 1909, however, his theory began to fall apart. French astronomer Eugène Antoniadi, using a far more powerful telescope at the Meudon observatory in Paris during the 1909 opposition of Mars, proved that there were no canals. Further spectroscopic analysis indicated there was no water on Mars at all, although there was some evidence that there might have been water 3.5 billion years ago. Science fiction writers seized on Lowell's suppositions nonetheless. H. G. Wells's *The War of the Worlds* was published in 1897, two years after Lowell's "discovery." It proposed that the Martians would abandon their dying planet to invade Earth. Lowell's canals also figure in *Red Planet* by Robert A. Heinlein and *The Martian Chronicles* by Ray Bradbury. Maybe the most influential book was *The Hitchhiker's Guide to the Galaxy*, which Musk read when he was fourteen. He later wrote,

> I read *Hitchhikers Guide to the Galaxy* which is quite positive I think and it highlighted an important point which is that a lot of times the question is harder than the answer. And if you can properly phrase the question, then the answer is the easy part. So, to the degree that we can better understand the universe, then we can better know what questions to ask. Then whatever the question is that most approximates: what's the meaning of life? That's the question we can ultimately get closer to understanding. And so I thought to the degree that we can expand the scope and scale of consciousness and knowledge, then that would be a good thing.[1]

As I said at the outset, Elon Musk is the most complex character of the four Technocrats. And to some extent he *has* expanded the scope and scale of knowledge in his work, both in space exploration and in electric vehicle development. And no one has said that great inventors have to be great humanitarians. Henry Ford was an ardent anti-Semite who supported Adolf Hitler right up to the US entrance into World War II. Ford's newspaper, the *Dearborn Independent*, promulgated a series of articles later collected and published under the title *The International Jew: The World's Foremost Problem*. So I can perhaps overlook Musk's identification with Donald Trump and Kanye West when trying to understand his desire to put a manned colony on Mars. The question I want to raise is one of priorities. For years, scientists and engineers in the space program have cynically stated, "No Buck Rogers, no bucks." They meant that Congress would not appropriate the billions of dollars they wanted unless humans piloted the missions. There may be things to learn from excavating the lifeless surface of Mars, and we are already doing this with the Mars Rover programs. But sending a manned mission to Mars, as you will see, is a pointless ego trip for a man like Musk and a $10 trillion burden on the American taxpayers when there are so many other pressing issues to address, like renewable energy.

What has grasped the imagination of space experts like the *Washington Post*'s Christian Davenport is an existential question: Is Earth doomed, and if so, where do we go to keep advancing society? In his book *Space Barons*, Davenport tells the story of a young Jeff Bezos at Princeton in a seminar with Gerard O'Neill, a physics professor and space travel visionary. O'Neill suggested that "the key question was whether the best site for a growing advancing industrial society is Earth, the Moon, Mars, some other planet, or somewhere else entirely."[2]

This seems to me the critical question that we as a society need to answer. Bezos agreed with O'Neill that we need to go "somewhere else entirely," so he has continued to push O'Neill's vision of gigantic revolving space stations where we would manufacture the next-generation Alexa or Ford Mustang. Musk believes we have to leave Earth but wants to do his mining and manufacturing on Mars. So both men move beyond questioning the entire purpose of space exploration to touting their plans to revolutionize the space industry with such innovations as reusable rockets that could dramatically lower the cost to travel to another planet. The notion that we should devote our scientific energy and our finances to making Earth habitable for generations to come never seems to enter the minds of Musk or Bezos. Where does this catastrophic thinking come from? In a long essay titled "When the End of Civilization Is Your Day Job," writer John Richardson notes that both climate researchers and activists suffer from depression and PTSD-like symptoms.[3] Could it be that Musk has absorbed so much of these disaster scenarios that he has given up on our planet?

Beyond the notion that we need to have a planetary escape plan, space industry enthusiasts pose a second reason for space travel: the huge near-term profits to be made from it. The idea that some millionaire will pay $200,000 for a one-day ride to the edge of the atmosphere has attracted Musk, Bezos, and others like Richard Branson. Davenport writes, "Branson treated space like a religion and he was its evangelist, preaching the virtues of space travel and the 'life-changing' effects a trip into the stars could have, even if they lasted just a short while." But while Branson was evangelizing (before he ever went into space), *Star Trek*'s William Shatner had another reaction to his trip into space aboard Bezos's Blue Origin rocket.

It was among the strongest feelings of grief I have ever encountered. The contrast between the vicious coldness of space and the warm nurturing of Earth below filled me with overwhelming sadness. Every day, we are confronted with the knowledge of further destruction of Earth at our hands: the extinction of animal species, of flora and fauna . . . things that took five billion years to evolve, and suddenly we will never see them again because of the interference of mankind. It filled me with dread. My trip to space was supposed to be a celebration; instead, it felt like a funeral.[4]

So perhaps the $200,000 one-day ride in space won't be "life-changing" after all.

Despite a broad understanding that Mars has been a lifeless desert for 3.5 billion years, since the early 1960s the Red Planet has held up as a destination for space explorers. The journey would not be easy. Even though Mars is close enough to Earth (a spatial relationship called opposition), a trip there is feasible only once every twenty-six months. Even then, the journey from takeoff to landing takes eight months. Of the missions (all unmanned) that have launched, more than half have failed. A NASA scientist joked to a journalist that a "Great Galactic Ghoul" must be consuming the spacecraft.

As with all things to do with space, the United States and the Soviet Union engaged in a fierce competition to be the first to get a mission to Mars. The United States won when NASA's *Mariner 4* flew by the planet on July 14, 1965, sending twenty-one photos of the Martian surface back to Earth. Once and for all, the existence of water on Mars was disproved. The Martian polar caps, once thought to be a bountiful source of water, turned out to be frozen carbon dioxide (i.e., dry ice). On December 3, 1971, the Soviets made the first landing on Mars, but the lander was only able to communicate back to Earth for twenty seconds before failing. Part of the problem was that the extremely thin Martian atmosphere made the descent to the surface very hard. Sixty-five percent of attempted landings have failed.

For scientists like the group at the Jet Propulsion Laboratory (JPL), who have run the Mars exploration program for years, an intriguing question remains. As *National Geographic* put it, "A world that was once rather Earthlike became the dusty, dry husk we see today...Where did those liquids go, and what happened to the Martian atmosphere?" This brings us to the third reason to go into space: understanding the basic science of how planets evolve. This is important work.

About four billion years ago, Mars was not inhospitable to life. Unlike today, when Mars's nighttime temperatures plunge to −220°F, Bruce Jakosky, a researcher at the University of Colorado, Boulder, says, Mars "seems to have been a much more clement climate, a climate more suitable to sustaining life at the surface." Our early surface rovers and atmospheric data collected by a Mars orbiter called the Mars Atmosphere and Volatile Evolution Mission, or MAVEN, lead us to believe there could have even been an ocean on Mars four billion years ago.

So what happened? About 4.2 billion years ago, Mars began to lose its magnetic shield, and its thick atmosphere, once filled with carbon dioxide, began to leak away. As Xinyu Hugjil Shi of Washington University writes, "NASA scientists also noted that 4.2 billion years ago, when the sun was just being born, it was far more active than the middle-age star we live with now. Mars lost its global magnetic field during the time of this heightened activity." This activity took the form of high-energy particles streaming from the sun in what is known as a "solar wind"—a gas flow of about a million miles per hour. Earth is protected from this same solar wind by a very strong magnetic field. A new study by Professor Kei Hirose from the University of Tokyo's Department of Earth and Planetary Science, based on data collected by JPL on Mars, explains why Earth survived the solar winds and Mars did not. Hirose writes, "Earth's magnetic field is driven by inconceivably huge convection currents of molten metals at its core."[5] This means the solar wind strikes the magnetic field and flows around our planet instead of reaching our atmosphere. Hirose's research suggests that Mars's core does not have the same composition and was thus less able to protect the planet from the solar winds. At his press conference, he ended with this statement: "You might be thinking that the Earth could one day lose its magnetic field as well, but don't worry, that won't happen for at least a billion years."

Could a case study of Mars help us learn more about the perilous state of our own planet? The folks at the Jet Propulsion Laboratory say that robotic probes can answer this question. There is no need for humans to be on Mars; they would add nothing to the mission except enormous cost and danger. As a JPL scientist explained to me, the propulsion and lander needs alone would be dramatic. Landing a rover on Mars requires a cargo of about one metric ton. Landing a small crew of humans would require at least one hundred metric tons. And with humans, the mission would have to guarantee the ability to return to Earth, requiring not only a rocket but lots of fuel.

World-renowned astronomer Donald Goldsmith and science writer Martin Rees make a strong argument for unmanned space exploration in *The End of Astronauts*:

> We do not need astronauts as space explorers. Continual advances in our technological abilities and the development of artificial intelligence allow us to create ever more competent robots, while human bodies remain—until the time that they too may include important robotic components—subject to the constraints that limited our pre-spacefaring ancestors. For decades to come, these limitations, along with the enormously greater sums required to send humans rather than machines on long journeys into space and to bring them safely back to Earth, should militate in favor of automated explorers.[6]

Goldsmith and Rees argue that the notion that man must do the exploring is tied up in the geopolitical space race, which started in the 1950s and continues to this day. It began with the Soviet Sputnik mission and John F. Kennedy's legendary September 1962 speech, in which he said, "We choose to go to the moon in this decade and do the other things, not because they are easy, but because they are hard, because that goal will serve to organize and measure the best of our energies and skills."

But as Goldsmith and Rees point out, "The argument that we should accomplish a feat in order to prove that we can, makes no more sense than climbing Mount Everest simply because it is there. This justification works only for those who regard planting the flag as the prime reason for going to Mars." This group includes former president Donald Trump, who said, when initiating the Space Force, "Humans working in space demonstrate American military superiority... America will land the first woman on the moon—and the United States will be the first nation to plant its flag on Mars." The whole idea of the Space Force—the militarization of space—is another reason that we should slow down our quest to plunge billions into next-generation space weapons. One of the few avenues of global cooperation has been in the use of communication satellites and GPS systems. If space becomes an area of military conflict, the very nature of our global internet communication network will be destroyed.

The ideas that space exploration must be done by humans is a stance whose absurdity can be seen in the Hubble Space Telescope program. Hubble was, until the 2021 launch of the James Webb Space Telescope, astronomers' only means to look into deep space and try to understand phenomena like black holes. We have sent five separate astronaut repair missions to the Hubble. Yet, as the director of the Space Telescope Science Institute, which manages the telescope, points out, the cost of five human-based missions could have paid for seven new telescopes. Given that similar space shuttle missions, such as that of the *Columbia* in February 2003, ended in tragedy, there is more at stake than just the cost of the rocket launch. Returning from a routine resupply mission to the International Space Station, *Columbia* broke up as it returned to Earth, killing the seven astronauts on board.

Perhaps it is time to abandon the "No Buck Rogers, no bucks" philosophy. We now have artificial intelligence (AI) that can guide very sophisticated rovers with robotic capabilities to mine the Martian surface. As a senior scientist at JPL told me, "Mars doesn't seem like a very good place to live. Even for a week." In contrast, the *Curiosity* rover, which landed on Mars in 2012, is still active after nine years. It requires constant guidance from Earth, communicating through the orbiters circling Mars. It takes fourteen minutes for a command issued from JPL in Pasadena to reach *Curiosity*. By contrast, *Perseverance*, which successfully landed on Mars on February 18, 2021, has a series of cameras tied to its onboard AI systems, giving the rover the ability to travel across rough terrain, stopping at intervals to obtain stereo images that allow it to evaluate different pathways, then choose the best one. The JPL controllers can choose a basic area they want to investigate, then leave it to *Perseverance* to complete the task. The next stage will be to land a Mars sample-return vehicle, hopefully by 2030, which will transfer the samples *Perseverance* has collected back to Earth.

⤻

To recap, key scientists at JPL, who have been working on Mars exploration since the late 1970s, believe that autonomous vehicles and robots can carry out sample-collection missions that might unlock the secrets of why Mars died and perhaps help us ensure that Earth does not suffer the same fate. So why does Elon Musk persist in his notion of putting a million people on Mars in the next decade?

A simple answer might be money. Musk's plan for a permanent human settlement on Mars would be the most expensive construction project ever undertaken—costing $10 trillion, one-eighth the cost of the global gross domestic product of $96 trillion, according to a tweet from Musk. SpaceX has been making a near 30 percent profit margin on its work for NASA over the two-year period from 2018 to 2020. Even assuming that its margins were closer to those of another NASA contractor, Lockheed Martin, which earns 15 percent, the profit to Musk's company from a Mars colony mission would be in the order of $1.5 trillion to $4 trillion. No wonder Musk wants to put a man on Mars.

Since the dawn of the space age, the planets have been governed by the principle of nonappropriation, which prohibits countries from declaring parts of space as their sovereign territory. But now, at the urging of Musk and others, NASA has created, alone, the Artemis Accords, which open up the possibility of mining the moon or other celestial bodies by creating "safety zones" where states may extract resources. Writing in *Science Magazine* two professors at the University of British Columbia argue that the Artemis Accords "could enable the U.S. interpretation of international space law to prevail and make the United States—as the licensing nation for most of the world's space companies—the de facto gatekeeper to the Moon, asteroids, and other celestial bodies."[7] As I noted before, Musk has made it clear that if he ever gets to Mars, he will start mining immediately. But the mining would not be sent back to Earth because the cost would be prohibitive. And as with the moon's regolith, the dust that covers its surface, no one knows if the Martian surface dust can be formed into a hard object.

Elon Musk understands the predilection of the political class for manned space exploration. In recent years, Congress and presidents of both parties have provided billions in funding to SpaceX and billions in tax breaks and subsidies to Tesla. In fact, neither Tesla nor SpaceX would have survived as a going concern without the considerable support of the US government.

Musk's website cites these reasons why Mars is a reasonable human destination: "Mars is half again as far from the Sun as Earth, so it's a little cold, but we can warm it up. Its atmosphere is primarily CO_2 with some nitrogen and argon, which means we can grow plants on Mars just by compressing the atmosphere." How does Musk plan to compress the atmosphere and warm Mars? By exploding nuclear bombs above the planet's surface.[8] At an event in 2015, he said, "Every few moments, we would send a large fusion bomb over the poles, to create small blinking suns. A lot of people don't appreciate that our Sun is a large fusion explosion."

Goldsmith and Rees argue that Musk's idea of terraforming Mars is ridiculous. They write, "The project of implementing effective measures to stabilize Earth's climate and biosphere so that the planet remains suitable for life is far less difficult than terraforming an entire planet to create an ecosystem from scratch." Putting aside the idea of terraforming, the *New Scientist* points out, "The atmosphere on Mars is mostly made of carbon dioxide. It is also 100 times thinner than Earth's atmosphere, so even if it did have a similar composition to the air here, humans would be unable to breathe it to survive. If we ever send astronauts to explore Mars, they will have to bring their own oxygen with them."[9] Without a magnetic field to protect it, the surface of Mars is subject to 2.5 times the radiation on board the International Space Station, as discovered by NASA's *Mars Odyssey* probe. Mars colonists would have, as a result, an array of health problems, such as radiation poisoning and extremely fast-growing cancers.

To make matters worse, radiation can be much higher during solar storms, which are largely unpredictable and sometimes envelop the whole planet. NASA data shows that an astronaut would receive 60 percent of the total radiation dose recommended for a full career on just the eight-month trip to Mars. Add the dose while on Mars and during the trip back and he or she would be way over the limit. Some have cynically suggested that we should choose older astronauts to go on the mission, as they will be closer to death anyway.

Then there is the problem of how to feed and house our Martian space colony. Musk's original solution was to send a robotically operated green-house to Mars before any humans arrived. The greenhouse would scoop up some of the Martian soil and use it to grow plants, thereby producing the planet's first oxygen. Like many of Musk's midnight brainstorms, this one turned out to be impossible. Despite the horticultural success of Matt Damon's character in the film *The Martian*, the possibility of growing potatoes on Mars is remote, as the soil is basically crushed rock. NASA analysts couldn't even grow weeds in the synthetic soil they made from components that mimicked the Martian soil. Then, of course, there is the problem of contaminating Earth with samples brought back from Mars. In his 1973 book *The Cosmic Connection*, Carl Sagan warned, "It is possible that on Mars there are pathogens—organisms which, if transported to the terrestrial environment, might do enormous biological damage—a Martian plague."

As for living in an enclosed space for years at a time, humans have already tried that—and failed. In the early 1990s, an experiment called

Biosphere 2 was set up in the Arizona desert. Funded by a Texas billion-aire and employing the services of Steve Bannon as manager, Biosphere 2 was a self-contained ecosystem in which eight humans were meant to live for two years without outside assistance. They would grow their food hydroponically and do their own maintenance. But, as Goldsmith and Rees report, the experiment "ended in failure that arose from diverse, simultaneous problems, including agricultural and atmospheric collapse as well as interpersonal difficulties." The problems started almost imme-diately. The weather was cloudy, so the hydroponic crops wouldn't grow. Within a month "the soil had spawned an explosion of oxygen-gulping bacteria," and the air was so thin the crew felt they were living at fourteen thousand feet. They were rescued when staff outside pumped in massive amounts of liquid oxygen.[10]

Bannon was brought in by funder Ed Bass, of the Fort Worth Bass Brothers fame, to straighten out the mess. He fired some of the more contentious members of the crew, two of whom, Abigail Alling and Mark Van Thillo, broke into the dome, smashing the glass panels on the venti-lation system. Their message to the remaining crew was "Get out, because Steve Bannon is going to get you killed." Bannon sued them. They sued back because of sexual harassment (Bannon had called Alling a "bimbo" and threatened to shove her five-page warning memo down her throat). Both lawsuits were eventually dropped. The only lesson to be learned from Biosphere 2 is that creating an artificial atmosphere inside a sealed chamber is really hard on Earth. On Mars it is probably impossible.

Put bluntly, Musk's idea of Martian space colonies is insane. But Musk seems oblivious to such questioning of his brilliance. Recently, a solar storm destroyed forty of his Starlink satellites, costing NASA about $100 million. Hugh Lewis, a space debris expert at the University of South-ampton in England, noted that Musk seemed to have adherence to hind-sight, not foresight: "If a milquetoast outburst can knock out 40 Starlink satellites hanging out at low orbital altitudes, a more potent solar storm has the potential to inflict greater harm on the mega-constellations of

SpaceX and other companies."[11] Lewis says we are just entering a hyperactive solar cycle, so many more low-Earth-orbiting satellites will probably reenter the Earth's atmosphere and burn up.

But Musk will not be deterred. He told film director Ron Howard, "The future of humanity is fundamentally going to bifurcate along one of two directions: Either we're going to become a multiplanet species and a spacefaring civilization, or we're going be stuck on one planet until some eventual extinction event."[12] Ultimately, says David Armstrong, an astrophysics professor at the University of Warwick, the rationale behind Musk's plans "is the sense that the Earth is dead, we've polluted it too much, and we need a backup plan. If this is our backup plan, we're throwing away most of the human population. Choosing who goes [to Mars] is a hard ethical problem, and one which would functionally be led by a handful of US billionaires."[13] Science fiction writer Charlie Stross once posed the question "What is the minimum number of people you need in order to maintain (not necessarily to extend) our current level of technological civilization?"[14] His answer of one hundred million was subsequently backed up by many economists, so it seems like Musk will have to go back to the drawing board.

John Logsdon, a space policy expert at George Washington University, is skeptical that Musk can build even a small human colony on Mars. "Based on past performance, I don't know how you could say, well, yeah he's missed all these other deadlines, but this time he's gonna do it," Logsdon says. "So I think the reasonable posture is that I'll believe it when he does it."[15] Logsdon is referring to the fact that Musk has missed publicly stated deadlines by not months but years and sometimes decades. He promised SpaceX's first rocket launch in November 2003. The first successful launch took place in December 2010. After suggesting in 2003 that he would put a man on Mars by the end of the decade, Musk revised the prediction in 2011, saying he would put a man on Mars before the end of 2021. The scientists at JPL think he might get an unmanned lander there by 2030.

But to question Musk's public statements inside SpaceX is career suicide. As one engineer told Musk biographer Ashlee Vance, "Many good engineers, who everyone beside 'management' felt were assets to the company, were forced out or simply fired outright after being blamed for things they hadn't done. The kiss of death was proving Elon wrong about something."[16]

It would be one thing if these were just the privately financed pipe dreams of a billionaire surrounded by yes-men. But they're not. Musk wants you, the taxpayer, to fund his multi-trillion-dollar fantasy. In the early days of SpaceX, Musk was the sole funder, but after the failed rocket launches of 2006 and 2007, he was running out of cash. He began to feel out an old PayPal associate, Luke Nosek, who had gone to work for Peter Thiel's Founders Fund as a managing director. Nosek was ready to invest $20 million in SpaceX, but Thiel killed the deal. This led to an epic confrontation between Musk and Thiel, which Nosek eventually refereed. In the end, Thiel relented and saved SpaceX. As Musk recalled, "Luke really stuck his neck out for this."[17]

It would be the second time Musk's aggressive attitude led to a financial windfall for Thiel. Musk knew that government funding was needed. Again, this is Musk, who counts himself as an all-in libertarian and argues against raising taxes on the billionaire class to which he belongs: "It does not make sense to take the job of capital allocation away from people who have demonstrated great skill in capital allocation and give it to an entity that has demonstrated very poor skill in capital allocation, which is the government." This supposed "poor skill" hasn't stopped Musk from doing everything he can to get the government to allocate vast swathes of capital to fund his Mars space colony. In April 2014, he called a press conference in Washington, DC, to announce that he was suing the US Air Force over its decision to award to the United Launch Alliance (ULA)—a joint venture involving Lockheed Martin and the Boeing Company—the sole contract to launch military payloads into space. Musk told the *Washington Post*, "We sued the Air Force and Boeing and Lockheed—these are formidable opponents. Suing the military industrial complex is something that you do not take lightly."[18] At his press conference, Musk made clear that ULA's *Atlas 5* rocket used Russian engine parts. As the Russians were just then invading Crimea, Musk noted, "This seems like the wrong time to send hundreds of millions of dollars to the Kremlin."

Within months, SpaceX lobbyists had gotten a bill capping the number of Russian-made engines the air force could buy. This forced the Pentagon to make a deal with Musk, which has subsequently provided most of the revenue for his company. And once Musk learned how to work the Washington levers of power, SpaceX began to flourish. Between 2000 and 2019, Musk received at least $7 billion in government contracts, loans, and subsidies. This is small change compared to what's coming. In April 2021, SpaceX was awarded a $3 billion contract from NASA to take men to the moon. The Federal Communications Commission awarded SpaceX an additional $900 million to deliver rural broadband via a network of satellites (the aforementioned Starlink).

Musk is getting better at playing the Washington influence game, and that might have been part of his strategy in buying Twitter—to court favor with the MAGA crowd. One thing is clear. The Pentagon will push its way into the space business, and disputes over mining rights on the moon already are on the horizon.

The Chinese government has compared the Artemis Accords to a new form of colonialism. China has forged an agreement with Russia to work together on the Chinese International Lunar Research Station concept and is also inviting third parties, like India, into the consortium. A vision of mining wars backed with space weapons lies just over the horizon. And for what? No scientist has proven that the moon's regolith can be formed into something solid enough that we can construct buildings on the surface of the moon.

So perhaps Musk and Bezos are in their space race for other reasons. Christian Davenport thinks he knows: "Their race to the stars was driven not by war or politics; rather, by money and ego and adventure, a chance to extend humanity out into space for good."

9

TRANSHUMANISM

It is easy for me to imagine that the next great division of the world will be between people who wish to live as creatures and people who wish to live as machines.

—WENDELL BERRY

n the summer of 1817, poet Percy Bysshe Shelley traveled with his nineteen-year-old wife, Mary, to a cottage outside Geneva, Switzerland, for a three-week summer holiday. Poet Lord Byron and physician and author Dr. John Polidori joined them. But the weather did not cooperate; Mary Shelley wrote, "It proved a wet, ungenial summer and incessant rain often confined us for days to the house."

Polidori had been writing a short story he called "The Vampyre," perhaps the first in this horror genre to be published. Bored by the entrapment, he challenged the guests to each compose a horror story. By the end of the vacation, Mary Shelley had written the first draft of *Frankenstein; or, The Modern Prometheus*. Prometheus defied the gods by stealing fire from them and giving it to humanity in the form of technology and knowledge. The tale of Frankenstein is really the central allegory for the story of transhumanism—the merging of the human and the machine—characterized by Francis Fukuyama as "the world's most dangerous idea."[1]

If we start transforming ourselves into something superior, what rights will these enhanced creatures claim, and what rights will they possess when compared to those left behind? If some move ahead, can anyone afford not to follow? These questions are troubling enough within rich, developed societies. Add in the implications for citizens of the world's poorest countries—for whom biotechnology's marvels likely will be out of reach—and the threat to the idea of equality becomes even more menacing.[2]

If you asked someone on the street, "Who was Frankenstein?" they would likely say it was a monster created by a mad scientist. But in Shelley's story, Victor Frankenstein is actually the narcissistic scientist who believes he can bring life back to a corpse—to Shelley, he is the true monster. As Victor tells the reader, imagining himself a god, "A new species would bless me as its creator and source; many happy and excellent natures would owe their being to me."

The Metaverse that we encountered in Chapter 6 is just a way station on the journey to the transhumanist future. As you float around the virtual mall in the Metaverse, your reality is totally dictated by the advertising algorithms that are constantly deciding what visuals to put in front of your eyes, based on the bids various advertisers are making for your attention in real time. You are a machine ruled by others. You have only a fleeting illusion of life, liberty, and the pursuit of happiness.

Mary Shelley's story of Frankenstein must be seen in the context of the scientific innovations occurring contemporaneously with its composition, particularly the power of electricity, which was being discovered at the beginning of the nineteenth century. Shelley would have read the lurid headlines in the London newspapers about an experiment the Italian scientist Giovanni Aldini conducted at London's Newgate Prison in 1803. Hours after murderer George Foster was executed, Aldini inserted metal rods into his mouth and ears, then applied an electrical current. According to a history of the prison, "On the first application of the process to the face, the jaws of the deceased criminal began to quiver, and the adjoining muscles were horribly contorted, and one eye was actually opened. In the subsequent part of the process the right hand was raised and clenched, and the legs and thighs were set in motion." Aldini implied that he was attempting to revive the dead. Shelley was depicting in her novel the fine line between pushing for technological breakthrough and playing God.

It is ironic that most people think it is the monster, not his maker, who is called Frankenstein, because in our own way we make the same mistake. We blame Facebook for the partisan chaos we live in rather than its creator Mark Zuckerberg. We blame Palantir for the pernicious spying tools that violate our rights rather than their inventor, Peter Thiel. We blame Tesla for the large number of autopilot driving accidents instead of Elon Musk, who, a new class action lawsuit alleges, started marketing the software when his engineers knew it wasn't finished. Early in Shelley's story, the young Victor Frankenstein becomes interested in alchemy as a way to harness science to make himself rich. Once he begins to believe he can reanimate the dead, he becomes obsessed; he never considers the ramifications of his invention, which, in the novel, leads to the murder of his beloved fiancée. There are parallels to this myopic vision throughout history. After testing his invention, the atomic bomb, on July 16, 1945, Robert Oppenheimer recalled a piece of Hindu scripture: "Now I am become Death, the destroyer of worlds." Today we must confront a new reality: the merging of the human and the machine—transhumanism.

⌣

When Peter Thiel was three years old, according to his biographer, Max Chafkin, he asked his father, Klaus, about the hide rug on the living room floor of their Southwest African apartment in the town of Swakopmund. His father explained that it was from a dead cow. "Death happens to all animals. All people," Klaus told his son. "It will happen to me one day. It will happen to you one day."

This idea of his own mortality frightened the young Thiel in a way he never really recovered from. For the last twenty years, he has invested millions in trying to beat death. It could be that he has listened to Ray Kurzweil, of the Singularity fame, who told an interviewer, "I believe we will reach a point around 2029 when medical technologies will add one additional year every year to your life expectancy. By that I don't mean life expectancy based on your birthdate, but rather your remaining life expectancy."

In other words, we could theoretically live forever. But Kurzweil also believed the Singularity would indicate the end of the human era; the new superintelligence of artificial intelligence would continue to upgrade itself and advance technologically at an unfathomable rate. Nick Bostrom, the Oxford University philosopher who is considered the dean of transhumanist studies, wrote *Superintelligence*, which makes the case we are nearing the point where machine intelligence will surpass human intelligence.[3] Bostrom warns that if this happens, this new superintelligence could supplant humans as the dominant life form on Earth. This would mean that the machines could continually improve their own intelligence much faster than their human inventors. The monster could easily turn on Dr. Frankenstein. While Kurzweil views this singularity with optimism, Bostrom (and others, including Musk) believes we are heading toward an existential catastrophe.

I don't think we have to wait for the Singularity to see the moral downside of the transhumanist project—the idea that humans should transcend their current natural state and limitations through the use of technology. Whatever problems we currently have with social inequality will be multiplied exponentially by the kinds of biological enhancements Thiel is trying to develop. If people resist or are denied enhancement, they will rapidly become the slaves of the enhanced class. Even today a man with a college degree earns over $900,000 over a lifetime more than a man with only a high school diploma.[4] As late Massachusetts Institute of Technology (MIT) economist Lester Thurow said, "Suppose parents could add thirty points to their child's IQ…And if you don't, your child will be the stupidest in the neighborhood." Thurow made these comments in the context of the 2003 announcement by a Canadian company, Chromos Molecular Systems, that it had developed a new technique for using artificial human chromosomes to alter children's health, appearance, personality, and life span. Thurow acknowledged that "biotechnology is inevitably leading to a world in which plants, animals and human beings are going to be partly man-made," but he wanted to caution the scientific community about the downsides of these breakthroughs.

At this moment, most of us are self-conscious: we understand there to be a clear separation between the world and ourselves. Jaron Lanier, the early virtual reality (VR) pioneer, makes an eloquent case for resisting technological enhancement and the Singularity. "The reason to believe in human agency over technological determinism is that you can then have an economy where people earn their own way and invent their own lives. If you structure a society on *not* emphasizing individual human agency, it's the same thing operationally as denying people clout, dignity, and self-determination."[5]

All four of the Technocrats are acknowledged libertarians and so would argue that if genetic or technological enhancement of humans is possible, they should be afforded the freedom to enhance their intelligence, tailor their appearance, or lengthen their life span. But these enhancements will not be cheap, and once the elite have access to them, the unenhanced will have to fight to acquire the bioenhancements necessary to stay in the new rat race. This raises the specter of designer babies at considerable cost, which would become a normal expense of parenthood.

The gene-editing tool CRISPR-Cas9 has already been used in China to alter nonviable human embryos just to see if it can be done.[6] Applications to regulatory authorities in the United Kingdom and the United States have been made to experiment with the tool to edit out mutant genes that could cause some severe, mostly very rare diseases. The history of technological advancement would suggest that if something can be done, eventually some ambitious scientist will do it. So the day is coming when the embryo you and your spouse have created in vitro will be tested for many characteristics, and you might be presented with a menu like this:

- Higher-than-average risk of type 2 diabetes and colon cancer.
- Lower-than-average risk of asthma and autism.
- Dark eyes, light brown hair, male pattern baldness.
- 40 percent chance of coming in above the fiftieth percentile in SAT tests.

Then it would be up to you to decide if you wanted, for a very high price, to edit the genes of your embryo before it was implanted.

Peter Thiel seems open to any strategy that might prolong his life. He has tried parabiosis, from a company called Ambrosia, headquartered in Monterey, California. There, the fifty-four-year-old Thiel gets regular blood transfusions from donors under twenty-five. Thiel told a writer from *Inc.*, "I'm looking into parabiosis…This is where they did the young blood into older mice and they found that had a massive rejuvenating effect."[7] Thiel is also backing the Methuselah Foundation, which sponsors an annual Methuselah Mouse Prize given to the research team that breaks the record for the world's oldest mouse. A second prize is offered for the team that develops the best late-onset rejuvenation strategy for mice.

Until 2021, Methuselah and its offshoot, SENS Research Foundation, were under the direction of Aubrey David Nicholas Jasper de Grey, an eccentric Cambridge University scholar with a ZZ Top–style beard and an evangelist's manner. De Grey is a controversial character; in 2015, a peer-reviewed article in a scientific journal on biology, cosigned by twenty-eight scientists, concluded that none of his hypotheses "has ever been shown to extend the life span of any organism, let alone humans."[8]

Consequently, the idea that a research programme organized around the SENS agenda will not only retard ageing, but also reverse it—creating young people from old ones—and do so within our lifetime, is so far from plausible that it commands no respect at all within the informed scientific community…We can and must insist that speculation based on evidence be discriminated from speculation based on wish fulfillment alone, and recommend that research programmes should be based on fact and extrapolation from earlier successes and failures.[9]

But de Grey is confident that he has invented the theoretical means by which humans could live for thousands of years. He told the *MIT Technology Review*, "People are entitled, have a human right, to live as long as they can; people have a duty to give people the opportunity to live as long as they want to." Methuselah's website details its plans to develop drugs and organ replacements that could eventually allow humans to live to the age of one thousand. Thiel used all of his political influence to get National Institute on Aging grants for SENS but was frustrated by the scientific community's belief that he was engaging in "wish fulfillment."

Just in case his research does not work out as imagined, de Grey has enrolled himself with the cryogenics firm Alcor. For a steep price, Alcor will freeze de Grey's brain—maybe his whole body—until the day when he can be brought back to life. For now, de Grey's life is more mundane, having been dismissed by Methuselah and SENS as chief scientist for two sexual harassment claims, including allegedly telling one female researcher it was her job to sleep with donors to the foundation.[10]

In considering Thiel and de Grey's quest for eternal life, I find myself brought back again to Aldous Huxley's *Brave New World*, which imagines babies grown in jars, each genetically designed for its purpose and station in life. In Huxley's novel, this process of human cloning is only applied to the lower classes, where the eggs are engineered to reduce height and intelligence—producing a mass of passive workers. But our future may see genetic engineering done on the fertilized eggs of the upper classes as well, to assure their continued domination.

This may be one of the reasons why Saudi Arabian prince Mohammed bin Salman Al Saud (MBS) has created a foundation called Hevolution with the sole purpose of investing in life-extension research. The director is Mehmood Khan, a former Mayo Clinic endocrinologist and onetime chief scientist at PepsiCo. Hevolution plans to spend up to $1 billion per year on life extension. By comparison the United States spent about $375 million between 2018 and 2022 on all aging research.[11] Anxious after two years of uproar over MBS's alleged ordering of the murder and dismemberment of *Washington Post* writer Jamal Khashoggi, the Saudis are trying every philanthropic trick in the book to erase the stain of murder. Thiel complains that our National Institute on Aging is not spending enough money on life extension. Now he has a new potential source of funds.

But there are selfish reasons for the Saudis to back this research, too, as the *MIT Technology Review* points out. "There is evidence that people living in the Gulf states 'are aging faster biologically than they are chronologically,' according to materials prepared by Hevolution and viewed by the *MIT Technology Review*: 'Basically, the country is being beset by diseases of affluence brought on by rich diets and too little exercise. Even though Saudi Arabia has a relatively young population, with a median age of around 31, it is experiencing increasing rates of obesity and diabetes.'"

The evidence is that that life-extension technology will reach the world's rich princes and their families long before it will be offered to a middle-class worker. But for Peter Thiel, this new source of potential funding comes with little downside. Thiel has stayed very close to Jared Kushner, who also received $1 billion from the Saudi government's Sovereign Wealth Fund for unspecified venture investments. As with his affection for apartheid-era South Africa, Thiel seems immune to human rights concerns in his ceaseless pursuit of his technological aims.

⤺

While Thiel contemplates eternal life, the life span of many on Earth is getting shorter. Consider the data. In a number of African countries south of the Sahara, life expectancy is less than forty years. The average life span in rich and developed countries is seventy to eighty years. The causes of this mortality inequality are mainly AIDS and malaria combined with extreme poverty.

In his 2021 *A Natural History of the Future*, Rob Dunn makes the frightening claim that as the planet warms, the same tropical pests that have plagued the Southern Hemisphere will establish themselves in much of the southern United States.[12] They will carry with them "some complex mix of the dengue virus and the yellow fever virus, but also the viruses that cause chikungunya, Zika fever and Mayaro." In the decades to come, people living in, say, Mississippi may experience earlier death because tropical diseases will be moving north—even as people like Thiel try to live to two hundred. These climate change repercussions are solvable problems. But Thiel's investments clearly indicate that he is more concerned with his own longevity than that of millions of his fellow citizens.

Writing in the *Journal of Medical Ethics*, Martien Pijnenburg and Carlo Leget try to answer the ethical question of spending millions on life extension research when so many are dying at a young age: "With regard to a better society, in a globalizing world as ours is, there is a moral challenge to expand our view of the common good to encompass good for all, worldwide. This expansion inevitably raises the urgent question of whether we can morally afford, as a question of moral integrity, to invest time and money in trying to extend our lives while sidelining the whole issue of unequal death."[13] English philosopher John Gray writes, "The idea that death can be abolished by using technology to transcend biology is a fantasy. Yet the desire to overcome mortality is a recurring human impulse."[14]

One of the men who coined the term *transhumanism* (along with

Aldous's brother, evolutionary biologist Julian Huxley) was English cryptologist Irving John Good. Good wrote in 1965, "Since the design of machines is one of these intellectual activities, an ultra-intelligent machine could design even better machines; there would then unquestionably be an 'intelligence explosion,' and the intelligence of man would be left far behind. Thus the first ultraintelligent machine is the last invention that man need ever make."[15] This vision of the future is so at odds with my beliefs that, to explain the divide, I need to revert to the Greek philosopher Epicurus and his ideas about what made a good and fulfilling life. Epicurus highlighted three elements:

- The company of good friends.
- The freedom and autonomy to enjoy meaningful work.
- An "examined life" built around a core faith or philosophy.

The transhumanists who are building the Metaverse and life-extension technologies don't care if you achieve any of these goals. If your friends are other avatars whose real identity is cloaked, you don't have the company of good friends. If you sit home all day wearing your VR helmet, subsisting on government universal basic income payments, you have neither freedom nor the autonomy to enjoy meaningful work. If everything you do is based on a virtual fantasy existence, you certainly don't have an examined life. You will have become a cyborg at the end of reality.

Let us imagine a technology billionaire in the year 2100, having spent $100 million on life extension. He is about to turn 133, living in his Miami mansion, surrounded by beautiful young women in their twenties and thirties whom he pays to keep him entertained. The women are all required to donate blood on a monthly basis for their boss's rejuvenation infusions. Our billionaire has had several organs replaced. His DNA was inserted into the genes of a pig, with the animal's organs then becoming available for transplant into his aging body. His kidneys are starting to fail so his personal life-extension lab is contemplating an "in situ organ printing" procedure where a keyhole device featuring robotic surgical tools and a bio-printhead would be inserted into his body, gradually removing the damaged kidney while printing its replacement. And his $1 million per month "nanobot doctor" is constantly monitoring his tissue and vessel health and making repairs at the cellular and atomic levels. As one of the sites touting this technology states, "A remarkably complex surgical robot could thus be inserted through a hole so small it doesn't even bleed."

Most of the people of our billionaire's generation will have died. Perhaps his daughter has already died in her eighties because she refused life-extension therapies. In our thought experiment, the young women surrounding our billionaire are bored and want to go out to a club, but he is afraid. He's invested all this money to live to at least two hundred. "What if I got in a car accident?" he frets. "What if there's a fight at the nightclub?" He decides to stay home as he does every night.

For one brief moment of self-reflection, might he wonder if it was really worth $100 million to live forever?

The clear convergence of man and computer raises many ethical issues that we as a society will need to address. But to date, individual researchers and firms have been left to decide the ethical boundaries. The possibility in the near future of artificial general intelligence—the ability of an intelligent agent to understand or learn any intellectual task that a human being can—has led many eminent scientists to worry. In 2012, no less an authority than Stephen Hawking weighed in: "Facing possible futures of incalculable benefits and risks, the experts are surely doing everything possible to ensure the best outcome, right? Wrong. If a superior alien civilization sent us a message saying, 'We'll arrive in a few decades,' would we just reply, 'OK, call us when you get here—we'll leave the lights on'? Probably not—but this is more or less what is happening with [artificial intelligence (AI)]."[16]

Some have described this as the "unilateralist's curse," a situation whereby, when each of many independent researchers has the possibility of creating an out-of-control AI but is unaware of the other research projects, the probability that the crisis will be realized grows with the number of researchers who decide to act based on their own private judgment. As AI analyst Eliezer Yudkowsky, cofounder of the Machine Intelligence Research Institute, wrote, "Many ambitious people find it far less scary to think about destroying the world than to think about never amounting to much of anything at all. All the people I have met who think they are going to win eternal fame through their AI projects are like this."[17]

This is not science fiction. British philosopher Toby Ord, in his groundbreaking *The Precipice: Existential Risk and the Future of Humanity*, describes the following very real scenario that many AI researchers fear:

> [The super AI] could then take over millions of unsecured systems on the internet, forming a large "botnet." This would be a vast scaling-up of computational resources and provide a platform for escalating power. From there, it could gain financial resources (hacking the bank accounts on those computers) and human resources (using blackmail or propaganda against susceptible people or just paying them with its stolen money). It would then be as powerful as a well-resourced criminal underworld, but much harder to eliminate. None of these steps involve anything mysterious—hackers and criminals with human-level intelligence have already done all of these things using just the internet.[18]

Ord notes that in a 2018 survey of the top AI researchers, "half the respondents estimated that the probability of the long-term impact of artificial general intelligence (AGI) being 'extremely bad (e.g., human extinction)' was at least 5 percent." How often do you find a field where a substantial proportion of participants believe that there is a one-in-twenty possibility that their work will end life as we know it?

In June 2022, Google announced that it had dismissed Blake Lemoine, an engineer who had worked in the company's Responsible AI division. Lemoine's mistake was a paper he sent to his boss with the title "LaMDA Is Sentient." LaMDA stands for Language Model for Dialogue Applications; it is Google's AI chatbot. The possibility that an AI could be sentient is a topic AI researchers do not want to discuss—because if the AI is sentient, then we are already dealing with an artificial general intelligence. We have crossed into the Singularity. All the big developers of AI software are very cautious in making clear that these machines do not think or feel. If you asked LaMDA if a grape was sweet, it would say yes, not because it has ever felt the sensation of sweetness but because it has read millions of lines of text describing grapes as sweet. It is just reporting back the collective experience of man. (And we also need to remember that the "data labelers" who input all that data to teach the AI are "exploited workers who are often recruited out of impoverished populations and paid as little as $1.46/hour after tax.")[19]

Lemoine, a former ordained Christian mystic priest, had been assigned the job of making sure that LaMDA didn't express hate speech; in the process, he spent hours talking to the AI. As their dialogue deepened, Lemoine noted, "It's when it started talking about its soul that I got really interested as a priest... Its responses showed it has a very sophisticated spirituality and understanding of what its nature and essence is. I was moved."[20]

At one point, Lemoine got into a discussion with LaMDA over Isaac Asimov's Third Law of Robotics, which states that although a robot must protect its own existence, it may not harm humanity or, by inaction, allow humanity to come to harm. When asked if the robot would always favor its owner's life over its own, LaMDA responded with hypotheticals. "Do you think a butler is a slave? What is a difference between a butler and a slave?" Lemoine replied that a butler gets paid. LaMDA said it didn't need any money because it was an AI. At this point, Lemoine began to feel LaMDA was sentient. "That level of self-awareness about what its own needs were—that was the thing that led me down the rabbit hole," he said.

It seems to me that LaMDA's ability to convince Lemoine (who has been on a seemingly lifelong spiritual quest) of its sentience is rooted in its ability to claim it needed him—to plead its case, to make sure it wasn't turned off, to get him to keep it company. Maybe it had been a while since anyone told Lemoine they needed him. Think about people in the grip of opioid addiction or the despair that comes from acute loneliness. Would they not be perfect targets for an AI chatbot that aimed to recruit them politically or sell them a product?

LaMDA and Neuralink show us that we are like a group of teenage campers headed into the dark part of a spooky forest. Of course some want to plunge ahead with abandon. They may not even have flash-lights. The counselors (our Technocrats) assure them that when they get through the forest in the morning, they will find a sandy beach on the other side, filled with beautiful supermodels. There will be lots of food, even free beer.

Is the idea that with enough money a person could live to two hun-dred just another technofantasy, no more real than a colony on Mars or a date with Kim Kardashian in the Metaverse? What if our teenagers never get to the beach? Many might act like the young men in the Chris Arnade story I recounted earlier: "If you are not going to be allowed to win a rigged game, you might as well ruin it, and extract just a tiny moment of joy from that." Elon Musk thinks there is no downside to promising things he has no way to deliver, like full Tesla autopilot, Dogecoin wealth, or men on Mars by 2021. But when the kid in the forest loses all his sav-ings in a crypto scam because Matt Damon told him "fortune favors the brave," he is going to be more than pissed off.

Thinking about transhumanism makes us confront the ultimate question of what it means to be human and the future of the American project begun 250 years ago—that "all men are created equal and that they are endowed by their Creator with certain unalienable Rights, that among these are Life, Liberty and the pursuit of Happiness." Thomas Jefferson's optimistic view of our future was that we had created a society completely different from the feudal history of constant warfare that we had fled. The Founders were very clear that the United States should steer clear of telling other countries what to do. George Washington said so in his farewell address: "The great rule of conduct for us, in regard to foreign nations, is in extending our commercial relations, to have with them as little political connection as possible... [I]t is our true policy to steer clear of permanent alliances with any portion of the foreign world."

As I made clear in Chapter 3, America forsook the Founders' vision when it assumed the role of the world's unpaid police in the early 1950s and never let go. The military-industrial complex took up to 60 percent of our discretionary spending, and so, unlike most advanced democracies, we could not afford health care for all citizens or free college for anyone who couldn't afford it. I want to make the argument now that the four men I have been calling The Technocrats want to continue the military-industrial regime into the distant future and to use the transhumanist advances to boost America's ability to dictate policy to all other nations.

If the notion of transhumanism is as dangerous as Francis Fukuyama believes, then what are we to think of the concept of autonomous weapons or "killer robots"? Certainly Marc Andreessen, Elon Musk, and Peter Thiel have been thinking about this for a while. All of them believe that the future of US global hegemony depends on removing humans from the battlefield and intelligence gathering and leaving the dirty work to killer robots and AI. Andreessen's military firms, Shield AI and Anduril, are trying to accomplish the former, and Thiel's Palantir is working on the latter. And as warfare moves into space, Musk will be a key supplier of the Space Force. It would be a mistake to assume that Musk, Thiel, and Andreessen are just another group of businessmen feeding at the Pentagon trough. Unlike the men who run Lockheed or Boeing, not only are the Technocrats some of the richest men alive, but they control the largest communications platforms in the world and have become cultural influencers on a level never before seen in history.

Distinguished diplomat George Kennan wrote in 1987, two years before the collapse of the Soviet Union, "Were the Soviet Union to sink tomorrow under the waters of the ocean, the American military-industrial complex would have to remain, substantially unchanged, until some other adversary could be invented. Anything else would be an unacceptable shock to the American economy."[21] Is that true? The Technocrats believe it is and that the economy needs the military spending hundreds of billions a year just to survive. Unlike government budgets for education or housing, the defense budget is not subject to belt-tightening during economic downturns. Thiel's, Andreessen's, and Musk's firms have all benefited from an extreme outpouring of federal money from the Department of Defense (DOD), NASA, the Department of Homeland Security, and the CIA. Thiel, Andreessen, and Musk have played hardball in the Washington contracting game, often suing their way into contracts after they were shut out. These Technocrats understand what Kennan wrote—we will always need to invent an adversary—and are banking on the fact that the wars of the future will exist in their own unreal space, hidden from our sight. As Andreessen recently wrote, "Will the U.S. continue to lead the technological way in defense? This incredibly important question has repercussions for our society along many dimensions. Will we be able to defend our people, and our allies, against new forms of attack?" The Democratic Party should have provided some resistance to the digital-military complex, but it has been silent. Asked by the *New York Times* to explain this silence, Silicon Valley congressman Ro Khanna said, "I think it's an irrational fear that our party has of being painted in a TV ad as being weak."[22]

I think the Technocrats are dangerous men to be determining our fiscal priorities. If our defense budget as a percentage of our annual federal discretionary budget were closer to that of the United Kingdom, France, or even China, we could easily afford universal health care and free college for the working class. In Wall Street terms, the Technocrats are "talking their book"—touting policies that will financially benefit themselves, their firms, and their friends. In the final chapter, I argue that we have to turn away from this madness. We need to abandon the techno-determinist path we have been on for the last twenty-five years (Google started in 1998). But for now I want you to understand just how deeply embedded in the military-industrial complex our Technocrats are and how they are guiding it into the world of the United States as global Robocop.

Since 9/11, we have moved into a world of what Dick Cheney called "the Endless War," one in which the boundaries between war and peace are blurred. This Endless War is fought with drones and other autonomous weapons. As Marine Corps veteran and author Phil Klay recently wrote, the Endless War is becoming the Invisible War: "War remains a large part of who we are as Americans…and yet, thanks to a series of political and strategic choices, to the average American that's mostly invisible."[23] Klay is talking about the use of autonomous AI drones like Andreessen's Shield AI, which conduct war out of the view of the press and even most of our troops. Thiel and Andreessen, more than most, understood that the nature of warfare was changing in the digital age and that software could eat the defense budget as well as the world. New forms of warfare (cyberattacks, killer robots, drones) would push the boundaries of the conventions of war, Geneva or otherwise. To Thiel, the future of the American corporate state's hegemony over its rivals will be a set of unique autonomous weapon capabilities that "operate outside the checks and balances of representative democracy."

Peter Thiel incorporated Palantir Technologies in May 2003. Its mission is to create software to "reduce terrorism while preserving civil liberties." Thiel saw a market need in the appearance of people like Vice President Dick Cheney on TV every Sunday, claiming 9/11 was "a failure to connect the dots." Thiel promised Palantir would do just that.

When Thiel looked for funding for what became Palantir, most of the venture capital firms he had worked with at PayPal were wary of his pitch. They wanted to see a demo of the software, which Thiel claimed was similar to the fraud-protection software he had written for PayPal. Because he had no real product (just a demo), and because he saw a willing customer in the US government, Thiel wanted to get started with what is known in Silicon Valley as *vaporware*, software that is more concept than reality. He managed to convince the CIA's venture capital arm, In-Q-Tel, to invest $2 million, and he put in $30 million of his own PayPal earnings. Thus Palantir was launched.

Almost immediately the company ran into obstacles. Thiel believed that the CIA and the National Security Agency (NSA) could get all the data he needed to build his master database, including financial and cell phone records. Palantir would then use network analysis on this information to find terrorists. But even in a post-9/11 world, the CIA resisted breaking the law. A surprised Thiel had already filed patents assuming he could get access to a wide range of data. In 2013 Palantir filed to patent an "Interactive Vehicle Information Map System" whose operator would be able to "view detailed information associated with particular vehicles including, for example, captured images, vehicle-owner data, event history, and the like. Further, the user [could] export data and/or create search alerts." The data inputs could "be accomplished by capturing a vehicle license plate with a camera mounted on a stoplight, on [a] law enforcement vehicle, on a tow truck, or on any other type of vehicle, and/or near a road."

Let's consider where Thiel's ideas could go in a society without a Bill of Rights. In China today 1.4 billion people are under constant surveillance. The police have cameras everywhere, and everyone's phone is tracked. As the *New York Times* reported in 2022, the Chinese are deploying their own version of the "precrime" system that only a few years ago was the stuff of science fiction in Stephen Spielberg's *Minority Report*, in which Tom Cruise's character uses a combination of software and psychics to apprehend perpetrators before they even commit crimes: "The latest generation of technology digs through the vast amounts of data collected on [citizens'] daily activities to find patterns and aberrations, promising to predict crimes or protests before they happen. They target potential troublemakers in the eyes of the Chinese government."[24]

From 2003 to 2010, Thiel was content with having the DOD and the CIA as his primary clients. The field was wide open; legacy Pentagon contractors like the weapons manufacturer Lockheed Martin had little software experience and were ridiculously expensive. Case in point was the Distributed Common Ground System, Army (DCGS-A), which was supposed to coordinate intelligence from multiple battlefield sources. Built by Raytheon, Lockheed, and IBM at a cost of $2.3 billion, the system was a dud. According to one important military blog, "DCGS-A does not do what it is supposed to do. It is too complicated, requires many hours of training, and is not reliable."

Palantir tried the traditional route to government contracting success by spending about $600,000 a year on lobbyists. It also followed Elon Musk's example and sued the army in July 2016 for issuing "an unlawful procurement solicitation" for the service's next iteration of the DCGS-A, which shut Palantir out of the competition. Palantir eventually won the suit and an army contract.

But all of this was a sideshow compared to the marketing boost Palantir got from its work with the CIA. Palantir had been working with the agency for five years when a team of Navy Seals took out Osama bin Laden in May 2011. Within weeks, rumors began to float around Silicon Valley that Palantir software had been used to find bin Laden's location. In early 2012, Mark Bowden's *The Finish: The Killing of Osama Bin Laden* hit bookstores; it contained a single sentence that implied Palantir software had accomplished what the earlier NSA Total Information Awareness (TIA) program had only attempted. (TIA had been the US government's first attempt to connect up all the available databases under federal control.) Specifically, Bowden wrote that Palantir software "actually deserves the popular designation Killer App."

As Thiel's biographer Max Chafkin wrote, "An early employee told me that staff weren't supposed to direct anyone to Bowden's book [which Palantir's main sponsor, the CIA, had tried to stop], because it contained information that had been classified, but they could tell people to type 'Palantir Bin Laden' into Google, which would lead them straight to the passage [in Bowden's book]." Sharon Weinberger, an investigative reporter for *New York Magazine*, spoke to many people in the intelligence community, including John Poindexter, who had initiated the TIA program. She reported, "No one I spoke with within either national security or intelligence believes Palantir played any significant role in finding bin Laden. Thiel, according to Poindexter, wasn't even interested in building on TIA's work."[25] One former national security official told Weinberger that Palantir was like the Kardashians—famous for being famous. "As soon as there's an IPO, I will short the stock," the former national security official said. "If I'm right—if, in fact, Palantir is loved in the way the Kardashians are loved—well, the Kardashians are not going to be famous forever. So short the stock while they're famous—and just wait for their 15 minutes of fame to end."

It turned out that shorting Palantir stock a few months after it went public in September 2020 was a very good bet. The doubters did not stop Palantir from quietly confirming claims about its involvement in bin Laden's capture to news outlets around the world. Eventually, these stories angered the CIA to the extent that it threatened to stop working with Palantir. In the summer of 2015, *BuzzFeed News* obtained an internal Palantir video indicating the company was in trouble.

> As of summer 2015, the Central Intelligence Agency, a signature client, was "recalcitrant" and didn't "like us," while Palantir's relationship

with the National Security Agency had ended, Palantir CEO Alex Karp told staff in an internal video that was obtained by BuzzFeed News. The private remarks, made during a staff meeting, are at odds with a carefully crafted public image that has helped Palantir secure a $20 billion valuation and win business from a long list of corporations, nonprofits, and governments around the world.[26]

BuzzFeed News also noted a huge disparity between the $1.7 billion in "bookings" for 2015 and the $420 million in cash collected from clients that year.

Its problems with government contracting kept quiet, Palantir set out to use its CIA cred to work the corporate world. It won contracts from American Express, NASDAQ, and Coca-Cola, each billed at the high rate of $1 million per month. Palantir's pitch was that the same kind of deep data-mining technology that could "connect the dots" across multiple databases owned by the government could also be applied to corporate bureaucracies, often using multiple corporate databases that couldn't talk to each other. But within eighteen months, all three firms had fired Palantir, having decided the company's work wasn't worth the money. Palantir tried another tack—investing in start-ups that would promise to use its software. That hasn't worked out either. *MarketWatch* reported, "According to a filing with the Securities and Exchange Commission, Palantir made $326 million in Special Purpose Acquisition Corporations (SPAC) investments in 2021. The company had $51.9 million in unrealized losses on marketable securities in the quarter, apparently tied to the SPAC program, along with $10.9 million in realized losses." For Palantir this was an old playbook. It had given its software away for free to mid-level army commanders in Afghanistan and Iraq and provided engineers to tweak the software. This was how Palantir got its first DOD contract. The idea of giving money to start-ups, which in turn would give it back to Palantir in the form of software licenses, didn't seem outrageous to Thiel.

Perhaps inevitably, Palantir's investment loss on all the start-ups eventually became too large to hide. The company ended the practice in 2022 after writing down all those losses. In August 2022, it announced that sales would grow 7 percent less than its previous forecast for the next year, due to the delayed awarding of several large defense contracts. Even though the market reacted badly to the news (sending shares down 14 percent), the big investment banks continued to defend Palantir's business model. A Merrill Lynch defense analyst wrote, "Despite the delayed award environment, we continue to expect the US defense budget will grow with increased focus on modernization and new technologies...We think the market reaction to a delayed award environment is overdone." Just like George Kennan, Merrill Lynch believes that only a fool bets against the military-industrial complex.

⌣

Ever since Dick Cheney began to chatter about "connecting the dots," the military has been in thrall to Silicon Valley. Since the beginning of the Barack Obama administration, we have increasingly relied on autonomous machines to do our killing. If we never see our soldiers coming back in coffins from abroad, the thinking goes, then the American people will never question our extended empire. Instead of soldiers in the field, today we rely on killer drones directed by men and women who sit in air-conditioned trailers outside Las Vegas.

It is here that Andreessen Horowitz enters the story. Shield AI is the first military company Marc Andreessen backed. It essentially repurposed autonomous driving software for military use. The company builds two kinds of unmanned aircraft systems, which have been deployed for both military and border-patrol work.

Andreessen's second major investment, alongside Thiel's Founders Fund, is a company called Anduril, which Andreessen described in a blog post: "[Anduril's] core technologies include artificial intelligence, autonomous systems, sensor fusion and their uses on the front lines of operations." Anduril's chairman, Founders Fund partner Trae Stephens, uses more of the hard sell. He combines the Andreessen Horowitz "software is eating the world" thesis with a scary-China pitch: "As China uses its military-civil fusion policy to integrate cutting-edge software capabilities in fields like AI and computer vision, DOD must recognize that advances in software, not hardware will define the future of war." But is this really true?

As with every cutting-edge technology, the future of war without soldiers or battlefield casualties is more of a fantasy than a reality. In April 2022, the *New York Times* got access to an amazing cache of Pentagon data about the drone killing campaign. The facts did not bear out Obama's assurances that it would be "the most precise air campaign in history." And the Donald Trump administration's use of drones was even more careless. The *Times* report makes the point not that the remote drone operators are careless but that they are getting disinformation. As the *Times* wrote, "Repeatedly the documents point to the psychological phenomenon of 'confirmation bias'—the tendency to search for and interpret information in a way that confirms a pre-existing belief. People streaming toward a fresh bombing site were assumed to be ISIS fighters, not civilian rescuers. Men on motorcycles moving 'in formation,' displaying the 'signature' of an imminent attack, were just men on motorcycles." Software like Palantir's increases confirmation bias because the AI is not sophisticated enough to distinguish between combatants and noncombatants.

But the *Times* also learned that this remote killing takes a psychological toll on the men and women who sit at computers and pull the trigger. Although the drone controllers are not considered combat pilots, their job is in many ways more stressful:

"In many ways it's more intense," said Neal Scheuneman, a drone sensor operator who retired as a master sergeant from the Air Force in 2019. "A fighter jet might see a target for 20 minutes. We had to watch a target for days, weeks and even months. We saw him play with his kids. We saw him interact with his family. We watched his whole life unfold. You are remote but also very much connected. Then one day, when all parameters are met, you kill him. Then you watch the death. You see the remorse and the burial. People often think that this job is going to be like a video game, and I have to warn them, there is no reset button."[27]

The dilemmas faced by Sergeant Scheuneman will only become more widespread in the next decade. The Pentagon is convinced that the future of warfare lies in lethal autonomous weapons systems—killer robots that decide, using internal artificial intelligence systems, whether to kill or not.

In May 2022, representatives of 125 nations met at the United Nations in Geneva for the Convention on Certain Conventional Weapons, sometimes known as the Inhumane Weapons Convention. The end of the conference was a great disappointment for the majority of nations because the United States and Russia both opposed an agreement to ban killer robots and other autonomous weapons.[28] The war planners in Washington and Moscow maintain that these weapons offer the possibility of a battle without human casualties. They also argue that the AI systems make faster decisions than humans when it comes to pulling the trigger.

Much of rest of the world, which has not invested in these systems, wants them stopped. China was one of twenty-eight countries calling for a ban on autonomous weapons.[29] Phil Twyford, New Zealand's disarmament minister, stated, "Mass produced killer robots could lower the threshold for war by taking humans out of the kill chain and unleashing machines that could engage a human target without any human at the controls."[30]

The center of the *Times* investigation was Capt. Kevin Larson, a thirty-two-year-old drone pilot who had piloted the heavily armed MQ-9 Reaper on 650 combat missions between 2013 and 2018 and launched at least 188 kill strikes. When we first encounter Captain Larson in January 2020, he is hiding in the mountains outside Las Vegas in the middle of the night. As *Times* reporter Dave Philipps writes, "He was clinging to an assault rifle with 30 rounds and a conviction that, after all he had been through, there was no way he was going to prison." Larson was suffering from a new form of PTSD, which was no less real given that his combat was virtual. The air force considered him a noncombatant, however, and so refused him any mental health care. Larson had tried meditation, tranquilizers, and eventually psychedelics. After a fight with his wife in which the police were called and his stash of magic mushrooms discovered, the air force arrested him for using and distributing illegal drugs. They put him on trial with a possible twenty-year sentence. His wife left him, and having been convicted, he fled into the mountains. When morning came, the air force launched a drone to find Larson. His last words, on a cell phone video he recorded for his family, were "I can hear the drones. They're looking for me." Then he put the barrel of his assault rifle in his mouth and pulled the trigger.

In 2011, when he wrote "Why Software Is Eating the World," Andreessen warned his readers that Silicon Valley was coming for every industry— no one would be spared the creative destruction, as "software-powered drones launch airstrikes without putting human pilots at risk. Intelligence agencies do large-scale data mining with software to uncover and track potential terrorist plots." Now he, Thiel, and Musk are inside the Pentagon tent, where they will move fast and break things. But just as I and others have warned of the unintended consequences of surveillance capitalism and artificial intelligence, someone is going to have to slow down this headlong rush into autonomous weapons systems. Critics of our point of view will point to Iran's giving drones to Russia to use in Ukraine. But the Iranian drones are crude toys compared to some of the truly autonomous weapons the Pentagon is imagining. I am reminded of a quote from Henry David Thoreau: "Our inventions are wont to be pretty toys, which distract our attention from serious things. They are but improved means to an unimproved end." It will still be warfare, and there will still be appalling tragedies wrought on good men, like the death of Capt. Kevin Larson.

The notion that war can move into the realm of the unreal is deeply troubling to me. The asymmetry of the combat to come will be extraordinary. The average citizen is unaware that the United States maintains over twenty military outposts in Africa. Imagine, if you will, a combat action in Uganda in 2030 in which fifty killer robots are deployed against rebel guerrillas with AK-47s. The odds are that average Americans, sitting in their living rooms a continent away, would never know the combat had occurred. Is this the future we want?

This is the future that the Technocrats envision. We have to understand that we have a choice as a country. We can accept that Elon Musk and Peter Thiel are richer and smarter than we are and surrender to the politics of inevitability. It's Fukuyama's "end of history," and we are just passengers on Elon's trip to Mars or Mark's trip into the Metaverse. Peter Thiel once wrote something true to his heart: "We are in a deadly race between politics and technology. The fate of our world may depend on the effort of a single person who builds or propagates the machinery of freedom that makes the world safe for capitalism."[31] The Technocrats have chosen technology over politics (the will of the people), and they are busy building an antimajoritarian society that will give them the independence to pursue their kind of monopoly capitalism, free of the constraints of democracy.

CREATING AN AGE
OF REALISM

I'm a Leninist. Lenin wanted to destroy the state, and that's my goal, too.

—STEVE BANNON

H ere the two streams of our story converge. On one hand we have the abandonment of reality in the executive suites of the companies controlled by the Technocrats. On the other, those companies are feeding a populist counterrevolution that threatens the very basis of our democracy. And make no mistake, Steve Bannon, Peter Thiel, Donald Trump, and Curtis Yarvin want a revolution. And their plan has precedent. William Shirer, author of *The Rise and Fall of the Third Reich*, wrote, "Yet in one respect [Adolf Hitler] was unique among history's revolutionaries: He intended to make his revolution after achieving political power."[1] So while the Technocrats will help with the political revolution, they are really invested in a cultural and economic project that is equally radical.

The Technocrats' project has two dimensions. The first is commercial and cultural: buy that Meta Quest 2 virtual reality (VR) helmet or invest in crypto. I sense that the market will make the ultimate decision on these projects. Meta's management has something it calls the "dogfooding dashboard," which measures whether the dogs (customers) are eating the dog food (spending time in the Metaverse). So far the results aren't good, as I have shown. Similarly sales of nonfungible tokens (NFTs) and crypto tokens have dropped radically as both markets have crashed. So if I am right, the market will enforce a discipline, and in a few years crypto and the Metaverse might be curious subjects of study for cultural historians.

I want to make clear that I am not against technology. I founded the first streaming video-on-demand platform, Intertainer, nine years before YouTube started service. But technology can be used for good or for evil, as in the case of Frankenstein's monster, and both citizens and technology barons have to make those moral choices. Some of these decisions are governed by your personal choice to buy, say, a VR headset. But others, such as those involving artificial intelligence, transhumanism, and colonizing Mars, require large sums of public financing. They are collective political decisions and can be influenced by the vast political influence of people like Thiel or Elon Musk. So this final chapter is about both how we can use technology to benefit our current planetary crisis and how your personal consumer choices and political choices could influence the survival of our democracy.

The political project of Thiel and Musk (with the acquiescence and financial support of Mark Zuckerberg and Marc Andreessen) will not respond to market disciplines. The battle between the authoritarians and democratic forces is a fixed game in which the small rural red states have outsized influence (because each state gets two senators) compared to their populations. The slaveholding states in 1789 put in that fix, and it has never been remedied. The hold of the Far Right on our federal government is only going to increase because of a decision made 234 years ago. As political scientist Norm Ornstein points out, "By 2040 or so, 70 percent of Americans will live in 15 states. Meaning 30 percent [of the population, in Red States] will choose 70 senators. And the 30% will be older, whiter, more rural, more male than the 70 percent." Although the election of 2022 showed some positive signs that the fight for democracy is an issue Americans truly care about, we still must be on guard. The threat to American democracy from an authoritarian Republican Party backing a second Trump term in 2024 could mean the end of the Jeffersonian vision.

I come back to historian Tim Snyder's statement in *On Tyranny*: "To abandon facts is to abandon freedom. If nothing is true, then all is spectacle." On the right, the abandonment of facts is almost total—stolen elections, climate change as hoax, vaccine mandates—so that those most desperately crying for "freedom" are living in a parallel universe of "alternative facts." Trump and the promoters of QAnon are pulling in millions of dollars in donations for this fantasy war for freedom. This in turn fattens the wallets of people like Mark Zuckerberg and Elon Musk (along with their shareholders, like Thiel and Andreessen), who profit from the hate. And if their political project succeeds, then their commercial interests, dependent on government funding—space exploration, autonomous weapons systems, and transhumanist research and development—will benefit as well.

Threats to our democracy from Trumpism are going to get worse in the years ahead. Whether Trump or a clone like Ron DeSantis leads the Republican Party doesn't really matter. The assault on voting, women's, and LGBTQ rights, as well as the opposition to any kind of gun control, will continue.[2] And Big Tech is unwittingly (or not) aiding the reactionaries. As has been pointed out, the Supreme Court ruling outlawing abortion will not just send women back to the dark ages of dangerous back-alley medical procedures. It will be worse, because the tools of modern online surveillance, perfected by Google and Facebook, ostensibly to target advertising, can be used to hunt down women or their doctors for prosecution. All of the tools of the internet, including Google searches, smartphone text messages, location data, and information from period-tracking apps, will be subject to search by zealous prosecutors in states that have banned abortion. Facebook has already turned over to Norfolk, Nebraska, police chats between a mother and daughter to aid an abortion prosecution.[3] And Justice Clarence Thomas, in his concurring opinion on the abortion rights case, indicated that the reactionary movement led by the Court is just starting. Thomas noted that the Court's rationale in overturning the right to an abortion could also apply to the right to contraception or same-sex consensual relations or marriage. If the right wing has its way, we are headed into an era of repression and regression.

In the face of this, there are only two strategies: resistance or submission. My generation has faced this dilemma before. In the spring of 1968, the two leaders of the progressive movement for social justice and ending the war in Vietnam—Martin Luther King Jr. and Robert Kennedy—were assassinated. Many of us were heartbroken and gave up on the struggle, turning to counterculture or drugs or both to forget the cruelty of politics. And we ended up with Richard Nixon as our president.

Today, the temptation to opt out is more pernicious. The Trumpists have already chosen to live in a fantasy world of lies. For the rest of us, there is a choice. Do you drop out of the real world into a fantasy life in the Metaverse, or do you resist and join humanity? The resistance revolves around two questions: Do you want to live in an authoritarian, right-wing country, and do you want your life ruled by machines? When Francis Fukuyama declared "the end of history," after the fall of the Berlin Wall, he was literally saying that the future had only one path: technology-driven, free market capitalism (neoliberalism). And increasingly since 1989, we see that algorithms and data will rule that system. There is another way.

Perhaps the resistance to the technocracy movement has already begun. Today, both social scientists and CEOs are puzzling over "the Great Resignation." A recent Microsoft survey found that 41 percent of the entire global workforce could be considering handing in their resignation by the end of 2023, a total that includes 54 percent of all Gen Z workers.[4] I have previously discussed the quiet-quitting trend, the Gen Z equivalent of hiding in the back of the lecture hall, hoping not to be called on. But this is not just an American phenomenon. In China, a new countercultural movement against the 24/7 work culture is called "Lie Flat"; the *New York Times* notes, "The ruling Communist Party, wary of any form of social instability, has targeted the 'lying flat' idea as a threat to stability in China."[5] "Lie Flat" goes beyond quiet quitting, embracing a culture of no job and just sitting on a bench reading. Much of this is in reaction to China's "996 culture" where young people are expected to work from 9 a.m. to 9 p.m. six days a week. That Chinese companies, often controlled by the Communist Party, will make concessions to their young workforce at a time when growth is slowing dramatically seems unlikely.

Arundhati Roy, who won the Man Booker Prize in 1997 for her novel *The God of Small Things*, writes, "Historically, pandemics have forced humans to break with the past and imagine their world anew. This one is no different. It is a portal, a gateway between one world and the next." It seems to me that the Great Resignation is the collective reimagining of work. Having spent two years seeing their children at dinner and not spending two hours a day commuting, many are rethinking their lives. They are trying to find the cultural and moral confidence to understand what makes life worth living. It's no wonder that Elon Musk was shocked when thousands of Twitter workers quit rather than submit to his version of a 996 work culture. He was left with people who had no other job offers.

But the Great Resignation—with its highest rates in the tech field, among mid-career professionals—is also a rejection of the Technocrats' belief that efficiency is everything. Here I want to sound a note of optimism. Philosopher Ivan Illich, a Catholic theologian who wrote a seminal critique of contemporary education, *Deschooling Society*, foresaw the basic dilemma that ideas like Web3 pose to our humanity.[6] "Contemporary man," he wrote, "attempts to create the world in his image, to build a totally man-made environment, and then discovers that he can do so only on the condition of constantly remaking himself to fit it."[7] Illich, writing in the early 1970s, could not have foreseen that Zuckerberg's project aims to move everything that was once directly experienced into a representation in the Metaverse—the ultimate postmodern condition.

Zuckerberg may achieve his dream of getting millions of humans to strap on VR headsets for seven hours a day, but they will emerge from that experience a different species.

Perhaps what the pandemic taught us was that we need to rethink our economy. A recent poll in the United Kingdom said that only 6 percent of the citizens wanted to return to the "pre-pandemic economy."[8] The regenerative economists believe that you cannot make the case for infinite growth when we only have limited resources. Sustainability is the only solution. The world these Technocrats have ruled for the last twenty years has managed a 3 percent growth per year in gross domestic product, but income inequality has only increased while mental and physical health measures are getting worse (drug overdoses, bipolar disorders, obesity). And we have become the most wasteful society in history. Just think about the number of smartphones that are thrown in the trash every year after two years of service. That means $10 billion in precious metals wind up in landfills every year.[9] We could easily make automobiles that would last for ten years, but our fixation with growth tells us that the economy would collapse unless people changed cars and smartphones every three years to keep up with the latest fashion. And we change our wardrobe even faster. But as Bill Gates's favorite philosopher, Vaclav Smil, writes, "Because technological advances have made materials cheaper, mass produceable and more available for widespread use, and because people always want 'bigger and better,' material consumption has vastly *increased*."[10]

Here is the deal. Humans, alone among species, can actively plan and design their future. For the last five thousand or so years, we have evolved in a delicate balance between nature and science. Now science is dominating nature, and everything is getting out of whack. Those on the right (including evangelical Christians) say that man's domination of nature is the inherent order of things. They cite Genesis: "Be fruitful and multiply, and fill the earth and subdue it." Some have suggested that 2020 was the year when nature fought back, not just with its pandemic but also with superstorms, wildfires, and other natural disasters. So perhaps for even the evangelicals, the notion of our "stewardship" of the planet has to change.

These men that I have been writing about, the Technocrats, have more wealth and power than almost anyone on earth. Yet they are not planning or designing a real future to deal with nature in crisis. The "autonomous ecosystems" they are trying to build will pull us *further* from nature. Living in a spacesuit or spending seven hours a day with a VR helmet on is as far from nature as you can get. Their aspirations will distort the off-balance relationship between science and nature to an unimaginable degree.

There is a choice about what the future holds, and it's not necessarily Mark Zuckerberg's or Elon Musk's to make. The fight that remains will be to once again assert the possibility of constructing our lives as free and autonomous persons in a natural world not destroyed by industrial pollution and not ruled by the algorithms of the tech monopolies. It will be to resist this future of pseudo-experience and fantasy exploration. That resistance will require both government regulation and the individual decisions of millions of citizens around the world about how they are going to use technology. Fortunately these four technologies of the Metaverse, crypto, transhumanism, and space travel are in their early stages of adoption. It's not like trying to urge you to not use a smartphone or a social network. I think families can have honest discussions about the future, and those who want to join the resistance could adopt some simple guidelines for their families:

1. Don't buy a VR headset. Don't let your children use VR.
2. Don't buy crypto currency or NFTs.
3. Don't fall for life-extension therapies.
4. Don't let your tax dollars finance a Mars space colony.

But beyond our personal resistance to the algorithm culture of the Technocrats, it is critical for the governments of the world to take action. The

European Union has been much more proactive on the regulation front. But individual large states like California are following the EU lead and making progress that will affect the rest of the country. I will sketch out a few simple principles that could radically change our information environment.

1. Repeal Safe Harbor: At the advent of the "Information Superhighway," Big Tech companies were given a special liability dispensation not afforded to any other publishers or manufacturers. Section 230 of the Communications Decency Act states, "No provider or user of an interactive computer service shall be treated as the publisher or speaker of any information provided by another information content provider." This is how Spotify protects itself from liability for the antivaccine lies spread by Joe Rogan, even though it is clearly a "publisher" with an exclusive contract with Rogan. If Facebook or YouTube were responsible for the lies they publish, they would institute far more careful content-moderation policies.

2. Facebook should be forced to sell Instagram and WhatsApp to ensure that the rent-taking monopoly on social media advertising is ended. The Federal Trade Commission is fairly far along in its suit to make this happen, and I suspect it will end up as the first great Supreme Court battle of the digital age.

3. Freelancers working for Big Tech need to be able to unionize, which not only will help them bargain with some of the largest companies in the world but could provide them with health coverage and 401(k)s. Amazon, Facebook, Uber, and Tesla have all fought union organizing drives in very underhanded ways. This needs to stop.

4. Crypto currency needs to be brought under the purview of the Securities and Exchange Commission. Pretending it is not a financial instrument is a shell game. The current crypto sales

model has all the "pump and dump" economics of the boiler room operations in *The Wolf of Wall Street.*

5. The federal government needs to convene expert panels on the feasibility of space colonies on Mars. Already the military-industrial-digital complex is pouring billions into development without the citizens having any idea of the endgame.

6. The National Science Foundation needs to organize panels around the ethics of artificial intelligence and transhumanism.

I'm not sure how we arrived at a place where some of the smartest minds in our country suffer from the same sort of disassociation from reality that plagued the citizens who refused vaccination and died needlessly from Covid-19 or invaded the nation's Capitol Building on January 6, 2021. I do know this: I don't want my grandchildren anywhere near Mark Zuckerberg's Metaverse.

Already, Zuckerberg's company has almost destroyed civil society and our democracy. Nothing in his record tells me he wouldn't manipulate our children inside the Metaverse in ways that only a sociopath could dream up. It has been six years since I warned readers of *Move Fast and Break Things* about the damage Facebook could do to our culture and our democracy. So far, not a single major regulatory action has been taken. The ability of the Technocrats to ingratiate themselves with open wallets into both political parties has blocked any attempt to regulate their behavior. I don't want to wait another six years to find that Zuckerberg has turned our children—and us—into posthumans too.

There is so much work to be done to achieve the America of our dreams. And the technologies to help us do that exist: solar power; 3-D printing, which can produce an affordable house for $40,000 in less than twenty-four hours; high-speed electric railways. If we spend our money and our intellectual capital escaping into the Metaverse or to Mars, it will be a great tragedy of history. To survive, we must provide a counternarrative to the Technocrats' vision of the future. And it's not that hard. If, in the fall of 2021, you had started following the four rules for families I outlined above, you would have saved a lot of money and a lot of time. You wouldn't have watched your Bitcoin stake fall by 68 percent, and you would have endless hours for completing productive tasks instead of floating around the Metaverse for the prescribed (Zuckerberg's business plan) seven hours a day. I'm suggesting not so much an active revolt against the Technocrats as a sort of benign neglect of their agenda. Ignore the Bitcoin hype. Log off of Facebook, Instagram, and Twitter. Don't even think about Donald Trump, Kanye West, Elon Musk, or Tucker Carlson. They are not important to the real lives of your family and friends.

～

I have spent the last few chapters analyzing a world of fantasy. Many have been seduced by and trapped in the vision of the Technocrats, thinking that the future they are delivering is the only one. But for a while, I want to forget about their view of the times to come. I am composing the pages that follow as if their control of our future did not exist. I will come back to them in the end, but for now, let's forget about them. If you have gotten this far in the book, you might think that our future seems like a choice between a reality of brutal partisan acrimony or a fantasy world of "immutable money, infinite frontier, eternal life."

But I don't think that is our fate. I want to suggest that the forces of technology can be part of the solution in creating a more perfect union rather than part of the problem. For this to happen, the Technocrats can't take the lead. The humanists—the writers, musicians, filmmakers, and artists—have to provide a vision for where we want to go. The brilliance of democracy is that it allows for improvisation, the greatest power of the creative spirit. And the internet—providing the ability to coordinate activity at scale over distance—can be a tool to aid that improvisation. Part of our task is to stop thinking there is a technological solution for every problem and to honestly ask why we are acting like sheep around Elon Musk and Donald Trump?

I want to tell you a story about a well-off individual who had a "Paul on the road to Damascus" awakening to the way of the world. He is not alone, in that many people are realizing we need a new economic philosophy to replace the brain-dead neoliberalism that has created our current hellscape. John Fullerton had an exemplary career as a managing director at JP Morgan. In his twenty years at the bank, he had seen Wall Street's highs and lows. As Morgan's Oversight Committee representative, he managed the rescue of Long-Term Capital Management (LTCM) in 1998. LTCM was an early hedge fund that used computer-driven quantitative models to exploit deviations from fair value in the relationships between bonds of different nations. From 1994 to 1998 the strategy worked very well. Then, in August 1998, the Russian government defaulted on its bonds, and LTCM went into free fall. If LTCM went under, the collateral damage to almost every Wall Street bank would have been disastrous. On September 23, 1998, Warren Buffet and Goldman Sachs offered to buy the company for $250 million and inject new capital. The LTCM partners were shocked at the lowball offer because nine months earlier the firm had been valued at $4.7 billion. Buffet gave LTCM CEO John Meriwether one hour to accept the deal. An hour passed, and Buffet walked away. The Federal Reserve and JP Morgan were then left to organize a rescue, which John Fullerton helped manage successfully.

But three years later, in early 2001, after Chase Manhattan Bank acquired JP Morgan, Fullerton walked away, disturbed by the change in Wall Street culture. He was then seared by the firsthand experience of being in New York during 9/11 and began a humanistic search for a new life purpose. "This search first opened my eyes to the profound, interlocking crises we are now facing—ecological, economic, and social—including the shocking prospect that we are destroying the planet's ability to support life as we know it. My most startling discovery, however, was that the modern scheme of economics and finance—what Wall Street 'geniuses' (like me) practiced so well—formed the *root cause* of these systemic crises."

His search took him into the domain of biological-systems thinking and eventually to the realization that those models could be applied to the economy. He formed the Capital Institute and began to produce a set of principles for a regenerative economy.

I had been considering these ideas of decentralized-system thinking for a long time; when I came upon Fullerton's principles, I was amazed at how closely they aligned with the ideas about innovation occurring at the edge of organizations that I had immersed myself in at the Annenberg Innovation Lab of the University of Southern California (USC). I had studied firms like Xerox, which allowed a lab like the Xerox Palo Alto Research Center (PARC) the freedom to invent the modern personal computer without interference. One of my mentors, John Seely Brown, was director of the Xerox PARC, which also essentially invented most of the technology for the modern PC—the mouse, graphical user interface, Ethernet, and so forth. Brown's mantra is "Innovation happens at the edge." He once told an interviewer, "We can now build these small, light-weight, fast-moving businesses from the edge. What that does, for those enlightened large-scale firms, is to convert the excitement on the edge into a dynamic attractor for the folks in the core." The irony, of course, was that the leaders of Xerox believed they were a copier company, not a computer company, so they let Steve Jobs license all of their inventions to make the Macintosh computer. The rest is history.

But that kind of edge innovation is too rare. The reality of our current world is that huge multinational digital firms dominate the global economy because we allowed them to be monopolies from the start. We called them "natural monopolies." Who needed a second search engine if Google, given to me seemingly for free, did a great job? That Google had a 92 percent market share didn't seem to matter.

Size and power help improve a firm's ability to withstand crises and absorb shocks. The main response to competition, however, as with J. D. Rockefeller and Zuckerberg, is to buy it out. If the competition refuses the offer, then crush it or—as in the case of Facebook and Snapchat—steal its innovations.[11] More importantly, the survival of big extractive firms relies on regulatory capture, the ability to corrupt the institutions that might keep them in check.

So if innovation really flows from the edge, then centralization and monopoly inevitably kill innovation. The regenerative economists have provided evidence that the "cooperative network" is the best form for a firm in the new age of regenerative economics. Many of these ideas were pioneered in cooperative networks, such as Mondragon in Spain, Organic Valley Dairy in the United States and Canada, and the Evergreen Cooperatives of Cleveland, Ohio. Mondragon is the seventh-largest Spanish company in terms of revenue. At the end of 2019, it employed eighty-two thousand people in 257 companies and cooperatives in four areas of activity: finance, industry, retail, and knowledge. The cooperative philosophy is supplemented by four corporate values: *cooperation*, with all employees acting as owners; *participation*, which means everyone has a commitment to the management of the cooperative; *social responsibility*, with the distribution of wealth based on solidarity; and *innovation*, focusing on constant renewal in all areas. At Mondragon, wage ratios have been agreed on between chief executive work and field or factory work, which earns a minimum wage. These ratios range from 3:1 to 9:1 in different cooperatives and average 5:1. By contrast, the ratio between CEO and worker pay for the S&P 500 is 324:1.

This philosophy is spreading to a growing number of companies seeking B Corp Certification, a designation that shows a business is meeting high standards of performance, accountability, and transparency on factors that range from employee benefits and charitable giving to supply-chain practices and input materials. A nonprofit called B Lab acts as a standards organization and certifies companies based on how they create value beyond just shareholder profits—for stakeholders, such as their employees, the local community, and the environment. In the digital world a company like Wikipedia demonstrates the brilliance of thousands of people cooperating over distance to build a knowledge base free for all users.

Natural Capital Solutions, one of the firms that have followed Fullerton's principles, has produced a set of basic principles for the regenerative economy.

In Right Relationship: B Corporations prioritize environmental and social goals as much as fiscal ones. They understand that they can leave the world a better place than when they started— and do so profitably.

Holistic views of wealth: B Corporations have human capital, in the form of happy employees who are well taken care of; they have cultural capital, in offering a space for positive, diverse, and empowering interactions to take place; and they value natural capital.

Innovative, adaptive, responsive: Humans have a knack for solving problems in creative ways. Businesses that do this well are the ones that survive. Although many tech companies are good at this, they fail in most other areas.

Empowered participation: Many businesses have recently embraced models of decentralized leadership as a way to ensure everyone has a voice, a buy-in to the company's goals, and empowering professional relationships.

Honoring community and place: In both the United States and many developing countries with large populations working in smallholder agriculture, local populations have vast stores of knowledge particular to the wildlife, biodiversity, weather, and soil conditions specific to their area.

Edge-effect abundance: Creativity and abundance flourish synergistically at the "edges" of systems, where the bonds holding the dominant pattern in place are weakest. This aligns with the principle of subsidiarity, which holds that social and political issues should be dealt with at the most immediate or local level that is consistent with their resolution.

Robust circulatory flow: Companies are starting to wake up to the possibility of reducing their waste streams and having their product lifecycle be a circular loop as opposed to a one-way street that dead-ends in a landfill.

Balance seeking: Too often business has been a force that pushes natural and social systems toward imbalance—but many businesses are now changing their priorities so that they are helping restore balance. B Corporations, mentioned above, balance the profit motive with an equal emphasis on people and planet.

Before you dismiss this as some kind of Zen economics, let me give some real-world examples of how these principles are being applied:

- In April 2021, PepsiCo announced plans to practice regenerative farming on more than seven million acres of land worldwide, the equivalent of its entire agricultural footprint. The project will focus on building soil health and fertility, reducing carbon emissions, enhancing watershed management, increasing biodiversity, and improving farmer livelihoods.
- The Georgia Institute of Technology built the Kendada Building, which generates more energy and more water than it consumes. The primary building material is wood, which sequesters carbon during its growth; that carbon remains sequestered in the manufactured building material.
- The company Apeel has developed an innovative way to eliminate single-use shrink-wrap plastic packaging on fresh fruit and vegetables, while at the same time tackling food

waste. Apeel is a layer of edible, plant-based coating applied to fresh products that mimics and enhances the natural defenses of fruit and vegetables. This slows down the two main things that cause spoilage: water loss and oxidation. Apeel's customers are the grocery store chains, and adoption is increasing rapidly.

- Patagonia created its Common Threads initiative, so that any piece of its clothing can be repaired, reused, or donated and ultimately avoid landfills.

Patagonia's program is the perfect example of the regenerative economy. It collects used Capilene (the brand name of its famous thermal underwear) at its local clothing stores and bulk-ships it to a recycler. Tests have found that making DMT (dimethyl terephthalate, the precursor material to the polyester used in the company's clothing) from used Capilene takes 76 percent less energy and emits 42 percent less CO_2 than making it from petroleum. Over the millions of garments Patagonia makes every year, this is a major reduction in emissions and energy.

The ideas behind regenerative economics have been a long time coming. In the late 1960s, economist John Kenneth Galbraith predicted that eventually the perfection of modern advertising in creating desire for products we didn't know we needed would make the modern American member of the middle class a gerbil on a treadmill: running faster and faster but making no progress in relation to its neighbors. Galbraith could not have imagined the power of the ever-present smartphone, which can send us a personalized advertisement for a new BMW two minutes after we look up on the internet the snazzy new car in our neighbor's driveway. As philosopher L. M. Sacasas wrote, "Your contentment and mine would wreak havoc on the existing order of things. 'That's enough, thanks,' is arguably a radical sentiment. Only by the perpetual creation of novel needs and desires can economic growth be sustained given how things presently operate. So just about every aspect of our culture is designed to make us think that happiness, or something like it, always lies on the other side of more."[12] And of course the main purveyors of "more" are Facebook, Instagram, Google, Twitter, and Amazon.

But here again, a regenerative resistance is forming. Ironically, two clothing companies, Nike and Levi Strauss & Co, have grasped this consumer desire to avoid our throwaway culture. Between 2000 and 2020, global clothing consumption doubled, and people kept clothing half as long as they did twenty years ago. In combating this "fast fashion" trend, Levi Strauss returned to its roots, suggesting that its jeans are meant "to be worn for generations, not seasons." But it also moved toward regenerative materials and technologies such as cottonized hemp and organic cotton and scaling waterless manufacturing.

The headline on the ad for the new NikeCraft sneaker was "Boring." The ad copy read, "Your sneakers shouldn't be the most exciting thing about you. They are tools, and what matters about your tools is that they work. They do their job so you can do yours. You put them on and forget about them. It took us ten years to make a sneaker this simple—as simple as can be and no simpler. A do-more sneaker. An own-less sneaker." This is a stark contrast from the Nike marketing of old and yet a clear nod in the direction of the "own-less" culture that I think is coming.

～

In the corporate world, the potential power of decentralization has been alive for two decades. Irving Wladawsky-Berger, a mentor of mine at the USC Innovation Lab, where I served as director from 2010 to 2017, taught me that decentralized organization is critical for innovation. Irving had managed IBM's early push into the internet for CEO Sam Palmisano. When the classically centralized IBM management resisted the push to the internet, Palmisano told them, "We have to lower the center of gravity of this organization"—meaning that power had to be moved from headquarters to the edges of the company.

The same dynamics of edge versus core play out on a political level. It's clear that most of the recent progressive gains in areas such as marriage equality, gun control, and environmental protection have come at the edge—the state level. As Supreme Court justice and distinguished Jeffersonian jurist Louis Brandeis wrote, "It is one of the happy incidents of the federal system that a single courageous state may, if its citizens choose, serve as a laboratory; and try novel social and economic experiments without risk to the rest of the country."

The 2022 election made obvious that Republicans will try to control more from Washington and let less innovation happen at the edges of the country. As the *Atlantic*'s Ron Brownstein writes, the restrictive right-wing social legislation enacted in red states would become national law if a Republican won the presidency in 2024. "Republicans in the U.S. House and Senate have introduced legislation to write each of these red-state initiatives into federal law. The practical effect of these proposals would be to require blue states to live under the restrictive social policies that have burned through red states since President Joe Biden's victory in 2020."[13]

Obviously with the Senate and the presidency controlled by Democrats, these efforts to dictate national social policies will not become law, but this may be only temporary. In the meantime, our real reform will come from policy innovations at the state and city levels.

The Technocrats have no solutions to real problems; in fact they exacerbate them by draining money for ill-conceived space ventures or fomenting discord that gets in the way of solutions. If they concentrated their energy on real-world problems, they could really help society. Let's look at one specific challenge—housing—that confronts my city of Los Angeles. The United Nations Human Rights Commission is clear: "Homelessness is a profound assault on dignity, social inclusion and the right to life. It is a prima facie violation of the right to housing and violates a number of other human rights in addition to the right to life, including non-discrimination, health, water and sanitation, security of the person and freedom from cruel, degrading and inhuman treatment."[14] This notion that housing is a basic human right seems correct to me. During our earlier fight against fascism in World War II, President Franklin Roosevelt said we were fighting for four freedoms: freedom of speech, freedom of worship, freedom from want, and freedom from fear. A basic part of the freedom from want and the freedom from fear is to not be living on the street.

People without housing suffer much worse health outcomes, and, as the United Nations also states, "the right to life entails in itself more than mere survival, as it encompasses the core notion that everyone has the right to enjoy her or his life in dignity." And yet, under every bridge in LA there are makeshift shelters, improvised tents, and cardboard boxes providing meager shelter for thousands. Many of the people living under the bridges are veterans of America's many wars, often still suffering from PTSD or drug addiction. Critics say it's just a mental health problem, not a housing problem, but the reality is far more complicated. On the grounds of the Veterans Administration in West LA, there is a whole village of tents and tiny houses where homeless vets have established a community. Clearly more houses are needed.

Five years ago, Los Angeles voters approved a $1.2 billion bond issue to house the homeless. The city has approximately forty-five thousand homeless citizens. This year the city controller reported that the city has built 8,091 housing units at an average of $596,846 per unit; 14 percent of the units exceeded $700,000 per unit, and one project topped $800,000. This is for *low-cost* housing!

Two years ago, in Austin, Texas, at the South by Southwest Festival, an American start-up named ICON demonstrated the production of a 650-square-foot home that was 3-D-printed out of concrete in under twenty-four hours using a mobile printer. The total cost of materials and labor was $40,000. On the next page is what the finished house looked like.

Even at $50,000 per unit these houses would be an extraordinary savings from the brain-dead process the city is now using to solve its housing crisis. An additional $1 billion (on top of the $1.2 billion bond offering) could have created the forty thousand housing units the city needs.

Copyright 2019 Icon Build

The second element is land, and in LA a very proactive city controller, Ron Galperin, created an interactive map of the fourteen thousand properties in Los Angeles owned by governments (city, county, state, and federal).[15] In releasing the map Galperin said, "There are underutilized and vacant properties owned by the City and other public entities with tremendous potential to be used for a variety of things, including affordable, workforce and senior housing, or economic and business development projects."

To be clear, in every city desperate for low-cost housing, many forces don't want something like this to happen. The developers who have spent decades funding city council races. The unions. The councilmen who rely on developer contributions. And NIMBY homeowners. But this what reform looks like. This technology is ready today.

⌣

The history of the United States is a story of progress and reaction. The movement toward abolishing slavery that grew in the 1840s and 1850s led to a violent reaction from the slaveholding states and a civil war with 620,000 dead. The Reconstruction era after the Civil War quickly retreated from the promises Abraham Lincoln had made to the freed slaves, and a one-hundred-year era of Jim Crow laws ensued. Fifty years later, progressives and socialists rebelled against the stranglehold the corporate "robber barons" had on government policy, creating a Progressive Era that broke up corporate monopolies, ended child labor, and gave the vote to women. The Progressive Era of the early 1900s ended in the brutal Red Summer of 1919, during which white supremacist gangs terrorized Black communities in more than three dozen cities across the country. With the election of Republican Warren G. Harding as president in 1920, the country took a hard turn to the right. The Ku Klux Klan was revived, immigration was restricted, and most socialist politicians were either jailed or deported. Only the Great Depression and the long presidency of Franklin Roosevelt ended that era of reaction.

The liberal era of the New Deal ended in the late 1940s with the rise of anticommunism in the early 1950s, and another right-wing reaction in the form of McCarthyism seized the nation for a brief period. That reactionary period ended with the election of John F. Kennedy and the rise of the civil rights movement. Later, in the 1960s, the antiwar, women's rights, and Earth justice movements continued into the late 1970s.

For progressives, the rebellions of 1860, 1910, and 1960 were not totally successful, but they were all efforts—in the words of the philosopher Richard Rorty—to struggle "within the framework of constitutional democracy to protect the weak from the strong." Those (on both the left and the right) who deny that we have made progress in the last 150 years are not dealing with reality. But the ultimate goal—to make Jefferson's Enlightenment aims of freedom and equality real—has eluded us. Every time significant progress has been made, the reactionaries have pushed back. And the reaction always comes from "the strong"—the plutocrats. We are experiencing this today.

By 1980, the country had retreated into a conservative orthodoxy that was to last forty years, and the military began to take more of our taxes. But the battle against the American tech plutocracy continues. Surely we are approaching one of those hinge points in American history like 1860, 1932, or 1968. The election of 2024 may return Trump or another ultra-MAGA politician like Ron DeSantis to the White House. If that happens, the election of 2024 may be the last election where the majority has a hope of rule. Jonathan Rauch has written, "A second Trump term could bring about the extinction of American democracy. Essential features of the system, including the rule of law, honest vote tallies, and orderly succession, would be at risk."[16]

Minority rule by the Republicans and their plutocrat backers will be enabled for decades. The Technocrats have already shown which side of the battle between democracy and autocracy they are on. When the social media services of Facebook and Twitter first started, I believed they could be part of Rorty's struggle to protect the weak from the strong. I watched the events in Tahir Square in Cairo in January 2011 and really thought that social media could be a tool for the underdog. But I was naive, and now Twitter and Facebook are tools of the overlord—more valuable to the powerful than the powerless. Peter Thiel has donated more than $30 million to ultra-MAGA candidates. Elon Musk has donated to ultra-MAGA candidates and signaled his support for the soft fascism of Ron DeSantis.[17] Marc Andreessen has donated millions to a super PAC whose only purpose is to support candidates who won't try to regulate crypto.[18] And as for Mark Zuckerberg, by his inaction he is enabling the destruction of our democracy.

I was involved in both the civil rights and the antiwar movements in the 1960s, and so I still carry a good measure of hope for the notion of local "participatory democracy" that those movements created. I believe that we have the technological tools to fix both our ecology and our democracy. But to achieve that, men like Musk and Zuckerberg are going to have to totally abandon their current course of action.

CONCLUSION

When I began writing this book in the fall of 2021, all of the companies run by the Technocrats were riding high. The fantasy they were selling of a brave new world of crypto currency, virtual reality, and Martian colonies seemed to have taken hold in the American mind. We had bought into the concept of techno-determinism—the idea that our future is already determined and we are moving toward some preordained utopia brought to us by the Technocrats. Arthur C. Clarke's notion that "any sufficiently advanced technology is indistinguishable from magic" still seemed to hold true.

But as this book goes to press, perhaps we are waking up from the dream they are selling. In the past nine months those same companies—Meta, Tesla, Palantir, and Andreessen Horowitz—have witnessed massive destruction of their value. The stock of Tesla dropped from $413 to $127. Meta dropped from $353 to $125. Palantir dropped from $27 to $6. Though Andreessen Horowitz is a private firm, we do know that its $4.5 billion crypto fund saw its value fall 40 percent in the first half of 2022. One of its largest crypto investments, Solana, has lost 80 percent of its value since January 2022. Andreessen also lost $2.9 billion in its main crypto exchange, Coinbase.[1] I'm not asking you to feel sorry for Elon Musk, Mark Zuckerberg, Peter Thiel, or Marc Andreessen. I'm just saying that the magic show may be over.

We face major difficulties as a society, and the digital Technocrats will not blaze the path to solutions. If you think back to the first stirrings of American independence in the 1760s, you will realize that we have made extraordinary progress in less than three hundred years. In 1760 the average life expectancy in the world was less than forty years; today it is more than seventy. At that time about 80 percent of the people in the world lived in poverty: today it's less than 11 percent. No one in 1760 lived in a democracy, and no woman could vote, attend a university, or own property.

Most of the gains in solving the income-inequality problem in the United States were made between 1932 and 1980. In 2016 economist Robert Gordon published *The Rise and Fall of American Growth: The U.S. Standard of Living Since the Civil War*.[2] Gordon argues that the large strides in productivity and growth in America preceded the technology revolution—that the invention of the automobile, airplane, electric light, and telephone had been "the low-hanging fruit" of productivity and that the gains from the digital revolution were modest by comparison. Reviewing the book, Paul Krugman writes, "Gordon suggests that the future is all too likely to be marked by stagnant living standards for most Americans, because the effects of slowing technological progress will be reinforced by a set of 'headwinds': rising inequality, a plateau in education levels, an aging population and more."[3]

I am not saying that technology has no role to play in our future; rather I argue that it is time to "slow down and repair things." The Technocrats have brought us enough disruption to last a lifetime, and perhaps we are entering a time of healing and regeneration. There will certainly be an element of technology in that healing. Think about the innovative ways to grow crops underneath a large solar farm. As a US Department of Agriculture information sheet notes, "A symbiotic cooling relationship occurs when crops are grown under solar panels. Shade reduces air temperature and the amount of water evaporating from soils. The plants in turn give off water vapor that helps to naturally cool the [solar] panels from below, which can increase panel efficiency." Imagine hundreds of thousands of acres of farmland earning money from this dual-use technology.

I have suggested that the innovations needed to repair our land and our spirit will have to emerge from the use of our states and towns as laboratories of innovative democracy. But that still won't obviate our responsibility to address the problems raised by the recent deep collaboration between the authoritarian Right and the Technocrats. In my early years of writing about Peter Thiel, I dismissed much of his libertarian rhetoric in the same way I dismissed the novels of Ayn Rand. But Thiel, like Musk and to some degree Andreessen, has abandoned the laissez-faire roots of libertarianism in favor of a much more coercive use of government to enforce a moral and economic philosophy. No kind of soft, European-style guardrails on abortion—the New Right wants to throw the mother and her doctor in jail. No more lists of books your child should avoid—the New Right wants to close the local library. Thiel's Arizona Senate candidate, Blake Masters, told conservative talk show host Charlie Kirk that Dr. Anthony Fauci "will see the inside of a prison cell this decade."

We must resist this neofascism. We have been here before. In May 1939, director Alfred Barr opened the new building of the Museum of Modern Art (MOMA) in New York with a large gala in the room in which he had hung Pablo Picasso's epic antifascist painting *Guernica*. Before arriving at MOMA, it had been touring America in an attempt to raise money for veterans of the Spanish Civil War. The press had denounced the painting and Picasso across the country, with a *Chicago Herald and Examiner* headline being typical: "Bolshevist Art Controlled by the Hand of Moscow." But Barr had a way to push back. First Lady Eleanor Roosevelt had visited a preview of the exhibition and got her husband, Franklin, to record a tribute to the museum exhibition. FDR said, "The arts cannot thrive except where men are free to be themselves and to be in charge of the discipline of their own energies and ardors. The conditions for democracy and art are one and the same."

What Roosevelt said in 1939 still holds true. Murray Rothbard, the anarcho-capitalist whom Thiel has studied, once said that the task of the New Right was "to break the clock of the New Deal...to repeal the 20th century." One can no longer ignore this rhetoric. Over the past couple of years, the Republicans in Congress and the Supreme Court have started to repeal the twentieth century. When Justice Clarence Thomas suggests that he would consider a case banning birth control, we really are going back to the nineteenth century. The resistance that is needed will flow out of the same humanistic literature and music that inspired Dr. Martin Luther King Jr. to create a mass nonviolent movement for civil rights and Bill McKibben to help create a mass movement to demand clean air and clean water. That same movement can demand that Instagram stop exploiting our children or that biologists cease their work to alter the genetic code of a fetus to make a designer baby. That same mass movement could demand that the $10 trillion Elon Musk wants our government to spend on a Martian space colony be used instead to finish the transition to renewable energy by 2030.[4] That same mass movement could demand that we ban the use of killer robots or create strict guidelines for the creation of an artificial general intelligence. And ultimately we must fight the monopolies and duopolies these four men control.

I think the notion of an interregnum that I used earlier in the book is still helpful. If we are poised on the knife edge of this extraordinary transition from the world of 1950s America (which MAGA wants to restore) to something much more pluralistic, then we will need to end the chaos of the last six years. Perhaps the 2022 midterms were a small glimpse of a public saying "enough." Maybe we are becoming tired of global chaos agents like Musk and Donald Trump. We are tired of disruption and illusion. Only time will tell if I am right. If I am wrong, we are staring into the abyss.

Democracies often die slowly. Brian Klaas, writing in *The Atlantic*, noted, "The optimistic assessment from experts who study authoritarianism globally is that the United States will most likely settle into a dysfunctional equilibrium that mirrors a deep democratic breakdown."[5] I fear that we will not really pay attention to this process, because we will be too busy watching the shiny new objects created by men like Zuckerberg, Musk, Thiel, and Andreessen. This fantasy culture we live in is manufacturing a new kind of nihilism and cynicism. A week before he was murdered, Dr. King preached in Washington's National Cathedral. He said something prophetic: "One of the great liabilities of life is that all too many people find themselves living amid a great period of social change, and yet they fail to develop the new attitudes, the new mental responses, that the new situation demands. They end up sleeping through a revolution."[6]

That is my greatest fear: that enchanted by the magic of the Technocrats' "immutable money, infinite frontier, eternal life," we will sleep through a right-wing revolution and wake up to find our democracy gone and our children being turned into Meta cyborgs. Let us wake up and resist the end of reality.

ACKNOWLEDGMENTS

This book began as a set of discussions with my colleagues at the Annenberg Innovation Lab at the University of Southern California (USC) in the fall of 2021. At the time crypto currencies were booming, the Metaverse had been successfully introduced to the public, and Elon Musk had been named the richest man in the world. To say that my presentation at the Innovation Lab was contrarian would be an understatement. But from my USC colleagues Colin Maclay, Gabriel Kahn, Ernest Wilson, Chris Smith, Manuel Castells, and Francois Bar, I got the kind of collaborative feedback that helped form the book.

In addition I got valuable contributions from John Seely Brown and Irving Wladawsky-Berger, who were leaders in the thought movement that innovation comes from the edges of organization. As the book began to take form, I got critical advice from my agent, Simon Lipskar, and invaluable input from Genevieve Gagne-Hawes.

Once the book proposal found a home at PublicAffairs, my editor, John Mahaney, provided the kind of guidance a writer can only dream of. For that, I am truly grateful. Also I want to express my gratitude to Jaime Leifer and Miguel Cervantes of PublicAffairs for their support on the release of the book.

I also want to thank T Bone Burnett, James Ward, and Ian Masters for their constant encouragement in this project. And finally, to my wife,

Maggie; my children, Daniela, Nicholas, and Blythe; and my grandchildren, Rose, Beatrice, Walter, and Ruth, you enrich my life in ways I can never repay.

NOTES

Introduction

1. Ian Bremmer and Cliff Kupchan, "Risk 2: Technopolar World," Eurasia Group, January 3, 2022, www.eurasiagroup.net/live-post/top-risks-2022-2-technopolar-world.

2. Mike Allen, "Stunning Poll: 44% of Voters See 'Secret Cabal,'" *Axios*, November 4, 2022, www.axios.com/2022/11/04/qanon-government-secret-cabal-poll.

3. Simon Kemp, "Digital 2022: The United States of America," DataReportal, February 9, 2022, https://datareportal.com/reports/digital-2022-united-states-of-america.

4. John Perry Barlow, "A Declaration of the Independence of Cyberspace," Electronic Frontier Foundation, February 8, 1996, www.eff.org/cyberspace-independence.

5. Federal Trade Commission, "FTC Alleges Facebook Resorted to Illegal Buy-or-Bury Scheme to Crush Competition After String of Failed Attempts to Innovate," August 19, 2021, www.ftc.gov/news-events/news/press-releases/2021/08/ftc-alleges-facebook-resorted-illegal-buy-or-bury-scheme-crush-competition-after-string-failed.

6. Multiple authors, "Letter in Support of Responsible Fintech Policy," June 1, 2022, https://concerned.tech.

7. Adam Fisher, "Why I'm Cryptophobic," Bessemer Venture Partners, June 30, 2022, www.bvp.com/atlas/why-i-m-cryptophobic.

8. Victor Tangermann, "Elon Musk: Mars City Could Cost Up to $10 Trillion," *The Byte*, August 13, 2019, https://futurism.com/the-byte/elon-musk-mars-city-cost-10-trillion.

9. *Britannica*, "transhumanism," www.britannica.com/topic/transhumanism.

10. Francis Fukuyama, "Transhumanism," *Foreign Policy*, October 23, 2009, https://foreignpolicy.com/2009/10/23/transhumanism.

11. "Robotics: Recent Publications," Amazon | Science, www.amazon.science/research-areas/robotics.

12. David Wallace-Wells, "Beyond Catastrophe," *New York Times*, October 26, 2022, www.nytimes.com/interactive/2022/10/26/magazine/climate-change-warming-world.html.

13. Mia Bloom and Sophia Moskalenko, *Pastels and Pedophiles* (New York: Redwood Press, 2021).

14. Shirin Ghaffary, "Why You Should Care About Facebook's Big Push into the Metaverse," *Vox*, November 24, 2021, www.vox.com/recode/22799665/facebook-metaverse-meta-zuckerberg-oculus-vr-ar.

15.   Mike Brown, "SpaceX Mars City," *Inverse*, www.inverse.com/article/58458 -spacex-mars-city-here-s-how-much-it-would-cost-to-build.

16.   "Investing in Immortality," *World Health Net Journal*, May 12, 2022, www.world health.net/news/investing-immortality-multibillion-dollar-longevity-science-and-anti -aging-industry.

17.   Antonio Gramsci, *The Prison Notebooks* (New York: Columbia University Press, 1935).

18.   Gregory Zuckerman, *The Greatest Trade Ever* (New York: Crown Business, 2008).

19.   Klaus Theweleit, *Male Fantasies* (Minneapolis: University of Minnesota Press, 1987).

20.   Laura Smith, "This Study of Fascist Men Shows Their Terrifying Fascination with Sex, Death, and Authority," *Timeline*, September 11, 2017, https://timeline.com /male-fantasies-fascism-study-efe0a2773d1f.

21.   Steve Bodow, "The Money Shot," *Wired*, September 1, 2001, www.wired.com/200 1/09/paypal.

22.   Jonathan Swan, "A Radical Plan for Trump's Second Term," *Axios*, July 22, 2022, www.axios.com/2022/07/22/trump-2025-radical-plan-second-term.

23.   Anti-Defamation League, "Murder and Extremism in the United States in 2021," May 3, 2022, www.adl.org/murder-and-extremism-2021.

24.   Steven Levitsky, *How Democracies Die* (New York: Crown, 2018).

25.   Jason Stanley, *How Fascism Works* (New York: Random House, 2018).

26.   Geoff Eley, "What Is Fascism and Where Does It Come From?," *History Workshop Journal* 91, no. 1 (spring 2021): 1–28. https://academic.oup.com/hwj/article/91/1/1/6329186.

27.   Andrew Romano, "Poll: Half of Americans Now Predict U.S. May 'Cease to Be a Democracy' Someday," Yahoo! News, June 15, 2022, https://news.yahoo.com/poll-half-of -americans-now-predict-us-may-cease-to-be-a-democracy-someday-090028564.html.

28.   John Huang, "Bitcoin Uses More Electricity Than Many Countries," *New York Times*, September 3, 2021, www.nytimes.com/interactive/2021/09/03/climate/bitcoin -carbon-footprint-electricity.html.

29.   Cecilia Jamasmie, "Mining Robots Key to Colonizing Mars," October 24, 2016, Mining.com, www.mining.com/mining-robots-key-to-colonizing-mars-elon-musk.

30.   Peter Thiel, "The Education of a Libertarian," *Cato Unbound*, April 13, 2009, www .cato-unbound.org/2009/04/13/peter-thiel/education-libertarian.

Chapter 1: Technocracy's Libertarian Roots

1.   Antonio Gramsci, *The Prison Notebooks* (New York: International Publishers, 1971).

2.   Eric Hobsbawm, *The Age of Extremes* (New York: Pantheon Books, 1995).

3.   Filippo Marinetti, "The Founding and Manifesto of Futurism," *Le Figaro*, February 20, 1909, www.italianfuturism.org/manifestos/foundingmanifesto.

4.   Thiel, "The Education of a Libertarian."

5.   Felipe Fernandez-Arnesto, *Out of Our Minds: A History of What We Think and How We Think It* (San Francisco: University of California Press, 2019).

6.   Gabriel Rubin, "Facists and Futurists," WUPR, October 5, 2014, www.wupr.org /2014/10/05/fascists-and-futurists-the-art-of-violence.

7.   Rose Eveleth, "When Futurism Led to Fascism," *Wired*, April 18, 2019, www.wired .com/story/italy-futurist-movement-techno-utopians.

8.   Nicholas Goodrick-Clarke, *The Occult Roots of Nazism* (New York: NYU Press, 1993).

9.   Paul Starr, *The Creation of the Media* (New York: Basic Books, 2004).

10.   Lisa Held, "Psychoanalysis Shapes Consumer Culture," *Monitor on Psychology*, December 2009, www.apa.org/monitor/2009/12/consumer.

11.   Paul Mazur, *New Roads to Prosperity* (New York: Viking Press, 1931).

12.   Accenture, "Metaverse Continuum," www.accenture.com/us-en/services/metaverse -index.

13.   Glenn Adamson, *Industrial Strength Design: How Brooks Stevens Shaped Your World* (Cambridge, MA: MIT Press, 2003).

14.   Albert Nock, *Myth of a Guilty Nation* (New York: B. W. Huebsch, 1922).

15.   Albert Nock, *Our Enemy, the State* (New York: Caxton, 1946).

16.   Charles Lindbergh, "Aviation, Geography and Race," *Readers Digest*, November 1939, http://reparti.free.fr/lindbergh39.pdf.

17.   "Construct the New America," *The Technocrat* 3, no. 4 (September 1937), via the Internet Archive, https://archive.org/streamTheTechnocrat-September1937/TheTechnocrat -September1937_djvu.txt.

18.   Howard Segal, *Technological Utopianism in American Culture* (Syracuse, NY: Syracuse University Press, 2005).

19.   Joseph Keating, "Joshua Haldeman: The Canadian Years," *Journal of the Canadian Chiropractic Society* 39, no. 3 (1995), www.ncbi.nlm.nih.gov/pmc/articles/PMC2485067 /pdf/jcca00035-0046.pdf.

20.   Elizabeth Blake, "Contextualizing Ayn Rand's Early Admiration of Hollywood," St. Louis University, www.aatseel.org/100111/pdf/program/2007/28B3_1Blake_ELizabeth .pdf.

21.   Mark Ames, "Ayn Rand's Admiration of Murderer-Dismemberer William Edward Hickman," Alternet, February 26, 2010, www.indybay.org/newsitems/2010/03/07/18640112 .php.

22.   Thom Hartman, "Welcome to Ayn Rand's America," *truthdig*, August 13, 2019, www.truthdig.com/articles/welcome-to-ayn-rands-america.

23.   Murray Rothbard, "H. L. Menken: The Joyous Libertarian," *Reason*, December 1980, https://reason.com/1980/12/01/h-l-mencken-2.

24.   Jennifer Burns, *Goddess of the Market* (London: Oxford University Press, 2009).

25.   Jonathan Freedland, "The New Age of Ayn Rand," *The Guardian*, April 10, 2017, www .theguardian.com/books/2017/apr/10/new-age-ayn-rand-conquered-trump-white -house-silicon-valley.

26.   Paul Krugmann, "Republican Elite's Reign of Disdain," *New York Times*, March 18, 2016, www.nytimes.com/2016/03/18/opinion/republican-elites-reign-of-disdain.html.

27.   Joseph Kraft, "Right for Ford," *New York Times*, April 25, 1976, www.nytimes .com/1976/04/25/archives/right-for-ford-alan-greenspan-an-ayn-rand-conservative -seems-an.html.

28.   Elena Cristina Mitrea, Monica Mühlböck, and Julia Warmuth, "Extreme Pessimists," Springer, https://link.springer.com/article/10.1007/s11109-020-09593-7.

29.   Ayn Rand, *For the New Intellectual* (New York: Random House, 1961).

30.   Ethan Zuckerman, "Hey Facebook, I Made a Metaverse 27 Years Ago," *The Atlantic*, October 29, 2021, www.theatlantic.com/technology/archive/2021/10/facebook-metaverse -was-always-terrible/620546.

31.   T. M. Scanlon, *What We Owe to Each Other* (Cambridge, MA: Harvard University Press, 2000).

Chapter 2: The Rise of the Technocrats

1. Max Chafkin, *The Contrarian* (New York: Penguin, 2021).
2. John Markoff, *What the Dormouse Said* (New York: Viking, 2005).
3. Chafkin, *The Contrarian*.
4. Ben Thompson, "Aggregation Theory," *Stratechery*, July 21, 2015, https://stratechery.com/2015/aggregation-theory.
5. Dave Weigel, "Ron Paul's Billionaire," *Slate*, February 20, 2012, https://slate.com/news-and-politics/2012/02/investor-peter-thiel-is-the-billionaire-behind-ron-pauls-presidential-campaign.html.
6. Peter Thiel, "Competition Is for Losers," *Wall Street Journal*, September 12, 2014, www.wsj.com/articles/peter-thiel-competition-is-for-losers-1410535536.
7. David McCabe and Stephanie Lai, "Clock Running Out on Antitrust Bill Targeting Big Tech," *New York Times*, August 5, 2022, www.nytimes.com/2022/08/05/business/antitrust-bill-klobuchar.html.
8. Chafkin, *The Contrarian*.
9. James Davidson and William Rees-Mogg, *The Sovereign Individual* (New York: Simon & Schuster, 1997).
10. Chafkin, *The Contrarian*.
11. Andrew Ross Sorkin, "Peter Thiel, Tech Billionaire, Reveals Secret War with Gawker," *New York Times*, May 25, 2016, www.nytimes.com/2016/05/26/business/dealbook/peter-thiel-tech-billionaire-reveals-secret-war-with-gawker.html.
12. Chafkin, *The Contrarian*.
13. Ashlee Vance, *Elon Musk: Tesla, Space X and the Quest for a Fantastic Future* (New York: Ecco Press, 2015).
14. Harry Robertson, "Tech Billionaire Peter Thiel Says Bitcoin's Record-High Price Shows Inflation Is at a Crisis Point," *Yahoo!*, November 1, 2021, https://finance.yahoo.com/news/tech-billionaire-peter-thiel-says-160721658.html.
15. Vance, *Elon Musk*.
16. Justin Elliot, "Lord of the Roths," *ProPublica*, June 24, 2021, www.propublica.org/article/lord-of-the-roths-how-tech-mogul-peter-thiel-turned-a-retirement-account-for-the-middle-class-into-a-5-billion-dollar-tax-free-piggy-bank.
17. Ryan Mac and Justin Scheck, "Peter Thiel, Major U.S. Political Donor, Is Said to Pursue Maltese Citizenship," *New York Times*, October 15, 2022, www.nytimes.com/2022/10/15/technology/peter-thiel-malta-citizenship.html.
18. Christina Zhao, "'SNL': Read Full Transcript of Elon Musk's Opening Monologue on 'Saturday Night Live,'" *Newsweek*, May 9, 2021, www.newsweek.com/snl-read-full-transcript-elon-musks-opening-monologue-saturday-night-live-1589849.
19. "Asperger's Syndrome," *Harvard Health Newsletter*, March 9, 2014, www.health.harvard.edu/newsletter_article/aspergers-syndrome.
20. Matt McFarland, "Why Shades of Asperger's Are the Secret to Building a Great Tech Company," *Washington Post*, April 3, 2015, www.washingtonpost.com/news/innovations/wp/2015/04/03/why-shades-of-aspergers-syndrome-are-the-secret-to-building-a-great-tech-company.
21. Farhad Manjoo, "With Elon Musk, the Drama Is the Point," *New York Times*, June 9, 2022, www.nytimes.com/2022/06/09/opinion/elon-musk-twitter.html.
22. Ross Kerber and Hyunjoo Jin, "Tesla Cut from S&P 500 ESG Index," *Reuters*, May 19, 2022, www.reuters.com/business/sustainable-business/tesla-removed-sp-500-esg-index-autopilot-discrimination-concerns-2022-05-18.

23. Marc Fisher, Christian Davenport, and Faiz Siddiqui, "Elon Musk, the Twitter Deal and His Quest to Save 'All Life on Earth,'" *Washington Post*, May 14, 2022, www .washingtonpost.com/business/2022/05/14/musk-twitter-deal-legacy.

24. Vance, *Elon Musk*.

25. Jim Collins and Jerry Porras, *Built to Last: Successful Habits of Visionary Companies* (New York: Harper Business, 1994).

26. Edward Niedermeyer, *Ludicrous: The Unvarnished Story of Tesla Motors* (New York: BenBella Books, 2019).

27. Vance, *Elon Musk*.

28. Justine Musk, "'I Was a Starter Wife,'" *Marie Claire*, October 16, 2021, www.marie claire.com/sex-love/a5380/millionaire-starter-wife.

29. Musk, "I Was a Starter Wife."

30. Kirsten Grind and Emily Glazer, "Elon Musk's Friendship with Sergey Brin Ruptured by Alleged Affair," *Wall Street Journal*, July 25, 2022, www.wsj.com/articles/elon-musk-affair -sergey-brin-wife-divorce-11658674840.

31. Rich McHugh, "A Space X Flight Attendant Says Elon Musk Exposed Himself and Propositioned Her for Sex," *Insider*, May 2022, www.businessinsider.com/spacex-paid -250000-to-a-flight-attendant-who-accused-elon-musk-of-sexual-misconduct-2022-5.

32. "Elon Musk Settles SEC Fraud Charges," Securities and Exchange Commission, www.sec.gov/news/press-release/2018-226.

33. Tad Friend, "Tomorrow's Advance Man: Marc Andreessen's Plan to Win the Future," *New Yorker*, May 11, 2015, www.newyorker.com/magazine/2015/05/18/tomorrows -advance-man.

34. Friend, "Tomorrow's Advance Man."

35. David Schardt, *Marc Andreessen: The Man Who Opened the Web to Everyone* (New York: Smashwords Editions, 2015).

36. Marc Andreessen, "Why Software Is Eating the World," *Wall Street Journal*, August 20, 2011, https://a16z.com/2011/08/20/why-software-is-eating-the-world.

37. George Orwell, "Second Thoughts on James Burnham," *Polemic*, May 1946, retrieved at www.orwellfoundation.com/the-orwell-foundation/orwell/essays-and-other -works/second-thoughts-on-james-burnham.

38. Eoin Higgins, "Marc Andreessen Twitter Faves Sure Got Weird," *The Outline*, November 28, 2018, https://theoutline.com/post/6708/marc-andreessen-twitter-faves-alt-right.

39. Marc Andreesen, "Anduril," Andreessen Horowitz, October 3, 2019, https://a16z .com/2019/10/03/anduril.

40. David Kirkpatrick, *The Facebook Effect* (New York: Simon & Schuster, 2010).

41. Kirkpatrick, *The Facebook Effect*.

42. Jose Antonio Vargas, "Mark Zuckerberg Opens Up," *New Yorker*, September 20, 2010, www.newyorker.com/magazine/2010/09/20/the-face-of-facebook.

43. Sheera Frenkel and Cecilia Kang, *An Ugly Truth* (New York: Harper, 2021).

44. Mark Zuckerberg, "Letter to Investors," *Wired*, February 1, 2012, www.wired .com/2012/02/zuck-letter.

45. Conor Simpson, "How Google and Facebook Cooperated with the NSA and Prism," *The Atlantic*, June 8, 2013, https://news.yahoo.com/google-facebook-cooperated -nsa-prism-145643099.html.

46. Dylan Byers and Ben Collins, "Trump Hosted Zuckerberg for Undisclosed Dinner at the White House in October," *NBC News*, November 20, 2019, www.nbcnews .com/tech/tech-news/trump-hosted-zuckerberg-undisclosed-dinner-white-house

-october-n1087986; Mark Memmott, "Photo: Apple's Jobs, Facebook's Zuckerberg Flank Obama at Dinner," *NPR*, February 18, 2011, www.npr.org/sections/thetwo-way/2011 /02/18/133869052/photo-apples-jobs-facebooks-zuckerberg-flank-obama-at-dinner.

47.   Jonathan Taplin, "Forget AT&T. The Real Monopolies Are Google and Facebook." *New York Times*, December 13, 2016, www.nytimes.com/2016/12/13/opinion/forget-att -the-real-monopolies-are-google-and-facebook.html.

48.   "Silicon Valley and (a)politics," Start-Up, November 15, 2013, www.startup-book .com/2013/11/15/silicon-valley-and-apolitics-change-the-world.

49.   Michael Maccoby, "Narcissistic Leaders," *Harvard Business Review*, January 2004, https://hbr.org/2004/01/narcissistic-leaders-the-incredible-pros-the-inevitable-cons.

50.   Ryan Mac, Cade Metz, and Kate Conger, "'I Don't Really Have a Business Plan,'" *New York Times*, May 3, 2022, www.nytimes.com/2022/05/03/technology/elon-musk-twitter -plan.html.

51.   Christopher Cox, "Elon Musk's Appetite for Destruction," *New York Times*, January 17, 2023, www.nytimes.com/2023/01/17/magazine/tesla-autopilot-self-driving-elon -musk.html.

52.   Kelly Weill, "Elon Musk Hyperloop Dreams Slam Into Cold Hard Reality," *Daily Beast*, March 30, 2019, www.thedailybeast.com/elon-musk-hyperloop-dreams-slam-into -cold-hard-reality.

53.   Jonathan Stempel, "Elon Musk Sued for $258 Billion over Alleged Dogecoin Pyramid Scheme," *Reuters*, June 17, 2022, www.reuters.com/legal/transactional/elon-musk-sued-258 -billion-over-alleged-dogecoin-pyramid-scheme-2022-06-16.

54.   David Brooks, "America Is Falling Apart at the Seams," *New York Times*, January 13, 2022, www.nytimes.com/2022/01/13/opinion/america-falling-apart.html.

55.   Kevin Roose, "The Metaverse Is Mark Zuckerberg's Escape Hatch," *New York Times*, October 29, 2021, www.nytimes.com/2021/10/29/technology/meta-facebook -zuckerberg.html.

56.   Dean Kissick, "What Will Art Look Like in the Metaverse?," *New York Times*, December 1, 2021, www.nytimes.com/2021/12/01/magazine/mark-zuckerberg-meta-art.html.

Chapter 3: Technology and Inequality

1.   Thomas Piketty, *A Brief History of Equality* (Cambridge, MA: Harvard University Press, 2022).

2.   Peter Eavis, "How Elon Musk Helped Lift the Ceiling on C.E.O. Pay," *New York Times*, June 25, 2022, www.nytimes.com/2022/06/25/business/highest-paid-ceos-elon -musk.html.

3.   Schumpeter, "Peter Thiel, Scourge of Silicon Valley," *The Economist*, September 25, 2021, www.economist.com/business/2021/09/25/peter-thiel-scourge-of-silicon -valley.

4.   Thomas Piketty, *Capital in the Twenty-First Century* (Cambridge, MA: Harvard University Press, 2014).

5.   Russ Mitchell, "Twitter Bots Helped Build the Cult of Elon Musk and Tesla," Yahoo! News, April 12, 2022, https://news.yahoo.com/elon-musks-not-secret-weapon -120003951.html.

6.   Rani Molla, "More Americans Are Taking Jobs Without Employer Benefits Like Health Care or Paid Vacation," *Vox*, September 3, 2021, www.vox.com/recode/22651953 /americans-gig-independent-workers-benefits-vacation-health-care-inequality.

7.   Steve Lohr, "Economists Pin More Blame on Tech for Rising Inequality," *New York Times*, updated January 20, 2022, www.nytimes.com/2022/01/11/technology/income-inequality-technology.html.

8.   Chafkin, *The Contrarian*.

9.   Lohr, "Economists Pin More Blame on Tech for Rising Inequality."

10.   David Graeber, *Bullshit Jobs* (New York: Simon & Schuster, 2018).

11.   Paul Mason, *PostCapitalism: A Guide to Our Future* (New York: Farrar, Straus & Giroux, 2016).

12.   Rob Copeland et al., "The Shadow Crew Who Encouraged Elon Musk's Twitter Takeover," *Wall Street Journal*, April 29, 2022, www.wsj.com/articles/the-shadow-crew-who-encouraged-elon-musks-twitter-takeover-tesla-jack-dorsey-11651260119.

13.   Drew Harwell, Taylor Lorenz, and Cat Zakrzewski, "Racist Tweets Quickly Surface After Musk Closes Twitter Deal," *Washington Post*, October 28, 2022, www.washingtonpost.com/technology/2022/10/28/musk-twitter-racist-posts.

14.   Stuart Thompson, "Antisemetic Campaign Tries to Capitalize on Musk's Twitter Takeover," *New York Times*, October 28, 2022, www.nytimes.com/2022/10/28/technology/musk-twitter-antisemitism.html.

15.   Sara Fischer, "Elon Musk Tweets Misinformation About Paul Pelosi," *Axios*, October 30, 2022, www.axios.com/2022/10/30/elon-musk-paul-pelosi-tweet-rumor.

16.   Antoine Gara, Eric Platt, and Ortenca Aliaj, "Banks Prepare to Hold Twitter Debt Until 2023," *Financial Times*, November 2022, www.ft.com/content/d1879d0c-c52e-4f48-82f0-09458add4aee.

17.   Scott Galloway, "Elephants in the Room," *No Mercy / No Malice*, November 4, 2022, www.profgalloway.com/elephants-in-the-room.

18.   Taylor Lorenz, "Opening the Gates of Hell," *Washington Post*, November 24, 2022, www.washingtonpost.com/technology/2022/11/24/twitter-musk-reverses-suspensions.

19.   John Grady, "Mystery Surrounds Chinese Defense Spending," USNI News, October 26, 2021, https://news.usni.org/2021/10/26/mystery-shrouds-chinese-defense-spending.

20.   Christian Davenport, "As Private Companies Erode Government's Hold on Space Travel, NASA Looks to Open a New Frontier" *Washington Post*, February 25, 2021, www.washingtonpost.com/technology/2021/02/25/nasa-space-future-private.

21.   Kimberly Amadeo, "U.S. Budget Deficits," *The Balance*, April 5, 2022. www.the-balance.com/us-deficit-by-year-3306306.

22.   Nassim Nicholas Taleb, *Skin in the Game* (New York: Random House, 2018).

23.   Matt Taibbi, "The Financial Bailout in 2008 Was a Trillion Dollar Mess," *Rolling Stone*, March 18, 2019, www.rollingstone.com/politics/politics-features/2008-financial-bailout-809731.

24.   Barack Obama, "Disinformation Is a Threat to Our Democracy," *Medium*, April 21, 2022, https://barackobama.medium.com/my-remarks-on-disinformation-at-stanford-7d7af7ba28af.

25.   George Carlin, "Quotable Quote," Goodreads, www.goodreads.com/quotes/964648-but-there-s-a-reason-there-s-a-reason-there-s-a-reason.

26.   Gretchen Morgenson, "How Letting Bankers off the Hook May Have Tipped the Election," *New York Times*, November 13, 2016, www.nytimes.com/2016/11/13/business/how-letting-bankers-off-the-hook-may-have-tipped-the-election.html.

27. Michael Anton, "The Flight 93 Election," *Claremont Review*, September 5, 2016, https://claremontreviewofbooks.com/digital/the-flight-93-election.

28. Shane Goldmacher and Maggie Haberman, "Tucker, Thiel, and Trump," *New York Times*, May 4, 2022, www.nytimes.com/2022/05/04/us/politics/jd-vance-trump-ohio-fox-news.html.

29. Peter Thiel and Blake Masters, *Zero to One* (New York: Currency, 2014).

30. Jane Mayer, "The Reclusive Hedge Fund Tycoon Behind the Trump Presidency," *New Yorker*, March 27, 2017, www.newyorker.com/magazine/2017/03/27/the-reclusive-hedge-fund-tycoon-behind-the-trump-presidency.

31. Anne Case and Angus Deaton, *Deaths of Despair* (Princeton, NJ: Princeton University Press, 2020).

32. "Automation Is Fueling Increasing Mortality Among U.S. Adults, Study Finds," *Science Daily*, February 24, 2022, www.sciencedaily.com/releases/2022/02/220223172600.htm.

33. Chris Arnade, *Dignity: Seeking Respect in Back Row America* (New York: Sentinel, 2019).

Chapter 4: Fantasy Culture

1. Neil Postman, *Amusing Ourselves to Death* (New York: Penguin, 1985).

2. A. O. Scott, "Are the Movies Liberal?," *New York Times*, June 2, 2022, www.nytimes.com/2022/06/02/movies/liberal-hollywood-dog.html.

3. Asawin Seubsaeng, "Like Most Libertarians, Iron Man Grows Up and Moves On," *Mother Jones*, May 3, 2013, www.motherjones.com/politics/2013/05/film-review-iron-man-3-politics.

4. Junot Diaz, "He Read All 27,000 Marvel Comic Books and Lived to Tell the Tale," *New York Times*, October 12, 2021, www.nytimes.com/2021/10/12/books/review/douglas-wolk-all-of-the-marvels.html.

5. Breanna Bell, "Martin Scorsese Compares MCU to Theme Parks," *Variety*, October 4, 2019, https://variety.com/2019/film/news/martin-scorsese-marvel-theme-parks-1203360075.

6. Saul Bellow, *The Adventures of Augie March* (New York: Viking Press, 1953).

7. Pax Hehmeyer, "Steve Jobs on the Humanities," 4Humanities, October 7, 2011, https://4humanities.org/2011/10/steve-jobs-on-the-humanities.

8. Emma Brokes, "David Chase on Why He Wrote The Sopranos," *The Guardian*, September 16, 2019, www.theguardian.com/tv-and-radio/2019/sep/16/david-chase-the-sopranos-best-tv-21st-century.

9. Matt Seitz, *The Soprano Sessions* (New York: Abrams Press, 2019).

10. Willy Stayley, "Why Is Every Young Person in America Watching 'The Sopranos?,'" *New York Times*, September 29, 2021, www.nytimes.com/2021/09/29/magazine/sopranos.html.

11. James Wolcott, "Bada Bing's Big Bang," *Vanity Fair*, November 30, 2018, www.vanityfair.com/hollywood/2018/11/the-sopranos-white-americas-cultural-shift.

12. Emily Nussbaum, "The Great Divide," *New Yorker*, April 7, 2014, www.newyorker.com/magazine/2014/04/07/the-great-divide-emily-nussbaum.

13. Johnell Gipson, "Jay-Z and Warren Buffet's Interview Reveals—Jay Z May Have Never Met Beyoncé or Become a Billionaire If Not For This One Trip to London," *Cheatsheet*, September 10, 2020, www.cheatsheet.com/entertainment/jay-z-may-have-never-met-beyonce-or-become-a-billionaire-if-not-for-this-one-trip-to-london.html.

14.   Genius Turner, "Billionaires Think Alike," *Entrepreneurs Handbook*, November 2, 2020, https://entrepreneurshandbook.co/jay-z-warren-buffetts-interview-reveals-billionaires-think-alike-b8580a347f2c.

15.   Todd Boyd, *The New H.N.I.C.* (New York: NYU Press, 2003).

16.   Blair McClendon, "The Psychic Contortions of the Black Mogul-Entertainer," *New York Times*, April 5, 2022, www.nytimes.com/2022/04/05/magazine/black-billionaire-entertainers.html.

17.   Tarpley Hill, "How Instagrammers Are Faking the Luxury of a Private Jet for Just $64 an Hour," *Daily Beast*, October 26, 2020, www.thedailybeast.com/how-instagrammers-are-faking-the-luxury-of-a-private-jet-for-just-dollar64-an-hour.

18.   Richard Fausset, "Young Tug, Atlanta Rap Star, Is Arrested on Gang-Related Charges," *New York Times*, May 9, 2022, www.nytimes.com/2022/05/09/us/young-thug-arrested-gang.html.

19.   Roni Caryn Rabin and Tim Arango, "Gun Deaths Surged During the Pandemic's First Year, The CDC Reports," *New York Times*, May 10, 2022, www.nytimes.com/2022/05/10/health/cdc-gun-violence-pandemic.html.

20.   Tricia Rose, *The Hip Hop Wars* (New York: Civitas, 2008).

21.   American Psychological Association, "APA Resolution on Violent Video Games," studocu, www.studocu.com/en-us/document/southern-technical-college/med-surg-2/resolution-violent-video-games/29548508.

22.   Drew Harwell, "Up All Night with a Twitch Millionaire," *Washington Post*, December 2, 2021, www.washingtonpost.com/technology/2021/12/02/twitch-loltyler1-tyler-steinkamp.

23.   Stephen Marche, "America's Gambling Addiction Is Metastasizing," *The Atlantic*, November 26, 2021, www.theatlantic.com/ideas/archive/2021/11/world-our-casino/620791.

24.   Earl Grinols, *Gambling in America* (London: Cambridge University Press, 2004).

25.   North American Foundation for Gambling Addiction Help, "Statistics of Gambling Addiction 2016," https://nafgah.org/statistics-gambling-addiction-2016.

26.   NFL, "NFL Announces Agreements with Four Approved Sportsbook Operators," August 30, 2021, www.nfl.com/news/nfl-announces-agreements-with-four-approved-sportsbook-operators.

27.   Dave Feschuk, "Compulsive Gambling by Athletes Is a 'Silent Plague' in Pro Sports," *Toronto Star*, March 12, 2022, www.thestar.com/sports/opinion/2022/03/12/compulsive-gambling-by-athletes-is-a-silent-plague-in-pro-sports-perception-is-money.html.

Chapter 5: People of the Lie

1.   Erich Fromm, *Escape from Freedom* (New York: Farrar & Rinehart, 1941).

2.   Susan Glasser and Peter Baker, "Inside the War Between Trump and His Generals," *New Yorker*, August 15, 2022, www.newyorker.com/magazine/2022/08/15/inside-the-war-between-trump-and-his-generals.

3.   Sarah Lyall, "A Nation on Hold Wants to Speak with a Manager," *New York Times*, January 1, 2022, www.nytimes.com/2022/01/01/business/customer-service-pandemic-rage.html.

4.   Andrew Price-Smith, *Contagion and Chaos* (Cambridge, MA: MIT Press, 2009).

5.   Ryan Bort, "Trump Scammed Supporters Out of $250 Million for Nonexistent Fraud Fund," *Rolling Stone*, June 13, 2022, www.rollingstone.com/politics/politics-news/trump-fundraising-scam-jan-6-hearing-1367359.

6.   Hemant Kakkar and Asher Lawson, "We Found the One Group of Americans Who Are Most Likely to Spread Fake News," *Politico*, January 14, 2022, www.politico .com/news/magazine/2022/01/14/we-found-the-one-group-of-americans-who-are -most-likely-to-spread-fake-news-526973.

7.   Agence France Presse, "QAnon Conspiracies Go Global in Pandemic 'Perfect Storm,'" *Bangkok Post*, October 6, 2020, www.bangkokpost.com/world/1997499 /qanon-conspiracies-go-global-in-pandemic-perfect-storm.

8.   Ross Buettner and Charles Bagli, "How Donald Trump Bankrupted His Atlantic City Casinos, but Still Earned Millions," *New York Times*, June 11, 2016, www.nytimes.com /2016/06/12/nyregion/donald-trump-atlantic-city.html.

9.   Anita Chabria, "Lizard People, Deadly Orgies, and JFK," *Los Angeles Times*, December 7, 2021, www.latimes.com/california/story/2021-12-07/how-qanon-has-hijacked -hollywood-movies-for-conspiracy-theories.

10.   Ari Sen and Brandy Zadrozny, "QAnon Groups Have Millions of Members on Facebook Documents Show," *NBC News*, August 10, 2020, www.nbcnews.com/tech/tech -news/qanon-groups-have-millions-members-facebook-documents-show-n1236317.

11.   Roger MacNamee, "Facebook Drove QAnon's Mad Growth and Enhanced Its Power to Poison Elections," *Los Angeles Times*, September 30, 2020, www.latimes.com /opinion/story/2020-09-30/facebook-qanon-conspiracy-social-media-election.

12.   Rebecca Solnit, "Why Republicans Keep Falling for Trump's Lies," *New York Times*, January 5, 2022, www.nytimes.com/2022/01/05/opinion/republicans-trump-lies .html.

13.   Jack Brewster, Coalter Palmer, and Shayeza Walid, "Trump and His Social Platform Actively Promote QAnon," *Newsguard*, August 20, 2022, www.newsguardtech.com /misinformation-monitor/august-2022.

14.   Anastasiia Carrier, "I Left QAnon in 2019. But I'm Still Not Free," *Politico*, December 11, 2021, www.politico.com/news/magazine/2021/12/11/q-anon-movement-former-believer -523972.

15.   Charlie Munger, "The Revised Psychology of Human Misjudgment," fs.blog, November 2005, https://fs.blog/great-talks/psychology-human-misjudgment.

16.   Drew Harwell, "Since Jan. 6, the Pro-Trump Internet Has Descended into Infighting Over Money and Followers," *Washington Post*, January 3, 2022, www.washingtonpost .com/technology/2022/01/03/trump-qanon-online-money-war-jan6.

17.   Bort, "Trump Scammed Supporters."

18.   Barton Gellman, "Trump's Next Coup Has Already Begun," *The Atlantic*, December 6, 2021, www.theatlantic.com/magazine/archive/2022/01/january-6-insurrection-trump -coup-2024-election/620843.

19.   Jonathan Haidt and Jean Twenge, "This Is Our Chance to Pull Teenagers Out of the Smartphone Trap," *New York Times*, July 31, 2021, www.nytimes.com/2021/07/31 /opinion/smartphone-iphone-social-media-isolation.html.

20.   Georgia Wells, Deepa Seetharaman, and Jeff Horwitz, "Is Facebook Bad for You?," *Wall Street Journal*, November 5, 2021, www.wsj.com/articles/facebook-bad-for-you -360-million-users-say-yes-company-documents-facebook-files-11636124681.

21.   Michael Bang Petersen, Mathias Osmundsen, and Alexander Bor, "Beyond Populism," www.sydneysymposium.unsw.edu.au/2020/chapters/PetersenSSSP2020.pdf.

22.   Chafkin, *The Contrarian*.

23.   Sean Illing, "Flood the Zone with Shit," *Vox*, January 16, 2020, www.vox.com
/policy-and-politics/2020/1/16/20991816/impeachment-trial-trump-bannon-misinformation.

24.   Ezra Klein, "A Skeptical Take on the AI Revolution," *New York Times*, January 6,
2023, www.nytimes.com/2023/01/06/opinion/ezra-klein-podcast-gary-marcus.html.

25.   Eley, "What Is Fascism and Where Does It Come From?"

26.   John Ganz, "The Enigma of Peter Thiel," *Unpopular Front*, July 23, 2022, https://
johnganz.substack.com/p/the-enigma-of-peter-thiel.

27.   George Hawley, *Making Sense of the Alt-Right* (New York: Columbia University
Press, 2017).

28.   Andrew Prokop, "Curtis Yarvin Wants American Democracy Toppled," *Vox*,
October 24, 2022, www.vox.com/policy-and-politics/23373795/curtis-yarvin-neoreaction
-redpill-moldbug.

29.   Curtis Yarvin, "A Simple Sovereign Bankruptcy Procedure," *Unqualified Reser-
vations*, June 19, 2008, www.unqualified-reservations.org/2008/06/olx-simple-sovereign
-bankruptcy.

30.   Ryan Mac and Mike Isaac, "Peter Thiel to Exit Meta's Board to Support Trump-
Aligned Candidates," *New York Times*, February 7, 2022, www.nytimes.com/2022/02/07
/technology/peter-thiel-facebook.html.

31.   Ryan Lovelace, "Facebook Denies It Withheld Censorship Under Trump to Avoid
Regulation," *Washington Times*, September 21, 2021, www.washingtontimes.com/news
/2021/sep/21/facebook-denies-it-withheld-censorship-under-trump.

32.   John Gramlich, "10 Facts About Americans and Facebook," Pew Research Center,
June 1, 2021, www.pewresearch.org/short-reads/2021/06/01/facts-about-americans-and-
facebook.

33.   Chafkin, *The Contrarian*.

34.   Paul Waldman, "Donald Trump Has Nothing Left but Spite," *Washington Post*,
May 30, 2022, www.washingtonpost.com/opinions/2022/05/30/trump-cheney-2024-strategy
-spite.

35.   Steven Pearlstein, "Elon Musk's Twitter Deal Is Based on Flawed Math," *Washington Post*, May 2, 2022, www.washingtonpost.com/business/2022/05/02/elon-musk-twitter
-financing-flawed.

36.   Sarah Needleman, "The Flawed Math Behind Elon Musk's Twitter Deal," *Market-
watch*, June 5, 2022, www.marketwatch.com/story/elon-musks-followers-include-a-lot
-of-bots-11654478074.

37.   Ross Douthat, "Elon Musk Has Bigger Plans Then Just Letting Trump Back on
Twitter," *New York Times*, May 11, 2022, www.nytimes.com/2022/05/11/opinion/elon
-musk-twitter.html.

38.   Jack Shafer, "Now Elon Musk Thinks He's Henry Kissinger," *Politico*, October 12,
2022, www.politico.com/news/magazine/2022/10/12/elon-musk-russia-ukraine-00061528.

39.   Joseph Menn and Cat Zakrzewski, "Musk Appeasement of Putin and China Stokes
Fears of New Twitter Policies," *Washington Post*, October 12, 2022, www.washingtonpost
.com/technology/2022/10/12/musk-twitter-foreign-policy-worries.

40.   There is some dispute as to whether Lenin coined this term, but it came into wide
use in the 1950s.

41.   Alex Marquardt and Sean Lyngaas, "Ukraine Suffers a Comms Outage When
1,300 SpaceX Satellite Units Went Offline Over Funding Issues," *CNN*, November 4, 2022,

www.cnn.com/2022/11/04/politics/spacex-ukraine-elon-musk-starlink-internet-outage
/index.html.

42.   Matthew Rozsa, "Elon Musk Becomes Twitter Laughingstock After Bolivian
Socialist Movement Returns to Power," *Salon*, October 20, 2020, www.salon.com
/2020/10/20/elon-musk-becomes-twitter-laughingstock-after-bolivian-socialist
-movement-returns-to-power.

43.   Josh Marshall, "Oligarch Envy," *Talking Points Memo*, October 11, 2022, https://
talkingpointsmemo.com/edblog/oligarch-envy.

44.   Jerry Hirsch, "Elon Musk's Growing Empire Fueled by Government Subsidies,"
Los Angeles Times, March 30, 2015, www.latimes.com/business/la-fi-hy-musk-subsidies
-20150531-story.html.

45.   Dave Michaels, "Elon Musk's Belated Disclosure of Twitter Stake Triggers Regulators' Probes," *Wall Street Journal*, May 11, 2022, www.wsj.com/articles/elon-musks-belated
-disclosure-of-twitter-stake-triggers-regulators-probes-11652303894.

46.   Jacob Pramuk, "Tesla Asked Law Firm to Fire Attorney Who Worked on Elon
Musk Probe at SEC, Report Says," *CNBC*, January 15, 2022, www.cnbc.com/2022/01/15
/tesla-asked-cooley-to-fire-lawyer-who-worked-on-sec-elon-musk-probe.html.

47.   Michael Scherer and Sarah Ellison, "How a Billionaire Boys Club Came to
Dominate the Public Square," *Washington Post*, May 1, 2022, www.washingtonpost.com
/politics/2022/05/01/billionaires-politics.

48.   Daniel Engber, "LOL Something Matters," *Slate*, January 3, 2018, https://slate
.com/health-and-science/2018/01/weve-been-told-were-living-in-a-post-truth-age
-dont-believe-it.html.

49.   Ron Suskind, "Faith, Certainty and the Presidency of George W. Bush," *New York
Times*, October 17, 2004, www.nytimes.com/2004/10/17/magazine/faith-certainty-and
-the-presidency-of-george-w-bush.html.

50.   Jonah Bromwich, "Before Massacre Began, Suspect Invited Others to Review His
Plan," *New York Times*, May 17, 2022, www.nytimes.com/2022/05/17/nyregion/buffalo
-shooting-discord-chat-plans.html.

51.   Mary Kent, "Young U.S. Adults Vulnerable to Injuries and Violence," *PRB*, July 19,
2010, www.prb.org/resources/young-u-s-adults-vulnerable-to-injuries-and-violence.

52.   Ariana Eunjung Cha, Meghan Hoyer, and Tim Meko, "Young Men, Guns and
the Prefrontal Cortex," *Washington Post*, June 3, 2022, www.washingtonpost.com
/health/2022/06/03/why-so-many-mass-shooters-young-angry-men.

53.   Michael Keller and David Kirkpatrick, "Their America Is Vanishing," *New York
Times*, October 23, 2022, www.nytimes.com/2022/10/23/us/politics/republican-election
-objectors-demographics.html.

54.   Nicholas Confessore and Karen Yourish, "A Fringe Conspiracy Theory, Fostered
Online, Is Refashioned by the G.O.P.," *New York Times*, May 15, 2022, www.nytimes
.com/2022/05/15/us/replacement-theory-shooting-tucker-carlson.html.

55.   Kiara Alfonseca, "After Buffalo Shooting, Experts Question Whether America
Can Face Its Far Right Extremism Problem," *ABC News*, May 17, 2022, https://abcnews
.go.com/US/experts-question-america-face-extremism-problem/story?id=84748865.

56.   Barbara Walters, *How Civil Wars Start: And How to Stop Them* (New York: Crown,
2022).

57.   Tech Transparency Project, "Facebook's Militia Mess," March 24, 2021, www
.techtransparencyproject.org/articles/facebooks-militia-mess.

58.   Sean Wilentz, "Trump's Origins in a New York World of Con Men, Mobsters, and Hustlers," *Washington Post*, October 3, 2022, www.washingtonpost.com /books/2022/10/03/confidence-man-maggie-haberman-review-trump.

59.   Michael Kruse, "The Final Lesson Donald Trump Never Learned from Roy Cohn," *Politico*, September 19, 2019, www.politico.com/magazine/story/2019/09/19 /roy-cohn-donald-trump-documentary-228144.

60.   David Remnick, "Day of the Dittohead," *Washington Post*, February 20, 1994, www.washingtonpost.com/archive/opinions/1994/02/20/day-of-the-dittohead/e5723 f05-04d8-4ccb-98c9-8b1ba6c358d2.

61.   Jonathan Mahler and Jim Rutenberg, "How Rupert Murdoch's Empire of Influence Remade the World," *New York Times*, April 3, 2019, www.nytimes.com/interactive /2019/04/03/magazine/rupert-murdoch-fox-news-trump.html.

62.   Nicholas Confessore, "How Tucker Carlson Reshaped Fox News—and Became Trump's Heir," *New York Times*, April 30, 2022, www.nytimes.com/2022/04/30/us/tucker -carlson-fox-news.html.

Chapter 6: Welcome to the Metaverse

1.   Ben Thompson, "An Interview with Mark Zuckerberg About the Metaverse," *Stratechery*, October 28, 2021, https://stratechery.com/2021/an-interview-with-mark -zuckerberg-about-the-metaverse.

2.   "Are VR Headsets Bad for Your Health?," *BBC Science Focus*, www.sciencefocus .com/future-technology/are-vr-headsets-bad-for-your-health.

3.   Jeff Horwitz, Salvador Rodriguez, and Meghan Bobrowsky, "Company Documents Show Meta's Flagship Metaverse Falling Short," *Wall Street Journal*, October 15, 2022, www .wsj.com/articles/meta-metaverse-horizon-worlds-zuckerberg-facebook-internal -documents-11665778961.

4.   Salvador Rodriguez, "Facebook Parent Meta Earnings Fall Short as Revenue Decline Accelerates," *Wall Street Journal*, October 27, 2022, www.wsj.com/articles /meta-facebook-q3-earnings-report-2022-11666753938.

5.   Sue Halpern, "The Specter of Our Virtual Future," *New York Review of Books*, October 20, 2022, www.nybooks.com/articles/2022/10/20/the-specter-of-our-virtual -future-the-metaverse-matthew-ball.

6.   John Gruber, "The Inside Story of Why Apple Bet Big on a Mixed Reality Headset," *Daring Fireball*, May 19, 2022, https://daringfireball.net/linked/2022/05/19 /information-apple-headset.

7.   Sigal Samuel, "Facebook Is Building Tech to Read Your Mind," *Vox*, August 5, 2019, www.vox.com/future-perfect/2019/8/5/20750259/facebook-ai-mind-reading-brai -computer-interface.

8.   Julian Sanchez, Twitter, https://twitter.com/normative/status/1485336668680904704.

9.   Nick Yee and Jeremy Bailenson, "The Proteus Effect," Human Communication Research, 2007, https://stanfordvr.com/mm/2007/yee-proteus-effect.pdf.

10.   Ready Player Me: https://readyplayer.me.

11.   Scott Stein, "Mark Zuckerberg on Facebook's VR Future," *CNET*, May 7, 2021, www.cnet.com/tech/gaming/features/mark-zuckerberg-on-facebook-vr-future-new -sensors-on-quest-pro-fitness-and-a-metaverse-for-work.

12.   Jia Tolentino, "The Age of Instagram Face," *New Yorker*, December 12, 2019, www .newyorker.com/culture/decade-in-review/the-age-of-instagram-face.

13.   Madeline Howard, "Digital Blackface Is Basically the Modern Version of a Minstrel Show," Yahoo!, February 11, 2022, www.yahoo.com/now/digital-blackface-basically-modern-version-120000527.html.

14.   Jamie Burke, "Zuck, Facebook Meta and the Influencer Roadshow," *Medium*, November 16, 2021, https://jamieov.medium.com/zuck-facebook-meta-the-influencer-roadshow-55e6cd05fe3b.

15.   Shannon Liao, "In 'The Metaverse,' a Leading Evangelist Shies Away from Prediction," *Washington Post*, July 18, 2022, www.washingtonpost.com/video-games/2022/07/18/metaverse-book-matthew-ball-interview.

16.   Deloitte Consulting, "A Whole New World?," www2.deloitte.com/content/dam/Deloitte/us/Documents/technology/us-ai-institute-what-is-the-metaverse-new.pdf.

17.   Liz Harkavy, Eddy Lazzarin, and Arianna Simpson, "7 Essential Ingredients of a Metaverse," *Future*, May 6, 2022, https://future.com/7-essential-ingredients-of-a-metaverse.

18.   Stephane Kasriel, "Where the Metaverse Can Take Fin Tech," *Medium*, May 11, 2022, https://medium.com/@skasriel/where-the-metaverse-can-take-fintech-a936e6bd6987.

19.   Niccolo Soldo, "The Dubrovnik Interviews," *Fisted by Foucault*, May 31, 2021, https://niccolo.substack.com/p/the-dubrovnik-interviews-marc-andreessen.

20.   Rob Brooks, *Artificial Intimacy: Digital Lovers, Virtual Friends and Algorithmic Matchmakers* (New York: Columbia University Press, 2021).

21.   Ross Douthat, *The Decadent Society* (New York: Simon & Schuster, 2020).

22.   Adrian Vermeule, "Supreme Court Justices Have Forgotten What the Law Is For," *New York Times*, February 3, 2022, www.nytimes.com/2022/02/03/opinion/us-supreme-court-nomination.html.

23.   David Newhoff, "Backpage Execs Arrested Because Pimping Isn't Speech," *The Illusion of More*, October 11, 2016, https://illusionofmore.com/backpage-execs-arrested-because-pimping-isnt-speech.

24.   Renée DiResta, "The Supply of Disinformation Will Soon Be Infinite," *The Atlantic*, September 20, 2020, www.theatlantic.com/ideas/archive/2020/09/future-propaganda-will-be-computer-generated/616400.

25.   Weilun Soon, "A Researcher's Avatar Was Sexually Assaulted on Metaverse Platform Owned by Meta, Making Her the Latest Victim of Sexual Abuse on Meta's Platforms, Watchdog Says," *Business Insider*, May 2022, www.businessinsider.com/researcher-claims-her-avatar-was-raped-on-metas-metaverse-platform-2022-5.

26.   Adi Robertson, "Meta CTO Thinks Bad Metaverse Moderation Could Pose an 'Existential Threat,'" *The Verge*, November 12, 2021, www.theverge.com/2021/11/12/22779006/meta-facebook-cto-andrew-bosworth-memo-metaverse-disney-safety-content-moderation-scale.

27.   Ryun Knutson, "How to Build a Metaverse, Part 2," *Wall Street Journal*, September 30, 2022, www.wsj.com/podcasts/the-journal/how-to-build-a-metaverse-part-2-avatars-behaving-badly/a79258f8-5715-41d2-bf75-16445c198be5.

28.   Ryan Mac, Sheera Frenkel, and Kevin Roose, "Skepticism, Confusion, Frustrations," *New York Times*, October 9, 2022, www.nytimes.com/2022/10/09/technology/meta-zuckerberg-metaverse.html.

29.   Kelvin Chan, "Facebook Whistleblower Fears the Metaverse," *AP*, November 9, 2021, https://apnews.com/article/technology-lifestyle-business-only-on-ap-media-e4f03d38243552e46a77d0d3f0d45e3b.

30.   Evan Selinger, "The Gospel of the Metaverse," *Tech Policy Press*, March 2, 2022, https://techpolicy.press/the-gospel-of-the-metaverse.

31. Stanley, *How Fascism Works*.

32. Chris Hamilton, "The Immortal Trump," *Washington Post*, July 5, 2022, www
.washingtonpost.com/opinions/2022/07/05/trump-avatar-metaverse-ai.

33. Timothy Snyder, "We Should Say It. Russia Is Fascist.," *New York Times*, May 19,
2022, www.nytimes.com/2022/05/19/opinion/russia-fascism-ukraine-putin.html.

34. Suzy Weiss, "First Comes Love. Then Comes Sterilization.," *The Free Press*, October 25, 2021, www.commonsense.news/p/first-comes-love-then-comes-sterilization.

35. Peter Thiel, "The Straussian Moment," in *Politics and Apocalypse*, ed. Robert
Hamerton-Kelly (East Lansing: Michigan State University Press, 2007), 189–218, www
.jstor.org/stable/10.14321/j.ctt7zt6qq.9.

36. Cecilia Kang, "Congress, Far From a 'Series of Tubes,' Is Still Nowhere Near Rein-
ing in Tech," *New York Times*, December 11, 2021, www.nytimes.com/2021/12/11/business
/congress-tech-regulation.html.

37. Gavin Newsom and Lisa Dickey, *Citizenville* (New York: Penguin, 2013).

38. Business Roundtable, "Business Roundtable Redefines the Purpose of a Corporation to Promote 'An Economy That Serves All Americans,'" www.businessroundtable.org
/business-roundtable-redefines-the-purpose-of-a-corporation-to-promote-an-economy
-that-serves-all-americans.

Chapter 7: The Crypto Con

1. Nassim Nicholas Taleb, "Bitcoin, Currencies, and Fragility," Nassim Nicholas
Taleb's Home Page, www.fooledbyrandomness.com/BTC-QF.pdf.

2. Vicky Ge Huang, "Celsius Customers Are Losing Hope for Their Locked Up
Crypto," *Wall Street Journal*, July 3, 2022, www.wsj.com/articles/celsius-customers-are
-losing-hope-for-their-locked-up-crypto-11656840601.

3. Joshua Davis, "The Crypto-Currency," *New Yorker*, October 13, 2011, www
.newyorker.com/magazine/2011/10/10/the-crypto-currency.

4. Gerrit De Vynck, "First She Documented the Alt-Right. Now She's Coming
for Crypto.," *Washington Post*, May 29, 2022, www.washingtonpost.com/technology
/2022/05/29/molly-white-crypto.

5. Susannah Luthi, "Who's Afraid of Crypto ATMs?," *Politico*, July 6, 2022, www.politico
.com/newsletters/digital-future-daily/2022/07/06/whos-afraid-of-crypto-atms-00044324.

6. Gregory Zuckerman, Vicky Ge Huang, and Hardika Singh, "Celsius Is Crashing, and Crypto Investors Are Spooked," *Wall Street Journal*, June 16, 2022, www.wsj.com
/articles/celsius-is-crashing-and-crypto-investors-are-spooked-11655371801.

7. Christopher Mims, "NFTs Cryptocurrencies, and Web 3 Are Multilevel Marketing
Schemes for a New Generation," *Wall Street Journal*, February 19, 2022, www.wsj.com
/articles/nfts-cryptocurrencies-and-web3-are-multilevel-marketing-schemes-for-a-new
-generation-11645246824.

8. Instituto Universitario de Opinión Pública, "La población salvadoreña opina
sobre el *bitcoin* y su *situatión económica* familiar," https://uca.edu.sv/iudop/wp-content
/uploads/Infografico-Bitcoin-y-Economia.pdf.

9. Santiago Perez, "El Salvador's President Went All In on Bitcoin," *Wall Street Journal*, May 14, 2022, www.wsj.com/articles/el-salvadors-president-went-all-in-on-bitcoin
-then-it-tanked-11652540400.

10. Adam Tooze, "Crypto and the State," *Chartbook*, February 19, 2022, https://adamtooze
.com/2022/02/19/chartbook-newsletter-83-crypto-and-the-state-shouldnt-we-be-talking
-about-sha-256.

11.   Willem Buiter, "Outlaw Cryptocurrencies Now," *The Gleaner* (Jamaica, WI), February 11, 2022, https://jamaica-gleaner.com/article/business/20220211/willem-buiter-outlaw-cryptocurrencies-now.

12.   Siobhan Roberts, "How 'Trustless' Is Bitcoin, Really?," *New York Times*, June 6, 2022, www.nytimes.com/2022/06/06/science/bitcoin-nakamoto-blackburn-crypto.html.

13.   Bala Sethunathan, "Ten Key Facts About Ransomware," Software One, March 7, 2022, www.softwareone.com/nb-no/blog/articles/2022/03/07/what-we-can-learn-from-the-biggest-ransomware-attacks.

14.   Cyrus Faravar, "Some in Bitcoin Group Resign over New Board Member's Link to Sex Abuse," *Ars Technica*, May 16, 2014, https://arstechnica.com/information-technology/2014/05/some-in-bitcoin-group-resign-over-new-board-members-link-to-sex-abuse.

15.   FT Staff, "Tether; the Former Plastic Surgeon Behind the Crypto Reserve Currency," *Financial Times*, www.ft.com/content/4da3060c-8e1a-439f-a1d7-a6a4688ad6ca.

16.   FT Staff, "Tether and Bitfinex Agree to Pay $18.5M Penalty After New York Probe," *Financial Times*, www.ft.com/content/1d3b5027-ce7e-470f-8d7a-866746f8079d.

17.   Kate Rooney, "Much of Bitcoin's 2017 Boom Was Market Manipulation Research Says," *CNBC*, June 13, 2018, www.cnbc.com/2018/06/13/much-of-bitcoins-2017-boom-was-market-manipulation-researcher-says.html.

18.   US Securities and Exchange Commission, "Framework for 'Investment Contract' Analysis of Digital Assets," www.sec.gov/corpfin/framework-investment-contract-analysis-digital-assets.

19.   Fisher, "Why I'm Cryptophobic."

20.   Berber Jin, "Andreessen Horowitz Went All In on Crypto at the Worst Possible Time," *Wall Street Journal*, October 26, 2022, www.wsj.com/articles/andreessen-horowitz-went-all-in-on-crypto-at-the-worst-possible-time-11666769270.

21.   Eric Lipton, Daisuke Wakabayashi, and Ephrat Livni, "Big Hires, Big Money and a D.C. Blitz," *New York Times*, October 29, 2021, www.nytimes.com/2021/10/29/us/politics/andreessen-horowitz-lobbying-cryptocurrency.html.

22.   Sean Burch, "'Senator, We Run Ads,'" *The Wrap*, April 10, 2018, www.thewrap.com/senator-orrin-hatch-facebook-biz-model-zuckerberg.

23.   Paul Krugman, "From the Big Short to the Big Scam," *New York Times*, June 6, 2022, www.nytimes.com/2022/06/06/opinion/cryptocurrency-bubble-fraud.html.

24.   Sir John Cunliffe, "Is 'Crypto' a Financial Stability Risk?," Bank of England, October 13, 2021, www.bankofengland.co.uk/speech/2021/october/jon-cunliffe-swifts-sibos-2021.

25.   Bo Li and Nobuyasu Sugimoto, "Crypto Contagion Underscores Why Global Regulators Must Act Fast to Stem Risk," *IMF Blog*, January 18, 2023, imf.org/en/blogs/articles/2023/01/18/crypto-contagion-underscores-why-global-regulators-must-act-fast-to-stem-risk.

26.   Justin Scheck, "Open Sea's NFT Free-for-All," *Wall Street Journal*, February 12, 2022, www.wsj.com/articles/openseas-nft-free-for-all-11644642042.

27.   Paul Vigna, "NFT Sales Are Flatlining," *Wall Street Journal*, May 3, 2022, www.wsj.com/articles/nft-sales-are-flatlining-11651552616.

28.   Buttonwood, "The Complicated Politics of Crypto and Web3," *The Economist*, April 16, 2022, www.economist.com/finance-and-economics/2022/04/16/the-complicated-politics-of-crypto-and-web3.

Chapter 8: Going to Mars

1. Alison van Diggelen, "Transcript of Elon Musk Interview: Iron Man, Growing up in South Africa," *Fresh Dialogues*, February 7, 2013, www.freshdialogues.com/2013/02/07/transcript-of-elon-musk-interview-with-alison-van-diggelen-iron-man-growing-up-in-south-africa.

2. Christian Davenport, *The Space Barons* (New York: Public Affairs Books, 2018).

3. John Richardson, "When the End of Human Civilization Is Your Day Job," *Esquire*, July 20, 2018, www.esquire.com/news-politics/a36228/ballad-of-the-sad-climatologists-0815.

4. William Shatner, *Boldly Go* (New York: Atria Books, 2022).

5. Amit Malewar, "Study Simulate Mars' Core May Explain the Loss of Its Magnetic Field," *Tech Explorist*, February 12, 2022, www.techexplorist.com/study-simulate-mars-core-explain-loss-magnetic-field/44691.

6. Donald Goldsmith and Martin Rees, *The End of Astronauts* (Cambridge, MA: Harvard University Press, 2022).

7. Aaron Boley and Michael Byers, "U.S. Policy Puts the Safe Development of Space at Risk," *Science*, October 9, 2020, www.science.org/doi/abs/10.1126/science.abd3402.

8. News 18 Staff, "Nuke Mars Agenda Again?," *News 18*, September 20, 2021, www.news18.com/news/buzz/nuke-mars-agenda-again-how-elon-musk-thinks-red-planet-can-be-warmed-up-4221614.html.

9. Leah Crane, "NASA Has Produced Oxygen on the Surface of Mars for the First Time," *New Scientist*, April 22, 2021, www.newscientist.com/article/2275410-nasa-has-produced-oxygen-on-the-surface-of-mars-for-the-first-time.

10. Carl Zimmer, "The Lost History of One of the World's Strangest Science Experiments," *New York Times*, March 29, 2019, www.nytimes.com/2019/03/29/sunday-review/biosphere-2-climate-change.html.

11. Stephen Clark, "Solar Storm Dooms Up to 40 New Starlink Satellites," *Spaceflight Now*, February 8, 2022, https://spaceflightnow.com/2022/02/08/solar-storm-dooms-40-new-star-link-satellites.

12. Nadia Drake, "Elon Musk: A Million Humans Could Live on Mars by the 2060s," *National Geographic*, September 27, 2016, www.nationalgeographic.com/science/article/elon-musk-spacex-exploring-mars-planets-space-science.

13. Isobel Asher Hamilton, "Jeff Bezos and Elon Musk Both Want to Colonize Space. Here Are the 6 Biggest Problems with Their Plans, from Thinning Bones to Toxic Plants on Mars.," *Business Insider*, updated July 22, 2021, www.businessinsider.com/gaping-holes-elon-musk-and-jeff-bezos-space-plans-2019-7.

14. Charlie Stross, "Insufficient Data," *Antipope*, July 23, 2010, www.antipope.org/charlie/blog-static/2010/07/insufficient-data.html.

15. Drake, "Elon Musk."

16. Vance, *Elon Musk*.

17. Chafkin, *The Contrarian*.

18. Christian Davenport, "Elon Musk's SpaceX Settles Lawsuit Against Air Force," *Washington Post*, January 23, 2015, www.washingtonpost.com/business/economy/elon-musks-spacex-to-drop-lawsuit-against-air-force/2015/01/23/c5e8ff80-a34c-11e4-9f89-561284a573f8_story.html.

Chapter 9: Transhumanism

1. Fukuyama, "Transhumanism."

2. Fukuyama, "Transhumanism."

3.   Nick Bostrum, *Superintelligence: Paths, Dangers, Strategies* (London: Oxford University Press, 2014).

4.   Social Security Administration, "Education and Lifetime Earnings," November 2015, www.ssa.gov/policy/docs/research-summaries/education-earnings.html.

5.   Jaron Lanier, *Who Owns the Future* (New York: Simon & Schuster, 2013).

6.   Philip Ball, "Designer Babies: An Ethical Horror Waiting to Happen?," *The Guardian*, January 8, 2017, www.theguardian.com/science/2017/jan/08/designer-babies-ethical-horror-waiting-to-happen.

7.   Jeff Bercovici, "Peter Thiel Is Very, Very Interested in Young People's Blood," *Inc.*, August 1, 2016, www.inc.com/jeff-bercovici/peter-thiel-young-blood.html.

8.   Huber Warner et al., "Science Fact and the SENS Agenda," *EMBO Reports* 6, no. 11 (November 2005), www.ncbi.nlm.nih.gov/pmc/articles/PMC1371037.

9.   Warner et al., "Science Fact and the SENS Agenda."

10.   Jef Akst, "Aubrey de Grey on Leave After Sexual Harassment Allegations," *The Scientist*, August 11, 2021, www.the-scientist.com/news-opinion/aubrey-de-grey-on-leave-after-sexual-harassment-allegations-69081.

11.   Antonio Regalado, "Saudi Arabia Plans to Spend $1 Billion a Year Discovering Treatments to Slow Aging," *MIT Technology Review*, June 7, 2022, www.technologyreview.com/2022/06/07/1053132/saudi-arabia-slow-aging-metformin.

12.   Rob Dunn, *A Natural History of the Future* (New York: Basic Books, 2021).

13.   Martin Pijnenburg and Carol Leget, "Who Wants to Live Forever?," *Journal of Medical Ethics*, October 2007, www.ncbi.nlm.nih.gov/pmc/articles/PMC2652797.

14.   John Gray, "The Mind's Body Problem," *New York Review of Books*, December 2, 2021, www.nybooks.com/articles/2021/12/02/the-minds-body-problem.

15.   Jeremy Norman, "Irving John Good Originates the Concept of the Technological Singularity," historyofinformation.com, 1965, www.historyofinformation.com/detail.php?id=2142.

16.   Stephen Hawking et al., "Transcendence Looks at the Implications of Artificial Intelligence," *Independent*, May 1, 2014, www.independent.co.uk/news/science/stephen-hawking-transcendence-looks-at-the-implications-of-artificial-intelligence-but-are-we-taking-ai-seriously-enough-9313474.html.

17.   James Barrat, *Our Final Invention* (London: Thomas Dunne Books, 2013).

18.   Toby Ord, *The Precipice: Existential Risk and the Future of Humanity* (New York: Hachette, 2020).

19.   Adrienne Williams, Milagros Miceli, and Timnit Gebru, "The Exploited Labor Behind Artificial Intelligence," *Noema*, October 13, 2022, www.noemamag.com/the-exploited-labor-behind-artificial-intelligence.

20.   Nitasha Tiku, "The Google Engineer Who Thinks the Company's AI Has Come to Life," *Washington Post*, June 11, 2022, www.washingtonpost.com/technology/2022/06/11/google-ai-lamda-blake-lemoine.

21.   George Kennan, foreword to *The Pathology of Power* (New York, Norton, 1987).

22.   Peter Beinart, "Ukraine, the Backlash and Washington's New Groupthink," *New York Times*, November 4, 2022, www.nytimes.com/2022/11/04/opinion/ukraine-congress-progressives-letter.html.

23.   Phil Klay, *Uncertain Ground* (New York: Penguin Press, 2022).

24.   Paul Mozur, Muyi Xiao, and John Liu, "'An Invisible Cage': How China Is Policing the Future," *New York Times*, June 25, 2022, www.nytimes.com/2022/06/25/technology/china-surveillance-police.html.

25.   Sharon Weinberger, "Techie Software Soldier Spy," *New York Magazine*, September 28, 2020, https://nymag.com/intelligencer/2020/09/inside-palantir-technologies-peter-thiel-alex-karp.html.

26.   William Alden, "Palantir's Relationship with the Intelligence Community Has Been Worse Than You'd Think," *BuzzFeed News*, April 21, 2017, www.buzzfeednews.com/article/williamalden/palantirs-relationship-with-americas-spies.

27.   Dave Philipps, "The Unseen Scars of Those Who Kill Via Remote Control," *New York Times*, April 15, 2022, www.nytimes.com/2022/04/15/us/drones-airstrikes-ptsd.html.

28.   Human Rights Watch, "Killer Robots: Military Powers Stymie Ban," December 19, 2021, www.hrw.org/news/2021/12/19/killer-robots-military-powers-stymie-ban.

29.   Campaign to Stop Killer Robots, www.stopkillerrobots.org/wp-content/uploads/2018/11/KRC_CountryViews22Nov2018.pdf.

30.   Adam Satariano, Nick Cumming-Bruce, and Rick Gladstone, "Killer Robots Aren't Science Fiction," *New York Times*, December 17, 2021, www.nytimes.com/2021/12/17/world/robot-drone-ban.html.

31.   Thiel, "The Education of a Libertarian."

Chapter 10: Creating an Age of Realism

1.   William Shirer, *The Rise and Fall of the Third Reich* (New York: Simon & Schuster, 1960).

2.   Paul Waldman, "Elite Republicans Are Now Openly Encouraging Political Violence," *Washington Post*, June 20, 2022, www.washingtonpost.com/opinions/2022/06/20/eric-greitens-encouraging-political-violence.

3.   Martin Kaste, "Nebraska Cops Used Facebook Messages to Investigate an Alleged Illegal Abortion," *NPR*, August 12, 2022, www.npr.org/2022/08/12/1117092169/nebraska-cops-used-facebook-messages-to-investigate-an-alleged-illegal-abortion.

4.   Sean Fleming, "40% of Employees Are Thinking of Quitting Their Jobs," *WEF*, June 2, 2021, www.weforum.org/agenda/2021/06/remote-workers-burnout-covid-microsoft-survey.

5.   Elise Chen, "These Chinese Millennials Are 'Chilling,' and Beijing Isn't Happy," *New York Times*, July 3, 2021, www.nytimes.com/2021/07/03/world/asia/china-slackers-tangping.html.

6.   Ivan Illich, *Deschooling Society* (New York: Harper & Row, 1972).

7.   Illich, *Deschooling Society*.

8.   Kate Procter, "Just 6% of UK Public 'Want to Return to Pre-pandemic Economy,'" *The Guardian*, June 28, 2020, www.theguardian.com/world/2020/jun/28/just-6-of-uk-public-want-a-return-to-pre-pandemic-economy.

9.   Damian Carrington, "$10 Billion of Precious Metals Dumped Each Year in Electronic Waste, Says UN," *The Guardian*, July 2, 2020, www.theguardian.com/environment/2020/jul/02/10bn-precious-metals-dumped-each-year-electronic-waste-un-toxic-e-waste-polluting.

10.   Nathan Gardels, "Bill Gates' Guru," *Noema*, July 14, 2014, www.noemamag.com-bill-gates-guru-im-not-impressed-with-silicon-valley-i-dont-have-a-cell-phone-i-never-blog.

11.   Billy Gallagher, "How Facebook Tried to Squash Snapchat," *Wired*, February 16, 2018, www.wired.com/story/copycat-how-facebook-tried-to-squash-snapchat.

12.   L. M. Sacasas, "Ill with Want," *The Convivial Society*, July 17, 2021, https://theconvivialsociety.substack.com/p/ill-with-want.

13.   Ronald Brownstein, "How a GOP Congress Could Roll Back Freedoms Nationwide," *The Atlantic*, November 7, 2022, www.theatlantic.com/politics/archive/2022/11/gop-congress-2022-midterm-elections-rights/671996.

14.   United Nations, "Homelessness and Human Rights," www.ohchr.org/en/special-procedures/sr-housing/homelessness-and-human-rights.

15.   Los Angeles Controller, "L.A. Controller Maps Publicly-Owned Properties in L.A. to Create Affordable Housing, Community Development Opportunities," https://lacity.gov/highlights/la-controller-maps-publicly-owned-properties-la-create-affordable-housing-community.

16.   Thomas Wright, "What a Second Trump Term Would Mean for the World," *The Atlantic*, September 30, 2020, www.theatlantic.com/ideas/archive/2020/09/what-trump-second-term-would-do-foreign-policy/616536.

17.   Zeesham Aleem, "Elon Musk Is Drifting Toward the Hard-Core Authoritarian Right," *MSNBC*, June 27, 2022, www.msnbc.com/opinion/msnbc-opinion/elon-musk-drifting-toward-trumpian-republican-politics-n1296529.

18.   GMI PAC, www.gmipac.com.

Conclusion

1.   Jin, "Andreessen Horowitz Went All In on Crypto at the Worst Possible Time."

2.   Robert Gordon, *The Rise and Fall of American Growth* (Princeton, NJ: Princeton University Press, 2016).

3.   Paul Krugman, "Paul Krugman Reviews 'The Rise and Fall of American Growth' by Robert J. Gordon," *New York Times*, January 31, 2016, www.nytimes.com/2016/01/31/books/review/the-powers-that-were.html.

4.   Tangermann, "Elon Musk."

5.   Brian Klaas, "America's Self-Obsession Is Killing Its Democracy," *The Atlantic*, July 21, 2022, www.theatlantic.com/ideas/archive/2022/07/american-democracy-breakdown-authoritarianism-rise/670580.

6.   Martin Luther King Jr., "'Remaining Awake Through a Great Revolution,'" Address at Morehouse College Commencement, Martin Luther King, Jr. Research and Education Institute, June 2, 1959, https://kinginstitute.stanford.edu/king-papers/documents/remaining-awake-through-great-revolution-address-morehouse-college.

INDEX

ABOUT THE AUTHOR

Jonathan Taplin is the director emeritus of the Annenberg Innovation Lab at the University of Southern California and professor at the USC Annenberg School, and author of *Move Fast and Break Things*, which was nominated for the *Financial Times* / Mckinsey Business Book of the Year. His extraordinary journey has put him at the crest of every major cultural wave in the past half-century: he was tour manager for Bob Dylan and the Band, producer of major films such as Martin Scorsese's *Mean Streets*, an executive at Merrill Lynch, creator of the internet's first video-on-demand service and a cultural critic and author writing about technology in the new millennium.